TRAVEL THROUGH

THE OLD TESTAMENT

An extensive Old Testament Study and Reference Source
..............now in two volumes!

TRAVEL THROUGH

THE OLD TESTAMENT

REVISED AND EXPANDED

Volume One

Thomas L. Hiegel

Table of Contents

LIST OF **ABBREVIATIONS**

OLD TESTAMENT ABBREVIATIONS

Gen	Genesis	SS	Song of Solomon
Ex	Exodus	Isa	Isaiah
Lev	Leviticus	Jer	Jeremiah
Num	Numbers	Lam	Lamentations
Deut	Deuteronomy	Ezek	Ezekiel
Josh	Joshua	Dan	Daniel
Jud	Judges	Hos	Hosea
Ruth	Ruth	Joel	Joel
1, 2 Sam	Samuel	Amos	Amos
1, 2 Kings	Kings	Obad	Obadiah
1, 2 Chron	Chronicles	Jon	Jonah
Ezra	Ezra	Mic	Micah
Neh	Nehemiah	Nah	Nahum
Est	Esther	Hab	Habakkuk
Job	Job	Zeph	Zephaniah
Ps	Psalms	Hag	Haggai
Prov	Proverbs	Zech	Zechariah
Ecc	Ecclesiastes	Mal	Malachi

GENERAL ABBREVIATIONS

AMP	Amplified Bible
BCE	Before the Common Era (B.C.)
CE	Common Era (A.D.)
cp, cps	Chapter , chapters
i.g.	"that is" "for example"
ESV	English Standard Version
HCSB	Holman Christian Standard Bible
NASB	New American Standard Version
NET	New English Translation NET Bible
NIV	New International Version
NLT	New Living Translation
NT	New Testament
OT	Old Testament
vol	In this Volume
v, vv	Verse (s)

AUTHOR'S PREFACE TO REVISED EDITION

This two-volume edition of *Travel Through the Old Testament* is the complete teaching course (revised, expanded, and updated), previously printed in three smaller volumes. It is the author's intent to present a basic, and yet thorough study course on the entire thirty-nine books of the Old Testament. The author maintains a conservative Bible-centered view of Bible interpretation. The first several pages include information concerning the Bible: (1) Why Study the Bible? (2) The Uniqueness of the Bible, and (3) Structure of The Old Testament.

In this survey and teaching course, we will "travel" through the thirty-nine books called The Old Testament. In Volume One, from God's original creation in the dateless past, through a visit with the Patriarchs, the deliverance and forming of a special people, Joshua is leading God's people into the Promised Land, and the periods of Judges and Kings. Volume Two will include Hebrew poetry, the dividing of the Promised Land into Israel and Judah, the exile of both nations, and the return to the Promised Land.

Our journey will generally be chronological, with an emphasis on history. Therefore, some of the Old Testament books will be referenced in more than one Section. The full index of word studies, Expanded Help Papers, Depth of Bible Words and Places, and outlines and keys for each book, will assist in locating the material for your in-depth study.

If you are thirsty for the water of the Word, you will benefit from this study. It is my desire for you to spiritually grow. To read and understand the Old Testament is the primary need of our generation and the generation to follow. This work will serve as a small library of Old Testament information. Both the scholar and the student will discover truths in this course that will assist in personal growth. In addition, an in depth Chronology of Old Testament Events and History may be found at the back of this volume.

The course could be utilized in most settings:
> Universities and Colleges
> Sunday School and Seminars
> Home Groups and Personal Studies
> Mid-week gatherings

The author may be contacted at ThomasLHiegel @ thomaslhiegel.com.

Will you join with me in the following prayer while "travelling" through this Course?

> *Every breath I take...is by Your grace*
> *Every step I take...is directed by You*
> *Every word I speak...is for Your glory*
> *Everyone I meet...is a neighbor to be loved*

Any claims, on my part, to be capable of deploying all, or most, of the methods of textural and historical criticism that are needed for this work would be unwarrantable. All that I offer is this man's research and view of the declarations, which the Old Testament writings illuminate.

Many sources were used in preparing the general outline during the four weeks following a heart attack in June, 2007. The work was completed in three volumes and printed in color during the following year. In 2016 the three original volumes were completely edited, greatly expanded, and combined into two black and white volumes.

Acknowledgments

The following are many of the sources of information used in addition to my personal commentary notes. These sources are given full appreciation for their contributions, many used with permission. Footnotes are included for additional recognition. The author owes a debt of gratitude to the following:

Allis, Oswald T., *God Spake By Moses,* Presbyterian and Reformed Publishing Co, Nutley, NJ, 1972

Anderson, Bernhard W., *Understanding The Old Testament,* Prentice-Hall, Inc, Englewood Cliffs, New Jersey, 1957

Brier, Bob, *Great Pharaohs of Ancient Egypt* (transcript of class), The Teaching Company, Chantilly, Virginia, 2004

Brown, William, *The Tabernacle: Its Priests and Its Services,* Hendrickson Publishers, Inc., Peabody, Mass, 1996

Dobson, Kent, *Teachings of the Torah*, Zondervan, Grand Rapids, Michigan, 2014

Edersheim, Alfred, Bible *History Old Testament*, Hendrickson Publishers, Inc., Peabody, Massachusetts, 2009

Feiler, Bruce, *Walking The Bible*, HarperCollins Publishers, New York, 2002

Geisler, Norman L, *A Popular Survey of the Old Testament,* Grand Rapids, Baker Books, 1977

Grant, Michael, *The History of Ancient Israel,* Michael Grant Publications Limited, 1984

Harris, Katharine, *Nelson's Foundational Bible Dictionary,* Thomas Nelson, Nashville Tennessee, 2004

Harris, Stephen L., *Understanding the Bible,* The McGraw-Hill Companies, Inc., 2003

Hayford, Jack W., Thomas Nelson Publishers: *Hayford's Bible Handbook.* Nashville: Thomas Nelson Publishers, 1995

International Standard Bible Encyclopedia, revised edition, Copyright © 1979 by Wm. B. Eerdmans Publishing Co. All rights reserved.

Ironside, H. A., *Joshua,* Loizeaux Brothers, Neptune, New Jersey, 1950

Ironside, H. A., *Esther*, Loizeaux Brothers, Neptune, New Jersey, 1983

Jones, Floyd Nolen, *The Chronology of the Old Testament*, Master Books, Green Forest, AR, 1993

Keller, Werner, *The Bible As History,* Barnes & Noble, Inc., 1995

KJV Bible Commentary, Nashville: Thomas Nelson, 1997, 1994

MacArthur, John, *The MacArthur Bible Handbook.* Nashville, Tenn.: Thomas Nelson Publishers, 2003

MacArthur, John, *The MacArthur Study Bible: New American Standard Bible.* Nashville: Thomas Nelson Publishers, 2006

MacDonald, W., *Believer's Bible Commentary,* Thomas Nelson Publishers, Nashville, 1990

McDowell, Josh: *Josh McDowell's Handbook on Apologetics* electronic ed. Nashville: Thomas Nelson, 1997

McClintock and Strong Encyclopedia, Electronic Database. Copyright © 2000, 2003, 2005, 2006 by Biblesoft, Inc. All rights reserved

Mears, Henrietta, *What The Bible Is All About,* Regal Books/Gospel Light, Angus Hudson London, 1999

Nelson's Illustrated Bible Dictionary, Copyright © 1986, Thomas Nelson Publishers

New American Standard Bible: 1995 Update. LaHabra, CA : The Lockman Foundation, 1995

NIV Archaeological Study Bible, Copyright © 2005, Grand Rapids, Zondervan

The Pulpit Commentary, Electronic Database. Copyright © 2001, 2003, 2005, 2006 by Biblesoft, Inc.

Purkiser, W.T. Demaray, C.E., Metz, D.C., & Stuneck, M.A., *Exploring The Old Testament,* Beacon Hill Press, Kansas City, 1955

Radmacher, Earl D.; Allen, Ronald Barclay; House, H. Wayne: *The Nelson Study Bible: New King James Version.* Nashville: T. Nelson Publishers, 1997

Richards, Larry: *Every Name of God in the Bible.* Nashville, Tenn.: Thomas Nelson, 2001 (Everything in the Bible Series)

Schultz, Samuel J, Smith, Gary V, *Exploring The Old Testament*, Crossway Books, Wheaton ILL, 2001

Stedman, Ray C., *Adventuring Through the Bible,* Discovery House Publishers, Grand Rapids, MI, 1997

Swindoll, Charles, *Job,* Copyright © 2004 Charles R. Swindoll, Inc., The W Publishing Group, Nashville

Thomas Nelson Publishers: *Nelson's Complete Book of Bible Maps & Charts: Old and New Testaments.* Rev. and updated ed. Nashville, Tenn.: Thomas Nelson, 1996

Ussher, James, *The Annals of the World*, 1658

Vine, W. E.; Unger, Merrill F.; White, William: *Vine's Complete Expository Dictionary of Old and New Testament Words.* Nashville: T. Nelson, 1996

Vos, H. F. (1999). *Nelson's new illustrated Bible manners & customs: How the people of the Bible really lived* (1). Nashville, Tenn.: T. Nelson Publishers.

Willmington, Harold L., *Willmington's Guide to the Bible*, Tyndale House Publishers, Inc., Carol Stream, Illinois, 1984

Wilkinson, B., & Boa, K., *Talk thru the Bible*, Nashville: T. Nelson, 1983

SECTION 1

Foundational Matters

ONE

Why Study the Bible?

1   A few remarks are appropriate concerning The Bible.

1.1. The Bible is the greatest, most unique book ever in existence.

1.2. All of it was breathed and birthed, by God. This is the foundation for this volume, *Travel Through The Old Testament.*

1.3. During this journey together, we will discover information about the contents of the Bible. Keep in mind, it is not the information, tables, and commentary presented, or even the instructor of a course, which gives direction to your life—rather it is your personal meditation in His Word along with a personal relationship to Him.

    1.3.1.   Keep at the forefront, the Bible *"is living and powerful"* (Heb 4:12).

    1.3.2.   Know that the Bible is *"a lamp"* to light where you are standing and a *"light"* to show you the way (Psalms 119:105).

1.4. There are hours of teaching, which could be presented concerning the Bible's uniqueness. This is not an all-inclusive attempt on the subject. In addition, the following thoughts are included as additional information to be used in your personal study. See the paragraph, "The Bible As a Book."

2   The following two assumptions are made as we begin this journey together.

2.1. One, you accept The Bible as His Word; (this name Bible comes from the Greek BIBLOS meaning book); so THIS book is called THE BOOK. How unique! No other writing in existence would dare claim such a name as THE BOOK. Therefore, we will understand that you accept the Bible as the inspired Word of God. Every word, every little jot and miniscule "mark," is breathed from God.

2.2. Two, we also move ahead with the understanding that you are a student who wants to LEARN—particularly about the Old Testament or Old Covenant. This is a study course, not to be entered with a casual manner or attitude. Discipline, which takes a great amount of effort, will be required in order to "graduate" with a new understanding of the Old Testament. Not all your questions will be answered in this journey, but if you stay with it, and do some homework, it will be a fulfilling journey that will help you the rest of your life.

3   With those two assumptions, we will proceed as though it we are in an entry-level college course. Perhaps you will see for the first time in your life, the great continuity of this exciting, true, and adventurous history.

3.1. This work is a journey through thirty-nine books, which make up the Jewish and Protestant Old Testament books. In addition, the additional books considered by Roman Catholics, will be considered.

3.2. This book is uniquely written in a "loose" outline form, because it is my life-long technique personally used for quick, simple reading. Generally (but not consistently), it is written using short statements, not long, eloquent sentences.

3.3. Included in this course are a variety of unique helps to assist in making your journey more beneficial:

    3.3.1.   *Key Words* to assist in understanding the Hebrew meaning.

    3.3.2.   *Author's Study Notes*, included in text and/or footnotes on each appropriate page.

    3.3.3.   *Jesus in each Book.* At the beginning of each Old Testament Book, you will be directed to Him.

    3.3.4.   The author has chosen to utilize the best available date for many events in the Bible, including the date of composition and actual period covered throughout each book. He uses the now accepted CE (Common Era) and BCE (Before the Common Era) in place of A.D. and B.C.

    3.3.5.   The author generally uses the appropriate abbreviation when referring to a Bible Book (e.g. Gen for Genesis).

    3.3.6.   *Expanded Help Papers* on various Bible topics are included for detail study.

    3.3.7.   *Depth of Bible Words and Places*.

    3.3.8.   Simplified/basic Outline of each Old Testament Book.

3.4. On a personal note, over 3,500 study and research hours have been invested in this work towards your growth in His Word. *"Study to show yourself approved...."* (2 Timothy 2:15).

The Bible As A Book (The Uniqueness of The Bible)

4   It's astounding, as you understand this. Perhaps you have looked at this before or read about it, however, it will always be a revelation,

no matter how often you review it, and is presented as the foundation of for this study.

4.1. Some have said "It's just another book" or "It's a book with some great teaching in it."

4.2. There are some believers who still question, "Is it God's Word?" or "How can I know for sure?"

4.3. We recognize the simplest way is to believe by faith. However, you can 'know that you know that you know' the Bible is the very Words of God! We have some facts, other than our faith, to KNOW this!

4.4. There are colleges and universities, even Christian by reputation, which do not believe in this Book. However, if any institution of learning would consider the evidence, would surely conclude that its authenticity and divine author make it not only unique, but also authentic.

4.5. If we would allow the Bible back into our schools, our nation would reverse its spiritual free-fall. Teaching this course—not as a forced religion—rather as a course about a book, would assist in a spiritual transformation.

    4.5.1.   It is a fact that a professor spent 42 years studying sacred Eastern books, comparing them to the Bible. His conclusion?

    4.5.2.   *"Pile them all up, if you will, on the left side of your study table; but place your own Holy Bible on the right side---all by itself, all alone and with a wide gap between them. For.... there is a great gulf between the Bible and the sacred books of the East which severs the one from the other utterly, hopelessly, and forever....a veritable gulf which cannot be bridged over by any science of religious thought."*[1]

    4.5.3.   Webster had to have had the Bible in mind when he penned down the definition for "unique." We take words for granted. We should examine this one closely. UNIQUE: 1. The One and only; single; sole. 2. Different from all others; having no like or equal.

4.6. The Bible truly is unique because of several factors. Thanks to Josh McDowell for much of the following information, which I have condensed along with some personal and updated material. I recommend his classic book.

THE BIBLE IS UNIQUE BECAUSE OF ITS CONTINUITY

---

[1] Quoted from *The New Evidence That Demands a Verdict*, Here's Life Publishers, 1972, p. 4

5   Written over a span of sixteen hundred years, from Genesis written about as early as 1600 BCE to Revelation and 3 John written around 96 CE.

5.1. Written over sixty generations.

5.2. Written by at least forty authors from every occupation.

    5.2.1.   Kings, peasants, philosophers, fishermen, poets, political leaders, scholars...on and on.

    5.2.2.   Moses trained in the great universities of Egypt, a political leader of his day.

    5.2.3.   Peter, that quick responder, with a hot temper, a fisherman.

    5.2.4.   Amos a herdsman.

    5.2.5.   Joshua, a military general.

    5.2.6.   Jeremiah a cupbearer.

    5.2.7.   Daniel, the prime minister.

    5.2.8.   Luke, a doctor.

    5.2.9.   Solomon, a king.

    5.2.10.   Matthew a tax collector.

    5.2.11.   And of course Paul, a Rabbi, brilliant scholar, and persecutor of Christians.

5.3. Written in different locations.

    5.3.1.   Moses in a wilderness.

    5.3.2.   Jeremiah in a dungeon.

    5.3.3.   Daniel on a hillside and in a palace.

    5.3.4.   Paul wrote from inside prison walls.

    5.3.5.   Luke while traveling.

    5.3.6.   John while exiled on the isle of Patmos.

    5.3.7.   Others while on military campaigns.

5.4. David wrote in time of war, Solomon wrote in times of peace.

5.5. Written on three continents, Asia, Africa, and Europe.

5.6. Written in three languages,

    5.6.1.   Hebrew, which eleven Kings called "The language of Judah."

    5.6.2.   A few portions in Aramaic, for a specific reason, a language of that day in the area written, and which evolved into Greek.

    5.6.3.   And, of course, the New Testament in Greek.

5.7. Consider the following additional story related by Josh McDowell:

    5.7.1.   A representative of the Great Books of the Western world was about to interview Josh McDowell to write a series for that organization. He spent five minutes talking about the great books of the western world.

5.7.2.　　　Josh challenged the man to take just ten authors, all from one walk of life, one generation, one place, one time, one mood, on one continent, writing in one language, and concerning just one controversial subject (the Bible speaks on hundreds with harmony and agreement).

5.7.3.　　　Then Josh asked him, "Would they agree"? The man paused and replied "Of course not." "What would you have?" And immediately the man replied "A conglomeration."

5.7.4.　　　Two days later, the man committed his life to Jesus, the theme of the Bible.[1]

THE BIBLE IS UNIQUE BECAUSE OF ITS CIRCULATION

6　The Bible has been read by more people and published in more languages than any other book ever printed.

6.1. More copies of the Bible have been produced, either in its entirety or in portions, than any other book in history.

6.1.1.　　　For example, the top selling books of all time include Don Quixote and The hobbit, each selling over 100 million copies. The Da Vinci Code, 80 million; the top six books in the Harry Potter series have sold 450 millions. The Bible has sold at least 3.9 billion copies.

6.2. The Bible was even the very first book ever printed! It was called the Latin Vulgate, printed on Gutenberg's press.

6.3. It was reported that in 1998, just one Bible society and its members, were responsible for distributing 20.8 million complete Bibles and another 20.1 million Testaments (Old or New). When portions of Scripture and extracts on particular themes are included, the total distribution of copies of the Bible or portions reached a staggering 585 million! (That's in a single year, by a single group). In 2014, 34 million full Bibles were distributed around the world just by Bible Societies.

6.4. Most books are never translated into another language. Among the books, which are translated, most of them are published in perhaps two or three languages.

6.4.1.　　　The Bible, or portions of it, has been translated into more than 2,200 languages, making it available to 90 percent of the world's population (www. biblesociety.org). No other book has been translated more than the Bible. Billions of copies are in

---

[1] Ibid, p. 7

circulation. See this author's *Partial History of the Written Word* in this volume.

6.4.2.   Around 250 BCE, the Hebrew Old Testament was translated into Greek (Septuagint) making it one of the first books translated. This was for Greek-speaking Jews in Alexandria who could no longer read Hebrew.

6.4.3.   Wycliffe Bible Translators has over six thousand people working with more than 850 different languages in fifty countries to produce different or revised versions.

6.4.4.   No other book in history comes close to comparing with the Bible in its translation activity.

THE BIBLE IS UNIQUE BECAUSE OF ITS SURVIVAL

7   First written on perishable materials, then copied and recopied for hundreds of years before the printing press, the Scriptures have never faced extinction.

7.1. No other ancient writing has more manuscript evidence of support. The Jews were given the responsibility to preserve God's Word—and then did it! Thank you.

7.2. Jews preserved the writings like no other manuscript. A special class of men within their culture had the duty of preserving these documents with absolute fidelity.

7.2.1.   The Masoretes counted the letters, syllables, and words to assure accuracy. If there was any difference, the work was destroyed. Whoever did this concerning the works of Plato or Shakespeare?

7.2.2.   Many enemies tried to burn, ban, or outlaw it, from the days of Rome to the present day of anti-Godly nations. Every copy of the Bible was ordered destroyed by fire in 303 CE by the Emperor of Rome, Diocletian.

7.2.2.1.   It is ironic, that twenty-five years later, Roman emperor Constantine ordered that fifty copies of the Scriptures be prepared at the government's expense!

7.2.3.   The Bible's enemies come and go, but the Bible stands. It is the most important single vehicle of our lives even above His Name (Psalms 138:2); Jesus said it will not pass away (Mark 13:31).

THE BIBLE IS UNIQUE BECAUSE OF ITS INFLUENCE

8   Cleland B. McAfee writes in *The Greatest English Classic:* "If every Bible in any considerable city were destroyed, the Book could be restored in all its essential parts from the quotations on the shelves of the city public library."

9   No other book in human history has inspired so many other books as the Bible. Its pervasive influence on western thought is undeniable.

9.1. Many literary texts draw on the Bible as its source of thought.

9.2. It also has had a great influence on the social and ethical plane, and on literary creation.

9.3. It has certainly had its impact on civilization.

9.4. The Bible presents the highest ideals known to man, ideals that have molded civilization.

9.4.1.   Introduce the Bible to any nation, tribe, or community, and in time that society will be influenced for good.

9.4.2.   It is no wonder entire denominations or other groups have as one of the primary goals, to distribute copies of His Word.

9.5. Theodore Roosevelt said, "A thorough knowledge of the Bible is worth more than a college education."

9.6. Napoleon Bonaparte said, "The Bible is more than a book, it is a living being with an action, a power, which invades everything."

10   These remarkable credentials of the Bible do not prove that it is true, but they do mean that it deserves serious consideration. Any sincere seeker after truth should look into this book for answers to the ultimate questions of existence. This course, Travel *Through the Old Testament,* will supplement your study of this unique "Book."

TWO

Structure of the Old Testament

1   Over the years, several stages in development of structure for the Old Testament, has taken place.
 1.1. The earliest and most basic structure was a two-fold format. The first five books were *The Law of Moses*, naming them after the great lawgiver of Israel. They are generally referred to as the *Torah* or Pentateuch (see cp THREE in this volume). All the other books were called *The Prophets*. This is one of the ways the New Testament refers to the Old Testament.
   1.1.1.   Matthew 5:17 *Do not think that I came to abolish the Law or the Prophets.*
   1.1.2.   Matthew 7:12 *In everything, therefore, treat people the same way you want them to treat you, for this is the Law and the Prophets.*
   1.1.3.   Matthew 22:40 *On these two commandments depend the whole Law and the Prophets.*
   1.1.4.   In the Old Testament Scriptures, there was a distinction made between the writings of "Moses" and "the Prophets."
      1.1.4.1.   Daniel writes in 9:11-13 *Indeed all Israel has transgressed Your law and turned aside, not obeying Your voice; so the curse has been poured out on us, along with the oath which is written in the law of Moses the servant of God, for we have sinned against Him. As it is written in the Law of Moses.*
      1.1.4.2.   Nehemiah 9:29-30 distinguishes between the two: *And admonished them in order to turn them back to Your law. Yet they acted arrogantly and did not listen to Your commandments 30 However, You bore with them for many years, And admonished them by Your Spirit through Your prophets.*
      1.1.4.3.   Zechariah 7:12 mentions *they could not hear the law and the words...by His Spirit through the former prophets.*
 1.2. We add that all the thirty-nine of the books with which we are familiar, were in this two-fold division. We are confident of that.

1.3. Jesus and the New Testament writers mention each of the accepted Old Testament books, other than Judges, Chronicles, Esther, and Song of Solomon. We also have fragments of thirty-eight (all the Old Testament except Esther), from The Dead Sea Scrolls. Therefore, from the first two-fold division we know we have all of His Word, which He destined us to have.

2. A three-fold structure developed in early Jewish circles and is used to this day.

2.1. The first division is the *Torah* comprising the five books of Moses (Genesis, Exodus, Leviticus, Numbers, and Deuteronomy).

2.2. The second division is *Prophets*, further subdivided into the four Former Prophets (Joshua, Judges, Samuel, and Kings), and the four Latter Prophets (Isaiah, Jeremiah, Ezekiel, and the Book of the Twelve Prophets). Also, the Latter Prophets were categorized in two groups, the "major" Prophets (Isaiah, Jeremiah, and Ezekiel), and the Twelve Minor Prophets collected into a single book.

2.3. The third division is called *Writings* comprising eleven books (Psalms, Proverbs, Job, Song of Songs, Ruth, Lamentations, Ecclesiastes, Esther, Daniel, Ezra-Nehemiah, and Chronicles. This is the arrangement regularly followed in printed editions of the Hebrew Bible.

2.4. Generally, the *Prophets* books were written by men holding a prophetic "office." The men who wrote inspired books, who had a "gift of prophecy" but not the office, David, Solomon, and Daniel, were listed in the third section called Writings.

THE SCRIPTURES OF THE JEWS

The Torah or Law (5)	The Prophets		The Writings (11)
	Former (4)	Latter (4)	
Genesis	Joshua	Isaiah	Psalms
Exodus	Judges	Jeremiah	Proverbs
Leviticus	Samuel	Ezekiel	Job
Numbers	Kings	12 Minor	Ruth
Deuteronomy			Song of Songs
			Lamentations
			Ecclesiastes
			Esther
			Daniel
			Ezra-Nehemiah
			Chronicles

2.5. The historian Josephus, writing in the first century CE used this three-fold division. Also, Jesus used this one time: Luke 24:44-45

> *"These are My words which I spoke to you while I was still with you, that all things which are written about Me in the Law of Moses and the Prophets and the Psalms must be fulfilled."*

3.   One more additional structure followed, one in which we use in most of our Bible studies in our day.

3.1. When the Hebrew was translated into Greek around 250 BCE, called the *Septuagint*, all the Old Testament books were rearranged according to subject matter.

      3.1.1.   It expanded the structure to four divisions. History and Wisdom were new categories. From the Septuagint forward, this four-fold structure was accepted. In 400 CE when the Hebrew was translated into Latin (The Latin Vulgate), the four-fold structure was used again.

OLD TESTAMENT STRUCTURE

LAW (5)	HISTORY (12)	WISDOM (5)	MAJOR PROPHETS (5)	MINOR PROPHETS (12)
Genesis	Joshua	Job	Isaiah	Hosea
Exodus	Judges	Psalms	Jeremiah	Joel
Leviticus	Ruth	Proverbs	Lamentations	Amos
Numbers	1 Samuel	Ecclesiastes	Ezekiel	Obadiah
Deuteronomy	2 Samuel	Song of Solomon	Daniel	Jonah
	1 Kings			Micah
	2 Kings			Nahum
	1 Chronicles			Habakkuk
	2 Chronicles			Zephaniah
	Ezra			Haggai
	Nehemiah			Zechariah
	Esther			Malachi

3.2. For this current study, *Travel Through The Old Testament*, the Prophets are divided into Major and Minor (the accepted structure has them combined).

3.3. Note that all thirty-nine books in our English Bibles are the same content as the twenty-four books used by Christ and identical to the earliest two-fold structure.

Depth of Bible Words and Locations
Canon of Scripture

A measuring rod or standard for books included in the Bible. The thirty-nine books of the Old Testament are historically accepted as meeting the standard. (Note there are also twenty-seven books accepted in the New Testament).

EXPANDED HELP PAPER
The Septuagint

The Septuagint, the standard Greek translation of the Old Testament, was composed to meet the needs of Greek-speaking Jews in Egypt during the Hellenistic period. This large Jewish community was concentrated in the city of Alexandria. The Jewish leaders located there began to translate the Old Testament into Greek in the third century BCE, completing their labor of love approximately in 132 BCE.

The standardized Greek text became known as the Septuagint (Greek for "seventy"). The Septuagint is often abbreviated LXX, the Roman-numeral notation for seventy. According to tradition, the Septuagint was prepared by seventy-two learned Jews during a seventy-day period, each working separately. The Lord so honored their effort, tradition goes, that when the scholars met, their translations were identical in every respect. However, in reality, the LXX took several centuries to complete, and as a translation, it varies in quality. Some parts are faithful renderings of the Hebrew, other parts are less so. In places, it seems to diverge from the Masoretic text. *The Masoretic Text* is the authoritative Hebrew and Aramaic text of the Tanakh or Jewish three-fold structure of the Scriptures. The entire work included the thirty-nine books, plus the books known in English as Deuterocanonical ("second canon"). Deuterocanonical is used to describe books not included in the Jewish Canon.

The importance of the LXX is that it is an ancient witness to the text of the Old Testament. Even in those places where the text differs from the Masoretic text, the percentage of difference is not great, and the differences do not represent significant changes in meaning.

Establishing the Journey

4. To emphasize the previous thought, the Old Testament is a collection of thirty-nine inspired books written in Hebrew (with only a few passages written in Aramaic)[1]

---

[1] Those include Jeremiah 10:11; Daniel 2:4-7:28; and two passages in Ezra, 4:8-6:18 and 7:12-26.

4.1. They were written by Prophets, Priests and many others over a period of 1,600 years. Refer to the previous notes on "The Uniqueness of the Bible" for additional detail concerning the writing of the Bible.

4.2. The Bible is the most unique book, in many ways, ever written. We can be absolutely sure, we have ALL of His Word, and nothing has been lost! God gave us, and preserved the exact material He planned.[1]

4.3. As we "travel-through" these thirty-nine books we will discover (or expand our thinking) on this magnificent story. The thirty second survey would look like this:

    4.3.1.   Creation of the universe

    4.3.2.   Fall of man

    4.3.3.   Judgment flood

    4.3.4.   Fathers of a chosen nation

    4.3.5.   History of that nation

    4.3.6.   430 years of exile in Egypt

    4.3.7.   40 years of wandering

    4.3.8.   Conquering of Canaan in 7 years

    4.3.9.   300 years of judges

    4.3.10.   United kingdom of three kings, 120 years

    4.3.11.   350 years of divided kingdoms

    4.3.12.   Followed by another exile, this one lasting 70 years

    4.3.13.   Concluding with a rebuilding of the nation over 140 years.

4.4. I personally use the five-fold structure, slightly expanded from the accepted four-fold structure mentioned earlier.

    4.4.1.   Five books of the Law, or Torah; the Pentateuch

    4.4.2.   Twelve books of history

    4.4.3.   Five books of wisdom

    4.4.4.   Five major prophets

    4.4.5.   Twelve Minor Prophets[2]

4.5. We also accept that ALL Scripture has but one theme.[3]

4.6. Everything revealed in Scripture, is associated with this theme. We accept,

    4.6.1.   There is one God

---

[1] We acknowledge the existence of many other excellent works, some entitled Apocryphal books. However, no books other than the thirty-nine (the same twenty-four of the Jewish Bible) are accepted as the divine canon of Scripture.

[2] Refer to the earlier chart which shows both the five categories used today and the three original categories used by the Jews.

[3] That theme is: "God has chosen to create and gather to Himself and for His glory a group of people to be His Kingdom, to praise and honor Him, and to serve Him forever."

4.6.2. The Bible has one Creator

4.6.3. The Bible is one book, "the Book"

4.6.4. The Bible has one plan of grace

5. Refer to the *Chronology of Old Testament History* in the Appendix, which is the author's conclusion and compilation of dates. He began with the dates of known events and established other dates to the extent of his research. The author accepts that an indefinite space of time intervened between the original creation of earth and the earth described in Gen 1:2. The author begins his dates with v2.

5.1. Absolute Chronology?

5.2. We of course know of very few "absolutes." Concerning many Biblical and historical events, there can only be "the most thought-out date which one concludes." This author used established dates from both the Scriptures and many other reliable ancient manuscripts. It is his conclusion that the Hebrew writers, directed by the Holy Spirit, and having access to the necessary oral and written records, generally preserved the exact dates for their history. The author of this volume established his foundation of dates, from the unbroken line of absolute dated events within the Scriptures. It is vital for every Christian to have a reliable chronology for his (her) study.

5.3. Several sources were considered in this compilation of both Biblical and historical events. Special mention is made of the most reliable chronologies of James Ussher[1], and Floyd Nolen Jones.[2] Many other works, too numerous to mention, were reviewed. It is well to note that several of the recent chronological charts, as well as a few of the chronologies reviewed, have in error established dates, which are contradicted upon a close study of the Scriptures.

5.4. The author's Chronology presented in this volume is his independent work. However, the results are highly dependent on Ussher's chronology. Ussher's dates have been slightly revised because of research and study of other methods of calculation.

5.5. Finally, a note concerning James Ussher, learned Archbishop of Armagh - the highest position in the Irish Anglican Church - scholar and historian of the first rank. He was one of the greatest scholars and theologians of his time. In his enduring search for knowledge, he travelled widely in Britain and Europe, seeking the earliest available manuscripts, buying those he could, and copying others. After his death, his extensive and valuable library formed the nucleus of the

---

[1] *The Annals of the World*, James Ussher, Archbishop of Armagh, 1658

[2] *The Chronology of the Old Testament*, Dr. Floyd Nolen Jones, Master Books, Green Forest AR, 1993

great library of Trinity College, Dublin. He had entered Trinity at age 13 where he prepared his detailed Hebrew chronology in Latin at age 15. No one could match him in debate. He was given a magnificent state funeral in Westminster Abbey where his epitaph reads, "Among scholars he was the most saintly, among saints the most scholarly."

5.5.1.   His research on biblical and secular world history, was incorporated into his *The Annals of the World*. He established the first day of creation as Sunday 23 October 4004 BCE. Other dates that he calculated included, Adam and Eve were driven from Paradise on Monday November 10 4004 BCE, and that Noah's Ark touched down on Mt Ararat on May 5 2348 BCE, "on a Wednesday." An authorized version of the Bible printed in 1701, incorporating his Annals, came to be regarded with almost as much unquestioning reverence as the Bible itself. To our current day, his dates are accepted by many scholars. However, during the mid twentieth century, proponents of evolution and textual criticism attacked the chronology foundation of Scripture. Dr. Floyd Nolan Jones notes that "this assault has resulted in clouding the minds of the human race against the veracity and accuracy of the Holy Writ and, subsequently, to God's claims on the lives of all mankind."[1]

5.5.2.   Again, it is stated; the author of this volume accepts the foundational dates in the Scriptures as Truth and uses them for the skeleton of his chronology. Ussher and Floyd Nolen Jones are most reliable in this topic of chronology. **See Chronology of Old Testament History, APPENDIX.**

---

[1] Ibid, p. iii

THREE

Old Testament History of Israel

1   The history of the Old Testament is one of my favorite personal areas of study. In this course, I will share considerable material and reference notes on the subject, in particular concerning God's chosen people/nation.

1.1. The Old Testament contains an outline of the history of Israel divided into clear segments of time, all of which we will review in this volume. We review the first period in the first five books, which are called the Pentateuch (see further detail on this unit, later in this chapter). The Pentateuch deals with the time before God's people settled in the land of Canaan.

1.1.1.   These first books are subdivided into definite periods of time, and we will see each of these periods.

1.1.1.1.   First, we find the 'patriarchs', who lived in the land of Canaan, before God's nation was recognized. (Gen. 12-50). Four of these patriarchs are detailed in our review of Genesis and are referred to as Four Great Men.

1.1.1.2.   Beginning in Exodus, we then review the period of a stay in Egypt followed by the Exodus from slavery (Ex. 1-15). The time of wandering in the wilderness follows (Ex. 16-18; Num. 10, 11-20, which is interrupted by the stay on Sinai (Ex.19:1-Num. 10:10). Finally the occupation of Transjordan, which is the land east of the Jordan River (Num.20:14-21.35). This entire history is prior to the crossing of the Jordan (Num.22-36).

1.1.1.3.   Deuteronomy then is presented almost as a separate book, (some believe even with a separate author—see JEDP theory). This was Moses' last instructions before entering the Promised Land

1.1.2.　　　The Scriptures then continue with the history of Israel **IN** its land. The book of Joshua is the occupation of the land and its division into tribes. The book of Judges depicts the first period after the settlement which tells of the loss of unity in leadership following the death of Joshua, a period of various judges.

1.1.3.　　　The books of Samuel begin another period, in that Saul is appointed king, (1 Sam. 1-15) followed by the monarchy passing over to David, which most of the two books of Samuel are devoted (1 Sam. 16-1 Kings 1).

1.1.4.　　　The first period of the monarchy ends with the death of Solomon (1 Kings 1-11).

1.2. The second phase of history opens with the division of the kingdom into two parts. Two nations are formed, Israel (ten tribes, northern kingdom) and Judah (two tribes, southern kingdom), sometimes at peace, other times in war. This period continues to the time when the northern kingdom was destroyed by the Assyrians in 721 BCE (1 Kings 12-2 Kings 17).

1.3. The last stage of the history of the state of Judah ends with the capture of Jerusalem, the destruction of the temple and the deportation of part of the population to exile in Babylon (2 Kings 18-25). We will visit each of these three periods of History in this survey volume.

1.4. At this period in Old Testament history, the Hebrew Bible breaks off with the books of Chronicles. These *review* the history from the beginning of the monarchy to the destruction of Jerusalem from a different perspective.

1.5. They end by reporting that Cyrus king of the Persians proclaimed the rebuilding of the temple in Jerusalem and allowed the Israelites to return to their own home (2 Chron. 36:22). The book of Ezra begins this way. There is no *detailed* account of the period of exile in Babylon. We no longer have a consecutive account for the following period, but only reports of the rebuilding of the temple (Ezra 3-6) and the comparatively brief periods of the activity of Ezra and Nehemiah (in the books which bear their names).

Pentateuch

2　Our travel through the Old Testament will begin by focusing on the first five books, the Pentateuch, as a unit.

3　Background material could fill several volumes. Since our purpose in this work is to "travel through" the individual books of the Old Testament, we will not cover the details concerning the method of gathering and establishing the canon. Nor will we detail each of the authors of the thirty-nine Christian books (or twenty-four Hebrew books, the TaNaKH). Neither is it our intent to include how the individual books were written, accepted into a canon, or the fact that many similar ancient books were rejected. These topics are each detailed in the author's book *The Essence of Christian Belief.*

4   However, we do need to offer an overview of the first five books of Scripture, as a unit. The Pentateuch or Torah was always the possession of all Israel. Even as they were dispersed to several areas of the world and took on elements of those societies. For example, a large group went North and brought in elements of Greek culture, a second group stayed East, never returning to Jerusalem, absorbing a Babylonian culture, and a third larger group gathered south in Egypt along the southern Mediterranean, especially in Alexandria. However, each of the groups still held the Torah as THEIR book. They somewhat always had "ownership."

4.1. The Torah was addressed to the entire people, who were to learn its contents and teach them diligently to their children. They were to read it publically when they assembled. For many years, the Torah (Pentateuch) alone was Israel's Bible. Just before Israel's move into the Promised Land, Moses established the process in which public reading would make its way into the hearts of people. Consider Deut 31:12 from a very literal translation,[1] *Assemble the men, women, and children, as well as the foreigners who live in your cities. Have them listen and learn to fear* <u>*Yahweh your Elohim*</u> *and faithfully obey every word of these teachings.* Amazing translation, *learn to fear* your personal God *Yahweh* and your God of power, *Elohim.* Two of God's revealed names, together. In addition, I note that these two names of God, used separately in various Scriptures, do NOT indicate two different authors, rather the identification of the characteristics of Yahweh.

4.2. Briefly on this, there were three separate *main* names of God revealed in the Old Testament. Those were Elohim, Yahweh, and Adonai'. Two of them are mentioned in the Deut 31:12 passage above.

4.2.1.   *Elohim* was the first of God's names, introduced in Gen 1:1 *"In the beginning, Elohim created..."* Elohim is the God of power, creator. Nothing existed as far as we know, except Elohim. Elohim then created. That name appears over 2100 times.

---

[1]Spangler, Ann, *The Names of God Bible,* Baker Publishing Group, Grand Rapids, MI, 2011

4.2.2.　　　Then *Yahweh*. We have that name in Gen 2:4 and all the way through Gen 2 as He started to reveal His personal name along with His name of power. I find it interesting to find that it was *Yahweh Elohim* who formed Adam and made Eve, who walked with them in the garden; and it is quite revealing that Satan always used the name *Elohim* in his conversation with Eve, never the personal name of Yahweh. *Yahweh* is found some 5200 times; more than all His other names combined! It is designated *LORD* in many English Bibles.

4.2.3.　　　Adonai', the third name, is the Owner of all things, found 137 times in the Old Testament. Designated in our English translations as *Lord*.

4.3. The Book of Nehemiah (cps 8-10 reports a public reading of the Torah in Jerusalem, probably in the year 444 BCE (Before the Common Era). This reading was conducted by Ezra the Scribe, with the aid of assistants who were to make sure that all those present, heard and understood what was read to them. A few days later, the entire people entered into a solemn undertaking to obey the Torah; this agreement was ratified in writing by the leaders. This reading is understood to be the event marking the completion of the written Torah in its present form. It also served as the event recognizing the Torah as the official "constitution" of the Jewish community.

4.4. The Pentateuch is vital to all of us, so I emphasize its importance, as a unit. There is a study commentary called *The Believer's Bible Commentary*,[1] a single volume but very valuable work. The writer makes this comment: *"Since the whole Old Testament, in fact the whole Bible is based on these first five books, the importance of the Pentateuch—can hardly be overstated."* Merrill Unger puts this very bluntly: *"The foundation of all revealed truth and of God's redemptive plan is based on the Pentateuch."*

4.4.1.　　　There are a few published, single volumes written on the Pentateuch, but at the same time, there are probably more volumes on Genesis and Exodus, as individual books, than any of the other thirty-seven Old Testament works. Even the most recent study Bibles include very little on the Pentateuch; most start with only Genesis. In fact, not one of my favorite study bibles has anything on the Pentateuch.

4.4.2.　　　The term *Pentateuch* comes from two Greek words *Penta* "five" and *teuchos* meaning "scroll." Originally, the word

---

[1] MacDonald, W., & Farstad, A. 1997, c1995. *Believer's Bible Commentary : Old and New Testaments* . Thomas Nelson: Nashville

had the meaning of "a five-scrolled (book). We also refer to these books as "Torah," which means "instruction."

4.4.3.   William Macdonald in the before mentioned *Believer's Bible Commentary* offers this:

"The Pentateuch is an essential introduction to the entire word of God. It opens up that which is afterwards unfolded."[1]

4.4.4.   These first five books in our Bible have several names when spoken of as a unit. We refer to them with "The Pentateuch." We could also refer to them as the "Book of The Law," the "Five Rolls" or as "Torah." At various times and locations they were referred to as "The Scrolls" or "the Books of Moses." I've also heard them called "Five Books of Torah." All correct, and generally refer to these five books.

4.4.5.   We would note Josh 8:34 *Joshua read all the words of the law;* 2 Chron 17:9 refers to *The Book of the Law of the Lord*. In addition, from the New Testament, Matt 12:5 *Or haven't you read in the Law...;* Luke 2:23 *....as it is written in the Law of the Lord;* Gal 3:10 *The Book of the Law*. While we cannot be positive that each of these Scriptures identifies the same five books and those only, we can have confidence with this conclusion.

    4.4.5.1.   An added note, not to confuse, rather to expand our understanding, "Torah" can have a very "broad" meaning. It can refer, to the entire Old Testament as well as the Hebrew traditions on law, and the Oral Law. The use of "Torah" isn't always specific enough. However, in most references, Torah refers to the five Hebrew scrolls, the Pentateuch.

    4.4.5.2.   I recently read of a woman living in Israel (actually the town of Bethel). She was asked why her family left America and moved to Israel. Her reply made it clear: *"We came here because God gave us this land. All of us stood at Sinai as a Jewish people, and we responded to God, 'we accept the Torah'."*

4.4.6.   These books, which were the very first divinely authored collection of Scripture, unveil God's plan, which never changed. We really should call the Pentateuch, *The Biography of Moses,* for it is his life, and how God directed him, which is detailed in these books.

4.4.7.   Practically every important Old Testament idea is introduced somewhere in the first five books of the Bible.

4.5. Let's look at the extent of time covered in these five books. Together, these books report history from the beginning of the earth to the time just prior to the Jews entering the Promised Land, about 2750 years of history. They conclude with the death of Moses. 2369 of those years is covered in the fifty cps of Genesis, while Exodus continues with the story in Egypt and advances by 400 years to Mt Sinai. 2700 years of history are reviewed in two books.

4.5.1.   Then comes Leviticus, similar length in pages, but covers a one-month period between Exodus and the next book, Numbers, Numbers goes from Mt Sinai to the end of the forty years of wilderness.

4.5.2.   Deuteronomy kind of back traces, taking place during the eleven months spent at Mt Sinai and tells of the final two months of Moses' life. The books are certainly uneven in the time covered.

4.5.3.   From the very time of the sin of Adam and Eve God began to give predictions of the coming Savior. I look at this as somewhat being hidden from Satan, but revealed to His own people. On various occasions, God would give new revelations of the line of descendants through which Christ would come. And Genesis will be vital in our understanding and tracing this. The blood is like a crimson chord running through the Old Testament

4.5.4.   The continuous story told in these five books was written on one long scroll, as early as the first century CE. Before that, the story was several smaller scrolls.

4.5.5.   In Genesis, the book opens with the history of creation, by God's breath and words—next the fall and judgment. God chose a man Abraham, his son Isaac, his grandson Jacob, and then Jacob's 12 sons, to be the channel through which He would bless the whole world. He made a covenant promise to His people. God's ultimate plan never changed. He did not decide to do something different as difficulties arose, or problems got in the way.

4.5.5.1.   God prepared Joseph to preserve His people, paving the way for a great deliverance.

4.5.6.   In Exodus, the chosen nation is in bondage; and the fullness of all that God is, (Ex 6 begins with Elohim speaking to Moses and tells him, "I am *Yahweh, I* appeared to Abraham and Isaac and Jacob as *El Shaddai.*" God goes on and says *"but I didn't make myself KNOWN to them by name."* This almighty one, revealed Himself to Abram, as *El Shaddai* first in Gen 17:1, and then 47 more times, 31 of those in Job. *El Shaddai* is the Almighty One; nothing is impossible with *El Shaddai*. A literal translation is God, "the Mountain One." Most of the gods of the ancient world were associated with mountains, so our God reveals that He made the mountains.

    4.5.6.1.   Exodus reveals how God took a giant step towards redemption. *Yahweh* chose Moses to deliver Israel from slavery. It records the escape of the Israelites and concludes with the cloud of the LORD, which led the people through the wilderness, and then descends upon the newly constructed tabernacle. The sign of God's presence would be the Ark of the Covenant.

4.5.7.   Leviticus, during an eleven-month period, expands the covenant law for this newly sanctified people in order to share in their new relationship. How can my people be holy, as I am holy? That theme is repeated over and over. From the cloud of God's Glory on the tabernacle, God summons Moses to the tent; And He presents to him the law. The law taught the Israelites how to approach God and how to live a healthy life.

    4.5.7.1.   Leviticus concludes with God's words *These are the commandments which Yahweh gave Moses on Mount Sinai, for the Israelites.*

4.5.8.   Numbers adds many more guidelines and regulations, for they needed instruction. These were His people, who in deed were to be different; not like the people they would meet in the Promised Land. He guides them through a wilderness on their way to a promised land. Day by day by day, He used a cloud, which was a speckle of His glory. The times when we view His light, are all a glimpse of glory.

    4.5.8.1.   Numbers begins with God commissioning Moses at the tabernacle, to take a census to prepare for war. It is easy to see where Numbers gets its name, for cp 1 and cp 26 offers an exact count of military eligible men, over 600,000 of them. Twelve tribes were bound for the Promised Land, but blood will be shed, so the army must prepare. Scared to face the enemy, doubts ruling, they wandered for forty years, with all the soldiers dying along the way, because of that disobedience. The final arrival on the plains of Moab, demanded a 2nd count, and there were almost the same number of soldiers in the 2nd generation.

4.5.9.　　　　Deuteronomy, the farewell address of Moses. A few of his addresses to the people, summarizing the desert journey, reminding that new generation of their heritage. As I read Deuteronomy I see Moses' heart weeping, as he desired to tell them what God had done for their fathers, and how they were to follow God's Law if they were to have success. Despite the fact that it was an eleven-day journey from Horeb to Barnea, the journey took forty years. So Moses preached the book of Deuteronomy as a sermon, preparing God's people to enter the land of covenant promise. Do not fail again, trust God. Moses says *"Love Yahweh your Elohim,* love your personal God, He's your creator of victory, *follow His directions, and obey his commands. Then you will live."* And these words from God, *I have offered you life or death, blessings or curses* (and then edges them on with a hint in humor, *choose life).*

Authorship: Moses or JEDP?

5　Let's look at the authorship of the Pentateuch. In addition, we will consider the two distinct views of that authorship, quite an interesting topic. Not a subject to pass over quickly.

5.1. Bible scholars have debated this question for many years, since a man named Julius Wellhausen concluded in the late 19th century, that Moses was not the sole writer. And so, the debate began. It is quite surprising the lack of information there is on the author of these books. Many commentaries and study books say little about it.

5.1.1.　　　　So on one side, many believe Moses authored all but a few verses of the books. Someone, perhaps Joshua, recorded the death of Moses, sometime in the 1400s BCE. In fact many of our Bibles, begin "The first book of Moses, called Genesis" followed by "The second book of Moses called Exodus" etc

5.1.2.　　　　Then the 2nd belief of many others, who say the material was written by different authors after Moses died. Their conclusion is based on the fact that there are definite differences in the style of writing, the usage of different names of God in specific passages and more importantly, several times, there are different versions of the same story.

5.1.3.　　　　Therefore, we answer those arguments, by realizing that God revealed Himself to people by revealing many names of His character, to make a point. In Gen 1 God is *Elohim,* the mighty Creator of everything and in Gen 2 God is Y*ahweh* the personal God who relates to humanity. That does not necessarily point to different authors, but to a single author referring to various names to describe different aspects of His character. Then, most writers use different linguistic expressions in different situations. However, we received these five books, whoever wrote them, and accept them as indeed the heart of Moses, received from the heart of Yahweh.

5.2. Let's review the two conclusions. Both Jewish and Christian tradition recognizes Moses as the single author of the Pentateuch, or at least most of it, as I mentioned. They also would agree the entire document bears his stamp and authority. I generally say, "This is the story of Moses" which was revealed and written by the inspiration of God.

5.2.1.   The testimony of the Bible itself strongly leads us to the conclusion of Moses being the author. Scripture must remain our guide. Let's look at the internal evidence for the Moses authorship. Ex 17:14 *Then the Lord said to Moses, "Write this in a book as a memorial and recite it to Joshua,* (those same words God said in 34:27 We could get picky here and ask "What book?" Did he write only SOME of the words? Pretty meticulous! In any case, we know Moses wrote a book!

5.2.1.1.   So Moses responds, Ex 24:4 *Moses wrote down all the words of the Lord.* He was WITH God for 40 days. In addition, later in Num 33:2 *Moses recorded their starting places according to their journeys by the command of the Lord.*

5.2.1.2.   In Leviticus, more than 25 times it is recorded *the Lord spoke to Moses,* such as 4:1.

5.2.1.3.   The entire Book of Deuteronomy begins with the claim that *These are the words which Moses spoke to all Israel*

5.2.1.4.   So we conclude that if he preached to them several sermons, the book must be his, not some priests who came along years later.2 Chron. the final book of the Hebrew Scriptures, in 25:4, it reads *as it is written in the law in the book of Moses*

5.2.1.5.   We read in Ezra 3:2 *Then Jeshua and his brothers the priests, and Zerubbabel and his brothers arose and built the altar of the God of Israel to offer burnt offerings on it, as it is written in the law of Moses, the man of God.*

5.2.1.6.   Another, of the many Old Testament references: 1 Kings 2:3 *Keep the charge of the Lord your*

God, to walk in His ways, to keep His statutes, His commandments, His ordinances, and His testimonies, according to what is written in the Law of Moses.

5.2.1.7.   Then let me share this in another way. The Pentateuch contains several "self-claims" as to the authorship of some of its "parts." There are two quite clear references to Moses as the author of an extended passage known as the "Book of the Covenant," which is Exodus 20-23; after writing this extensive covenant (which you can read), he makes it clear in Ex 24:4-7; Verse 4 begins *Moses wrote down all the words of the Lord* and says in v7 *Then he took the book of the covenant and read it in the hearing of the people.* So there is an entire passage of some 4 cps that the Bible says Moses wrote.

5.2.1.8.   Of course we also know the Scriptures state that Moses wrote the Ten Commandments at the Lord's direction; neat to read this in Ex 34:27-28 *Then the Lord said to Moses, "Write down these words, for in accordance with these words I have made a covenant with you and with Israel." 28 So he was there with the Lord forty days and forty nights; he did not eat bread or drink water. And he wrote on the tablets the words of the covenant, the Ten Commandments.*

5.2.1.9.   At least two other incidents are said to have been preserved in writing by Moses, we already read the one in Ex 17:14; another is in Num 33:2.

5.2.1.10.   Then just a quick mention from the New Testament; Luke 2:22 reads that the event concerning Mary's act of purification was *according to the law of Moses.*

5.2.1.11.   However, the most powerful argument for Moses authorship is the testimony of Christ. Mark 12:26 *have you not read in the book of Moses,* (there's that Book again; and Jesus was certainly present when God commanded Moses to write it), in the burning bush passage, how God spoke to him. Jesus confirms that Moses wrote Ex 3:1-3. Then Luke comments in Acts 3:22 that Deut 18:15 was authored by Moses and Paul in Rom 10:5 says Moses wrote Leviticus. Therefore, we have confidence that Moses wrote Ex. Lev. and Deut. from those passages.

5.2.1.12.   There are many other Scriptures, in both Old and New Testaments that confirm Moses as the author of much of the Pentateuch. The ones mentioned will suffice.

5.2.2.   Then, to be thorough and complete in our study, we consider a theory about the authorship of these five books. It's good to know about this very intriguing theory. And I don't dismiss it entirely. The theory makes a lot of sense.

5.2.2.1.   It is called the JEDP authorship (referred to as the Documentary Hypothesis). It is a theory that originated in the 18th century and theorizes that the Pentateuch can be understood most effectively by recognizing its composite nature. By the 19th century, this theory spread to Germany, Britain, and America. The thought is that Genesis, Exodus, Leviticus, Numbers, and Deuteronomy were not written by Moses; but by different writers after Moses.

5.2.2.2.   Four groupings of separate written and/or oral documents were collected and joined together forming the present text. These were written in the same order as the letters, JEDP. J the earliest writing, joined to E; D then was added to the JE writing; finally, the P source completed the Torah. Those four sources were collected between 850 and 445 BCE, edited, and joined during Ezra's day. So, as I mentioned already, a section that called God "Yahweh" was one source (J), and a section that used the name "Elohim" was a different writer, (E).

5.2.2.2.1.   Let me detail this for you. First came the Yahwist Source, called J.

5.2.2.2.2.   Just before God's land was divided, the people referred to God as *Yahweh or* sometimes mistranslated *Jehovah*. He was their personal God. God was *Yahweh* who walks and talks with them, with a stress on His blessings; they referred to those in the land as "Canaanites." They believed in a Man-God personal relationship, hardly ever mentioning any angels. These Scriptures refer to *Yahweh* (again, which was really *mistranslated* into English as Jehovah; that name is nowhere found in the Hebrew Scriptures). The *Yahweh* Scriptures, which focus around Judah, emphasize many cities of importance to the southern kingdom (i.e. Hebron). They were the entirety of the Scriptures at that time. For example, they began with Gen. 2:4b-25 that uses *Yahweh* throughout, and then most of cp 4. These oldest of the writings were compiled around 850 BCE from the earliest oral and written sources.

5.2.2.2.3.　However, the Kingdom divided about 931 BCE. And the North, called Israel, did not entirely accept the Scriptures that Judah had. Israel needed their own version according to what they believed; they referred to God as *Elohim*, the Creator, thus the Elohist or E writings were compiled. They collected a second narrative of the origins, a grouping of their stories about Abraham, Isaac, Jacob, etc. consciously a corrective to J's Judah-oriented account. Their material parallels narratives from J, adding traditions and focuses on traditions associated with their northern kingdom. Their work, in approximately 750 BCE included Gen 20-22. To them God was a God of fear. They referred to those in the land as "Amorites." Their Scriptures added many warnings and the dream passages; they pictured angels. They re-wrote many of the stories to suit their *Elohim*, causing there to be two versions of creation, two versions of Abraham and Isaac, etc. So here we have the "E" Scriptures. The 2nd oldest Scriptures compiled.

5.2.2.2.4.　At that time, the Southern Kingdom, Judah had the "J" Scriptures, the *Yahweh* passages. The Northern Kingdom, Israel had the "E" or *Elohim* Scriptures. The "J" and "E" accounts existed side by side for as long as the two Kingdoms lasted, until 721 BCE. The two sources were combined, probably when Israelite refugees fled to Jerusalem, bringing their E with them, following the northern kingdom's end—the JE Scriptures.

5.2.2.3.　Then during the period of the captivity of Judah, a group of Priests and Prophets decided that the people in Persia needed to be reminded of the consequences of the years of decline in their loyalty to *Yahweh*. They added material concerning their attempt to reform the bad practices they had brought from Judah; the result was the book of Deuteronomy: the "D" authorship around 620 BCE. A number of scholars maintain that the core of Deuteronomy, cps 12-26, may be the oldest part of all the Scriptures, to which the JE material was later added as an introduction. There is thought that the Deuteronomist Source had influence into other passages in Genesis, Exodus, Numbers, and later books of Joshua, Judges, and the Samuel and Kings Books.

5.2.2.4.   Then a final authorship took place, the Priestly Source, or P. A group of Priests, living during and after the Babylonian exile, used the name *Elohim* for the general name of God, and added a special name of God *El Shaddai*. To the Priests, they now portrayed *Yahweh* as the creator; mankind, created in God's image was to rule the earth. Their intent was to preserve and edit Israel's religious heritage. In addition, they added the genealogies and used a lot of dates and numbers. They inserted the vast body of legal material that extends from Exodus 35 through Leviticus to Numbers 10. They were responsible for the entire first chapter of Genesis, (so Gen 1 was written after Gen 2 and much of Genesis. They also included the account of Moses' death (Deut 34) and the detailed instructions of building the Tabernacle. Written after the fall of Judah in 587, around 500 BCE. We have the "P" source.

5.2.3.   This combination of efforts became the JEDP theory.

5.3. My personal conclusions? I accept that there's too much internal evidence of Moses' authorship to entirely accept the JEDP four-author hypothesis. In either case, let us always accept that God wrote His Word whether by Moses or by Moses and four other sources. Regardless of how men produced and preserved the Bible, it is truly a work of divine illumination.

SECTION 2
The Beginning of History
Four Great Events

Genesis 1-11 The period from Creation, (approx. 4004 to 2242 BCE)

Theme Statement: *"This is the account of heaven and earth"* (Gen 2:4)

THE KEYS IN SECTION TWO

Section 2: The Beginning of History-Four Great Events

Keys to Genesis—

A Key Word: God

The Key Verses (3:15; 12:3)

3:15 And I will put enmity
Between you and the woman,
And between your seed and her seed;
He shall bruise you on the head,
And you shall bruise him on the heel.

12:3 And I will bless those who bless you,
And the one who curses you I will curse.
And in you all the families of the earth will be blessed.

The Key Chapter (15)

The Key People in Genesis

Adam and Eve-the original human beings (1:26-5:5)
Noah-the faithful builder of the ark (6:5-9:29)
Abraham and Sarah-the parents of a nation called God's chosen people (12:1-25:9)
Isaac and Rebekah-the original members of a new nation (21:1-35:29)
Jacob-the father of the twelve tribes of Israel (25:21-50:14)
Joseph-the preserver of his people and the nation of Egypt (30:22-50:26)

Approximate DATES OF KEY EVENTS in Sections 2 and 3	
Undatable	Pre-Adam World
4004 BCE	Re-Creation
4004	The Fall
2344	The Flood
2242	The Tower
1997	Abraham is born in Ur of the Chaldeans
1921	Abraham is called to set out for Canaan
1896	Isaac is born to Abraham and Sarah
1837	Jacob is born to Isaac and Rebekah
1821	Abraham dies in Canaan
1745	Joseph is born to Jacob and Rachel
1728	Joseph is sold into slavery
1716	Isaac dies in Canaan
1706	Jacob and his family move to Egypt
1689	Jacob dies in Egypt
1635	Joseph dies in Egypt

FOUR

Creation

1   This section of our journey is entitled **THE BEGINNING OF HISTORY**. We will spend more time on the first book in the Bible, Genesis than any of the other thirty-eight books. Genesis is written in chronological order, which allows for an organized reading.

1.1. Genesis is from a Greek word meaning "beginning" or "generation." The beginning of all things. Certainly the beginning of generations, there are ten of them mentioned in Genesis.[1] Genesis covers the period from the creation through the death of Joseph in 1805 BCE (Before the Common Era, also B.C.). God's plan has never changed. He expanded His Kingdom of Heaven by making a colony called earth; Genesis 2:4 tells us *"This is the account of heaven and earth."* "Heaven and Earth" is mentioned, almost as though equating the two. Refer in this volume to "God's Kingdom."

1.2. As stated before, Genesis is the book of beginnings:

    1.2.1.   The beginning of the world
    1.2.2.   The beginning of the Human race
    1.2.3.   The beginning of sin
    1.2.4.   The beginning of redemption
    1.2.5.   The Family
    1.2.6.   Nations
    1.2.7.   The beginning of the Hebrew Nation
    1.2.8.   Government
    1.2.9.   Law
    1.2.10.   Sin
    1.2.11.   Judgment

1.3. There are several ways to outline Genesis; a relatively small summary outline of a specific book helps one to have an

---

[1] (1) 2:4 Heaven and earth; (2) 5:1 Adam; (3) 6:9 Noah; (4) 10:1 three Sons of Noah; (5) 11:10 the blood line son, Shem; (6) 11:27 Terah; (7) 25:12 Ishmael, Abraham's son; (8) 25:19 Isaac; (9) 36:1, 36:9 Esau; (10) 37:2 Jacob.

understanding and overview of the entire book. I suggest you memorize an outline for each of the thirty-nine books.

1.4. Note four ways to outline Genesis. Multiple outlines will not be prepared for most other books, however, this is Genesis—our goal should be to know this first book thoroughly. I suggest you choose one of these outlines to memorize.

A Basic Outline of Genesis
#1 KEY LOCATIONS[1]

1. Located in Mesopotamia, NE of Palestine, close to Armenia between the long widened area of the Tigris and Euphrates rivers. Cps 1-11. This covers the approximately first 1900 years of history.
2. Located in the Promised Land, approximately 200 years, 2090-1897 BCE, Cps 12-36.
3. Located in Egypt, approximately 100 years, 1897-1804 BCE, Cps 37-50.

A Basic Outline of Genesis
#2 KEY PEOPLE

1. Adam and Eve, Cps 2-5
2. Noah, Cps 6-9
3. Abraham &Sarah, Cp 21, parents of a chosen people
4. Isaac and Rebekah, Cps 26-27, members of a new nation
5. Jacob, Cps 34-34, father of the twelve tribes
6. Joseph, Cps 39-42, preserver of nations

A Basic Outline of Genesis
#3 KEY EVENTS

1. Creation
2. Fall
3. Flood
4. Separation of Nations
5. Covenant
6. Twelve Tribes

Author's Preferred Basic Outline of Genesis
For *Travel Through the Old Testament*

1. Four Great Events, Cps 1-11
    a. Creation

---

[1] Become oriented with the geography of Genesis. The three lands are Mesopotamia, Promise Land, and Egypt (see additional Expanded Papers on each); each is located SW of the other..

44

  b. Fall

  c. Flood

  d. Babel

 2. Four Great Men, Cps 12-50

  a. Abraham

  b. Isaac

  c. Jacob

  d. Joseph

1.5. We offer a KEY WORD in each book, along with the Hebrew meaning of that word. These will increase your knowledge of the Old Testament.

Depth of Bible Words and Places
Elohim

A Key Word in Genesis is the wonderful name we read as *God*, *"in the beginning God."*

  It is the Hebrew *Elohim,* the most used Hebrew term for God. Many times it was translated "the almighty God," and rightfully so. It was the fullness of God—a plural word perhaps indicating the Trinity, His fullness—GOD.

Jesus Christ, Son of God, is found in each of the thirty-nine Old Testament Books. In some cases He is found in a type, other times He has a form as a man. In many books, He appears several times. To increase your knowledge of the Old Testament, as we begin to review each of the thirty-nine books, I suggest that you look for the character and identity of Jesus. Enjoy finding Him in every book!

Jesus in Genesis...The Seed. Our accepted seed has provided the fruit of life for us. Genesis traces the line of Christ, *the seed* from Abraham through Isaac, Jacob, and Joseph. Genesis shows us how God had a plan to eventually deal a deathblow to the head of Satan. It is through Abraham's seed, God would reach out to save His people.

1.6. A few additional thoughts concerning His names:

 1.6.1. "*El,*" a root name for God, carries the important meaning of "god." Other cultures used this word when referring to their gods. It is used in a general sense of deity some 2,570 times in the Old Testament. The highest Canaanite god was EL, whose son was named Baal. So our God was specific in qualifying His name in Deuteronomy 5:9, *"I, the Lord* (Jehovah) *your God*

(Elohim), *am a jealous God* (El). When Abraham planted a tree at Beersheba, it is recorded in Genesis 21:33 *"...and there called on the name of the Lord* (Yahweh), *the Everlasting God* (El Olam)." El-Shaddai is the name with which God appeared to Abraham, Isaac, and Jacob, signifying God as a source of blessing.

1.6.2.	*Elohim,* pronounced el'-low-HEEM, one of the *three primary names* of God in the Old Testament, is the plural form of El, referring to our Supreme Being, the only true God, and the triune God of Genesis 1. This word appears only in Hebrew, no other language. No one using this name could mistake Him for any "el" of other nations or peoples. Nothing existed until Elohim created it. Elohim is used thirty-five times in the first thirty-six verses. This name is linked many times with the second name of God, YHWH.

1.6.3.	*Yahweh,* pronounced yah-WEH, the *second* of the primary names, is found 5,311 times in the Old Testament, more than twice as often as Elohim. It is unique among all names of God, for it is the one personal name of God in the Old Testament. This name is so significant that the translators of many English versions identify its every occurrence by printing it with all capitals, LORD. This name is from the Hebrew verb "to be." Yahweh is self-existent and possesses life in His self. Elohim is more of the general name of God concerned with creation and preservation of His works, while Yahweh is God revealing Himself in His personal attributes.

1.6.4.	The *third* of the primary names of God is Adonai, pronounced a-doe-NAI. He is the owner of all things, occurring 137 times in the Old Testament. Generally, translated as Lord (capital, followed by small letters). This is the name the Jews used when referring to YHWH, refusing to speak or read the name. This name conveys authority of the Master over each of His children.

1.6.5.	*"Lord God"* is formed by combining the two primary names of God, Yahweh, and Elohim. This combination occurs 595 times in the Hebrew Old Testament, and it is one of the most significant of the many and wonderful names of God.

1.6.6.	*"God Almighty"* is mentioned 48 times in the Old Testament, 31 of which are in Job.

1.6.7.	*"The Great God"* sums up the names of God. It is a phrase which is both a name and a description. Moses reminded the Israelites, *The Lord your God is God of gods and Lord of lords, the great God, mighty and awesome* (Deut. 10:17). Proverbs 26:10 assures us He is in fact *the great God who formed everything.*

EXPANDED HELP PAPER
Names of God in Each Chapter of Genesis

Genesis 1 *Elohim* used entirely, other than one time in 1:2 where *Ruach Elohim* is used.

Genesis 2 *Yahweh Elohim* used throughout.

Genesis 3 *Yahweh Elohim* used other than in 3:1b-4 where *Elohim* is used by Satan and Eve and one time used by God in v11.

Genesis 4 *Yahweh* used except one time in v25 when Eve responds with *Elohim.*

Genesis 5 *Elohim* used except one time in v28 where *Yahweh* is used.

Genesis 6 *Yahweh* used in vv 3 and 5; *Elohim* in all other verses.

Genesis 7 *Yahweh* used except one time in v 16a, *Elohim*

Genesis 8 *Elohim* used except in v20, *Yahweh.*

Genesis 9 *Elohim* used except in v 26a, *Yahweh.*

Genesis 10 Yahweh used the two times in v 9.

Genesis 11 *Yahweh* used throughout.

Genesis 12-13 *Yahweh* used throughout.

Genesis 14 *El Elyon* used except in v 22, *Yahweh El Elyon.*

Genesis 15 *Yahweh* (vv 1, 4-7, 18); *Adonai Yahweh* (vv 2, 8); *Elohim* (13, 18).

Genesis 16 *Yahweh* used except v 13b, *El Roi.*

Genesis 17 *Yahweh* 1a; *El Shaddai* 1b; *Elohim* in all other verses.

Genesis 18 *Yahweh* used throughout.

Genesis 19 *Yahweh* used except v29, *Elohim* (twice).

Genesis 20 *Elohim* used except v4 *Adonai* and v 18 *Yahweh.*

Genesis 21 *Yahweh* two times v 1a (first word) and v 33a; *El Olam* one time v 33b; *Elohim* all other times.

Genesis 22 *Elohim*, other than *Yahweh* in v 11, 14b, 15, 16, and *Yahweh Jireh* in v 14a.

Genesis 23 None

Genesis 24 a little confusing because of the various names used. *Yahweh* in vv 1, 21, 26 (except 26c, *Elohim*), 35, 40, 44, 48 (except 48c, *Elohim*) 50-52, 56; *Yahweh Elohim* in vv 3, 7a, 12, 42; *Elohim* in 7b.

Genesis 25 *Elohim* only in v 11; then *Yahweh* in all other verses.

Genesis 26 *Yahweh* used throughout.

Genesis 27 *Yahweh* vv 7, 20a, 27; *Elohim* vv 20b, 28.

Genesis 28 *El Shaddai* v 3; *Elohim* vv 4, 12, 13cd, 17, 20, 21b, 22; *Yahweh* vv 13ab; 16, 21a.

Genesis 29 *Yahweh* used throughout.

Genesis 30 *Elohim* used except vv 24, 27, 30 *Yahweh.*

Genesis 31 *Elohim* used except vv 3, 49 *Yahweh; El* in v 13.
Genesis 32 *Elohim* used except v9c *Yahweh.*
Genesis 33 *Elohim* used except v20a *El.*
Genesis 34 none.
Genesis 35 *Elohim* used except v1b, *El* and *El Shaddai* v11b.
Genesis 36-37 none.
Genesis 38 *Yahweh* used throughout.
Genesis 39 Yahweh used except v9, *Elohim.*
Genesis 40 *Elohim,* one time in v 9.
Genesis 41 *Elohim* used except v38, Ruach Elohim.
Genesis 42 *Elohim* two times vv 18, 28.
Genesis 43 *El Shaddai* in v 14.
Genesis 44 *Elohim* one time v 16.
Genesis 45 *Elohim* used throughout.
Genesis 46 *Elohim* in vv 1, 2, 3b; *El* in v3a.
Genesis 47 none.
Genesis 48 *Elohim* except v 3, *El Shaddai.*
Genesis 49 *Yahweh* in v 18, *El* in v 25a, and *Shaddai* in v 25b.
Genesis 50 *Elohim* used throughout.

Spoke to:
Eve as *Elohim* (Gen 3:3) and *Yahweh* (Gen 4:1).
Noah as both *Yahweh* and *Elohim* (Gen 9:26).
Melchizedek the priest, as *El Elyon* (Gen 14:19).
Hagar as *El Roi* (Gen 16:13).
Lot as *Yahweh* (Gen 19:14).
Sarah as *Yahweh* (Gen 16:2) and *Elohim* (Gen 21:6).
Abraham as *Yahweh El Elyon* (Gen 14:22), *Adonai Yahweh* (Gen 15:2), *Elohim* (Gen 20:13), *Yahweh, El Olan* (Gen 21:33), and *Yahweh Elohim* (Gen 24:7).
Isaac as *Yahweh* (Gen 27:27), *Elohim* (Gen 27:28), and *El Shaddai* (Gen 28:3).
Leah as *Yahweh* (Gen 29:32) and *Elohim* (Gen 30:18).
Jacob as *Yahweh* (Gen 27:20), *Elohim* (Gen 28:17), and *El Shaddai* (Gen 43:14).
Joseph as *Elohim* (Gen 39:9).

Key Names of God in Genesis:

Hebrew Name	Translated in most English Bibles
Yahweh	LORD

Creation

El, Elohim	God
Ruach Elohim	Spirit of God
El Elyon	God most High
Adonai	Lord
El Shaddai	God Almighty
El Olam	Everlasting God
El Roi	God Who sees me
Yahweh Jireh	the LORD will provide

The Names of God in the Old Testament
(Arranged chronologically)

Hebrew Name	Meaning	First Time	Total Times
Elohim, "God" el`-low-HEEM	Power and Might Creator; Eternal One	Gen. 1:1; Ps. 19:1	2,111
Ruach Elohim (ru-ACH)	The Spirit of God Associated with "life."	Gen. 1:2	14
Yahweh Elohim	Compound name	Gen. 2:4	211
Yahweh (YHWH) "LORD" *Jehovah* is a miss-translation (yah-WEH)	Personal name, His very nature; "to be" or "He is"; Owner; I AM	Gen. 4:1	5,181
El-Elyon (EL el-YOHN)	"The most high God"	Gen. 14:17-20; Isaiah 14:13,14	39
Yahweh El Elyon		Gen. 14:22	1
Adonai Yahweh		Gen. 15:2	270
El-Roi (El roe-EE)	"The strong one who sees"	Gen. 16:12	1
El-Shaddai (EL shad-DAI)	"God Almighty" Nothing is impossible; "The Mountain One"	Gen. 17:1; Ps. 91:1	48
Adonai "Lord" (a-doe-NAI)	The Lordship of God; Owner of all things; master; used when speaking of YHWH	Gen. 20:4; Ex 4:10, 15:17	137
El-Olam (EL o-LAM)	"The everlasting God"; Eternal God	Gen. 21:33; Isaiah 40:28-30	2
Yahweh –Jireh (yir-EH)	"The-Lord-Will-Provide"	Gen. 22:13,14	1
Ehyeh (eh-YEH)	"I Am" God Who always existed, and God Who is present with	Ex. 3:14; Hos 1:9	2

	His people		
Yahweh –Ropheka (ro-FEH-ka)	"The-Lord-our-Healer"	Exodus 15:26	1
Yahweh –Nissi (nis-SEE)	"The-Lord-Is-My-Banner"	Exodus 17:15	1
Ruach	"God, Spirit"	Num. 11:17	44
Ruach Yahweh	The LORD's Spirit	Judges 3:10	20
Yahweh –Shalom (sha-LOME)	"The-Lord-Is- Peace"	Judges 6:24	1
Yahweh Tsebaoth (tse-ba-OATH)	"The-Lord-of- hosts"	1 Samuel 1:3;Isaiah 6:1-3	230
Yahweh Elohim Tsebaoth		2 Sam. 5:10	13
Yahweh Elyon		Ps. 7:17	2
Yahweh –Roeh (roe-EE)	"The-Lord-my-Shepherd"	Ps. 23:1	3
Elohim Elyon		Ps. 57:2	2
Yahweh Adonay		Ps. 68:20	4
Adonay Yahweh Tsebaoth		Ps. 69:6	17
Elohim Tsebaoth		Ps. 80:7	2
El Yahweh		Ps. 85:8	1
Rophe (ro PHE)	Healer	Ps. 147:3	1
Yahweh –Tsidqenu (tsid-KAY-nu)	"The-Lord-our-Righteousness"	Jeremiah 23:6	3
Yahweh Shammah (SHAM-mah)	"The-Lord who-is-present"	Ezekiel 48:35	1
Adonay Elohim		Dan. 9:3	1
Ish (EESH)	Husband	Hosea 2:16	1
Adonay Yahweh Elohe Tsebaoth		Amos 3:13; 5:16	2
Yahweh Elohe Tsebaoth		Amos 4:13	4
Elohe Tsebaoth		Amos 5:27	1

EXPANDED HELP PAPER
Names

Names were particularly important in the biblical world. The *New International Encyclopedia of Bible Words* reminds us "in biblical cultures a name did more than identify; it communicated something of the essence, the character, or the reputation of the person or thing named."

This fact helps us understand why the Bible is so filled with many and wonderful names of God. Each name reveals something about the essential nature and character of God. Moreover, no single name or title could possibly sum up who He is. It is fascinating as we survey the Old Testament names of God to note that some names emphasize His power and excellence, others His relationship with human beings and still other names are descriptive, providing special information about who He is.

The prophet Isaiah reports a vision in which he "saw the Lord sitting on a throne, high and lifted up, and the train of His robe filled the temple" (Isaiah 6:1). In Isaiah's vision, seraphim were positioned around the throne, together crying *"Holy, holy, holy is the LORD of hosts; the whole earth is full of His glory!"* (v 3). Isaiah's reaction was one of awe and humility. Confronted by this revelation of God enthroned in heaven, the prophet cried, *"Woe is me, for I am undone! Because I am a man of unclean lips, and I dwell in the midst of a people of unclean lips"* (v 5).

Through his vision, a stunned Isaiah suddenly became fully aware of the vast gap that exists between any human being and God. We are made in the image of God, yet God remains unimaginably different from and greater than us. What theologians speak of as the transcendence of God was impressed upon the prophet, and Isaiah was immediately aware of how far he fell short of God's glory (Rom. 3:23).

Our God is high and lifted up. He is a God of power and excellence. He is so far above us that we can never truly fathom His greatness and majesty. Yet, through certain names in Scripture, we are invited to glimpse His greatness, and like Isaiah, we are called to bow down in wonder before Him. Here, then, are Scripture's exalted names of our God.

---

2   We begin Genesis with *FOUR GREAT EVENTS*. These four events are *THE BEGINNING OF HISTORY*. They comprise the first eleven chapters, and the time period of approximately 4,000 to 2 200 BCE, or 1,800 years. These first eleven chapters cover as much time as all the remaining thirty-eight books of the Old Testament! If these first eleven chapters were to have been lost, the rest of the Bible would be quite puzzling.[1]

2.1. This first section, FOUR GREAT EVENTS, has four key concepts, which are crucial in understanding the rest of the Bible.

2.1.1.   One, God created everything and is the only True God, the *Elohim* of Divine power and the *Yahweh* of personal relationship.

---

[1] Each Section in our course carries a theme. The theme will be stated on the first page of the Section.

2.1.2.　　　　Two, all people have rebelled against *Elohim* and have inherited a sinfulness from Adam and Eve's rebellion.

2.1.3.　　　　Three, God judges the actions of people and shows that human actions from flesh are unacceptable.

2.1.4.　　　　Four, God reveals His plan to save humanity from its own sinful deeds.

3　We consider the FOUR GREAT EVENTS

3.1. The first event was *CREATION* (1:1-2:25)[1]

3.1.1.　　　　Notice the way the Bible begins. Certainly no other book ever in existence COULD begin this way.[2]

3.1.2.　　　　No argument or proof of God is needed. It just begins with accepting that our existence depends on GOD — He WAS. God has no beginning. Certainly reminds us of His later name, I AM THAT I AM revealed in Exodus. It means, "I will be what I will be." Genesis begins with God, but as we will see, it ends with in a coffin. Genesis is a history of human failure, a flash of creation, but from there on we view the story of God bringing back a lost people to Himself.

3.1.2.1.　　　　Read about God from Psalms 90:2, *Before the mountains were born Or You gave birth to the earth and the world, Even from everlasting to everlasting, You are God.*[3]

Depth of Bible Words and Places
Create

A rare Hebrew word in the Old Testament, "bara." It is always used of an act of God, and implying the act was "out of nothing." No other individual in the Bible is said to "bara." The results of six days were accomplished only by *Elohim*. Another Hebrew word, used hundreds of times, meaning "made" could have been used, however He used *"bara."*

---

[1]Concerning the opening two verses of Genesis, there are two main views.

1. *Most generally* accepted is the view in which verse 2 describes "the earth" of undetermined age, consisting of unorganized matter before God transformed it in six creative days.

2. *A second view* is referred to as the "Gap-Restoration" view. See Expanded Help Paper on next page. This view states that v 1 is the original perfect creation, followed by a chaotic event resulting in verse 2. Then God restored the earth in six days.

[2] Genesis 1:1

[3]A.W. Tozer said *"In the beginning God....not matter, for matter is not self-causing. It requires a cause and God is that cause. In the beginning God, the un-caused cause of matter. There we must begin."*

EXPANDED HELP PAPER
The Gap-Restoration View of Genesis 1:1

To express a complete and fair view of creation, the gap view must be considered. This expanded view is presented for education and understanding of Genesis 1. It is presented in sermonic form, drawn from the personal library of the author. Very few tackle this controversial topic. However, at the least, it is quite informational. The author of this book began studying the view in 1970 and never stopped considering it. Let me offer, as you read it, if you can't follow it, or perhaps you disagree with it, don't go on. Allow me to note that, the authors of *Chronological Bible* by Reese, *Dake's Refererence Bible*, and *The Chronology of the Bible* by Frank Klassen, all are recognized as thorough scholars, have accepted this interpretation of scripture. In addition, C.M. Ward and Brad Strand considered the theory valid.

THE LIGHT WAS REMOVED. The verses in Genesis 1:1-2 are the foundation of the gap view of creation.

In the beginning God created the heavens and the earth. 2 The earth was formless and void, and darkness was over the surface of the deep, and the Spirit of God was moving over the surface of the waters.

First, please notice something very important in reading these verses—they do not say that God *created* the earth without form and void.

The Hebrew words used here (*tohu v'bohu*) which are translated "formless and void" mean, according to the Hebrew, "confusion, chaos, waste...." In other words, God did not create a mess, a disaster. Translators have used various words to clarify the meaning.

> Formless and void (HCSB)
> Without shape and empty (NET)
> Unformed and void (Jewish Bible)
> Waste and empty (Darby)
> An empty waste (AMP)
> Without form and void (KJV)

My study of these words has assisted in understanding these verses. Allow me to use the following example. You cleaned your house perfectly. The entire house is spotless. However, the next day, you walk down the hall and open the door to your teenager's room. And you yell out, "What have you done? This place has become (using these Hebrew words *confusion, chaos, and waste).* Clean it now." "It's a mess, a disaster." It was perfect but became a wasteland.

The Bible tells us very specifically in Isaiah 45:18 that God did not create the earth (and uses the same Hebrew word of Genesis v 2), *a worthless waste.*

For thus says the Lord — Who created the heavens, God Himself, Who formed the earth and made it, Who established it and did not create it to be a worthless waste; He formed it to be inhabited — I am the Lord, and there is no one else. (AMP)

From this, many who examine this view conclude that God did not create earth a chaotic mess. He created it as He always does a—perfectly. It was habitable and full of life at the very beginning.

This allows the possibility of dinosaurs being a part of life on earth in God's first work of creation. (My oldest grandson would love to hear me say that; he must have played with a least twenty dinosaur figures).

The big question among scientists has always been "What happened to them?" They have offered theory after theory; recently many have agreed on one theory—all the dinosaurs died at once, killed in one catastrophic event.

I recommend Strobel's book entitled "The Case for a Creator"[1] He noted that the majority of scientists today believe that something happened 'in the beginning'. Intelligence had to set it in motion. Something catastrophic happened between the first and second verses of Genesis to explain it. In one great climactic moment, judgment fell on "the world of Genesis," v1 and, as a result, *"the earth became without form, and void."* God did not create a mess.

In Jeremiah 4:23 the prophet records the moment which God allowed him to look back: *I looked on the earth, and behold, it was formless and void;* (again those same words of Gen 2 [tohu v'bohu]) *And to the heavens, and they had no light.*

God at some point, removed earth's light. Not the moon, not the stars. God removed Himself, His light, for "God is light" (1 John 1:5).

When God took Himself, the Light of Life, away from the earth, every living creature including the dinosaurs, died in an instant.

Jeremiah 4:26 records this judgment, which destroyed earth's cities and life, was the result of God's *"fierce anger."*

What caused such wrath? It was a rebellion so great that it split the angelic forces of heaven. A rebellion against God led by the most beautiful being God had created, the archangel Lucifer.

Isaiah 14:12-15 describes the event: *"How you have fallen from heaven, O star of the morning, son of the dawn! You have been cut down to the earth, You who have weakened the nations! 13 "But you said in*

---

[1] Strobel, Lee, *The Case for a Creator,* Zondervan, Grand Rapids, Michigan, 2004

your heart, 'I will ascend to heaven; I will raise my throne above the stars of God, And I will sit on the mount of assembly In the recesses of the north. 14 'I will ascend above the heights of the clouds; I will make myself like the Most High.' 15 "Nevertheless you will be thrust down to Sheol, To the recesses of the pit.

Like all of God's perfect creatures, Lucifer had been given a will. Instead of submitting that will to God, Lucifer was the first being ever to cross wills with the Father.

This passage in Isaiah reveals five "I wills" of Lucifer.

I will ascend

I will raise my throne

I will sit on the mount

I will ascend above

I will make myself like the Most High

He led a rebellion against God with the goal of taking over the very throne of God! And Jesus tells us what happened to the would-be usurper of God's throne: It's recorded in Luke 10:18 And He said to them, "*I was watching Satan fall from heaven like lightning.*"

God was so angry that He removed the Light from the earth where Lucifer's domain had been during the time before Genesis v1, and it became a mess, a disaster, an uninhabitable wasteland without form, and void.

3.1.3.   This portion of scripture, Gen 1:1 Answers the *agnostic* who says God and the beginning of the universe are unknowable,

      3.1.3.1.   Answers the *atheist* who denies the very existence of a Supreme God,

      3.1.3.2.   It answers *pantheism* which says the universe itself is God,

      3.1.3.3.   And it answers *polytheism*, which believes in many gods.

3.1.4.   The name of God in Gen 1:1 is a plural name, *Elohim*. See The Names of God in the Old Testament, in this volume, for additional information. This is the fullness of God, *all* of God introduced here as Creator, Power and Might. That name occurs 35 times in the 34 verses of the creation story.

3.1.5.   Hebrew texts highlight *"In the beginning."* That's how it was referred to; we refer today to Genesis, the Jews referred to

"In the beginning." The title of the books in the Old Testament, were not inspired. We will see more of this as we look at each book.

3.1.6.   Each day begins with the same three spoken words: *"let there be."* Nine times in the first chapter, He creates with these same three words.[1]

     3.1.6.1.   The days progressed with His creation. From earth to light, to water, to space, to plants; on to stars and planets, to fish, to birds, and climaxed with a being like God Himself, man. Note that light is mentioned, even before the "lights of a sun or moon or stars" were created. Also, each act of creation provided for the next creative act. Water—then fish—then plants, etc. Each was needed to sustain the next. A God of planning, perfection, and provision.

EXPANDED HELP PAPER
Day

The Hebrew word for day is *yom*, normally meaning a 24-hour day. Reckoned a day, from evening to evening, from the first appearance of the stars in the evening to the first appearance of stars next evening. We may refer to Gen 1:5, 8; Ex 12:18; and Lev 23:32. Days were numbered rather than being named, with the exception of the Sabbath. We read six times in Gen 1, *And there was evening and there was morning, one day.*
The Scriptures also uses the word "day" in a symbolic sense, as in "the day of the Lord" (Isa 2:12, 13:6, 9).

     3.1.6.2.   Here is revealed a great understanding. God **IS** light. He just allowed Himself to be unwrapped, and there was light as long as He was close to His earth. He'll be the light in heaven, no sun will be needed! Also, no sun was needed in the beginning of creation, but there was light!

3.1.7.   Notice something very important. Every act of creation, is initiated, is begun, by a container of spoken words.

---

[1] Vv 3, 6, 9, 11, 14, 20, 24, 26, 29. Also in cp 1, we see the expressive Hebrew. When God uttered *let there be*, it's really could be translated "*BE*." The single word (haw-yaw) simply means "*BE*." So, God commanded *"Light BE"* (and immediately in His "time," it BE'D!) HE, glory, light—was revealed, un-covered.

3.1.7.1.   God saw inside Himself, a picture of what He wanted—then the Trinity created everything. Elohim created.[1]

3.1.7.2.   Here's a note concerning a method to be used in understanding the creation:

3.1.7.2.1.   God the Father, the architect, *INITIATED* the plan. He visualized the end result and calculated it all out. He set this earth turning 10,000 miles an hour in one direction and 1,000 miles an hour in the other. He made sure that when the waters came in or when they went out, the earth would stand. He determined the perfect amount of mountains and valleys to make this planet stand.

3.1.7.2.2.   God the Son, the builder, *IMPLEMENTED* the plan. He took the vision of the Father, and put it in to action. The Son, the Living Word, carried the vision in the container of God's Words. The part of God, The Word, implemented, He was the one who became flesh.

3.1.7.2.3.   God the Holy Spirit, the beautifier, *EMPOWERED* the plan. The Holy Spirit brought into existence the plan carried by the Word.[2]

3.1.8.   As noted above, God in His divine wisdom masterfully created everything in relationship and order.[3]

3.1.8.1.   Man was created on the sixth day, a trinity being. He was created a spirit being, unlike other created beings. This creation was given a soul to reason, to will, to have emotions. Man was given intelligence, immortality, and perfect moral character. This spirit-man and his soul were placed in an earth suit, a body made

---

[1] An unknown writer said: *God the Father is the architect, God the Son, the builder, and God the Holy Spirit the beautifier, of the universe.*

[2] Understand that God has never changed. This is how His "image" is to walk. *Be ye imitators of God.*

Find His Word on any situation in life, envision it down inside, release it by saying it in faith, and trust the Holy Spirit to empower it into existence. Then keep believing and releasing that Word.

The instant you question why God has not answered you, or the moment you begin to accept the delay as a sign that God didn't want you to have what you prayed for, you are defeated. Leave the seed work.

If God promises you something from His Word, and you stand on that promise, He intends for you to have it! He is not a partner to trickery. He does not lie. Stand for what belongs to you! Stand firm on His Word and believe that you will see the answers to your Bibl e-based prayers.

[3] Day 1 light—Day 4 sun, moon, and stars

Day 2 sky—Day 5 birds and fish

Day 3 land and plants—Day 6 Animals man

from the elements of earth. He was a trinity being created in the likeness of God.

    3.1.8.2.   Creation ended. God stopped creating. And He rested the next day.

3.1.9.   We do not know how long a day was, but we don't have any reason to believe they were not 24-hour days. Exodus 20:8-11 suggests a 24-hour day, but there are other references where a day has nothing to do with hours. Therefore, we couldn't disprove that each day was "as a thousand years." God's unlimited power can indeed dispense what He wants in any time frame He wants.

3.1.10.   The story continues in the Garden of Eden, cp 2, where we are introduced to the very personal name of God, which later was revealed to Moses in Exodus 3:13-14.[1]

Depth of Bible Words and Places
Yahweh
Our English word for the Hebrew word for God. Also translated incorrectly "Jehovah." See previous Names of God for more information concerning His names; also refer to the following Expanded Help Paper, Jehovah.

3.1.11.   He's called Jehovah, a God who came down and loved man, cared for him. He's revealed as "Lord God," a personal, loving, and caring God.

    3.1.11.1.   Before this period, remember, those acts of creation always identified God as **Elohim**, "Mighty God," not a personal name.

    3.1.11.2.   In Genesis 1 He is full power, The Creator.

3.1.12.   The location of the garden seems to have two possibilities in Mesopotamia identified from the four rivers, which watered the garden. We know the Euphrates and Tigris, the two rivers still called by those names. Then the Pison and Gihon possible tributaries off the other two. Both a northern and southern location has been suggested.

    3.1.12.1.   A tablet found in 1885 CE identifies Mesopotamia as the most likely location.

---

[1]One of the study passions of life is to study the names of God. Each time a new name of God is revealed, it seems to have been given to meet a need at the specific time. Once that amplified name was given, showing an additional attribute of God, it was to be known from that instance, forward. By the time of the New Testament, we understand His fullness. In fact the name for Jesus "Yeshua," contains each of those names inside.

EXPANDED HELP PAPER
Jehovah[1]

The personal divine name YHWH has had an interesting history. In the Old Testament period, the Hebrew language was written only with consonants; vowels were not added until the Common Era, when Hebrew was no longer a living language. Based on Greek texts, which of course use both vowels and consonants, it is believed that the original pronunciation of the name was *Yah-WEH, Yahweh.* Notice the shortened form of the divine name in the exclamation, "Halleluyah-Praise Yah." However, because of its holy character, the name Yahweh was withdrawn from ordinary speech during the period of the Second Temple (*c.* 500 BCE and later) and the substitute Hebrew word, actually a title not a personal name-Adonai, or (The) Lord, was used, as is still the practice in synagogues. Scholars who translated the Hebrew Bible into Greek (the Septuagint) in the third century BCE adopted this synagogue convention and rendered YHWH as "(The) Lord." From this Greek translation, the practice was carried over into the New Testament.

The word Jehovah is an artificial form that arose from the *erroneous* combination of the consonants YHWH with the vowels of Adonai -written under or over the Hebrew consonants to indicate that the substitute is to be pronounced. The erroneous translation, Jehovah, is nowhere found in Hebrew Scripture. This hybrid form is often held to be the invention of Peter Galatin, confessor of Pope Leo X, in a publication dated 1518 CE, but in actuality, it can be traced back to a work by a certain Raymond Martin in 1270.

Jewish reverence for the Name has influenced numerous modern translations, which, like the Septuagint translators, follow the ancient synagogue practice and substitute Adonai, which translates as "The Lord" in English.

Depth of Bible Words and Places
Mesopotamia

Located in modern Iraq, the word means, "land between the rivers." The Euphrates River marks the eastern boundary of the land promised to Abraham (Genesis 15:18). Only briefly did Israel's boundary extend that far (1 Chronicles 18:3). Most scholars have arrived at the conclusion that Genesis 2-11 is set in Mesopotamia, more specifically in southern Iraq and extending into south western Iran and northeastern Kuwait. In light of this, it is perhaps not surprising to learn that there is an

---

[1] Much of the above is compiled using *Understanding the Old Testament*, Bernhard W. Anderson, Prentice-Hall, 1986, p. 61.

area north of the Persian Gulf where the Tigris, Euphrates, and Karun Rivers converge that is called the "Garden of Eden. The government of Iraq has recently sought to protect it.

This area has a long, rich history. They witnessed the birth of the Sumerian culture. In the first millennium BCE, this area was called the Sealand, and later it came to be known as Chaldea. The Chaldeans resisted Assyrian domination; however, Sennacherib, the son of Sargon II, destroyed the city of Babylon in 689 BCE because of the ongoing rebel lion, and hunted the Chaldean rebels in the marshes. Also see *Three Lands,* in this volume.

EXPANDED HELP PAPER
The Land of Ancient Israel (a detailed history)

1. Jericho (see information on Jericho elsewhere in this volume), located twelve miles north of the Dead Sea and one mile from the modern city which bears the name, emerged as early as *c.* 7000 BCE according to the earliest of records. (Note that the author recognizes Ussher's chronology, which does not agree with this early date).

2. The area was surrounded by a semi-tropical oasis, which provided a clean, abundant water supply. Jericho, even at this early date, produced its own food and made unique pottery. A population of 2000 was protected by a massive wall.

3. The first group of "outsiders" spread into Jericho, Egypt, and Mesopotamia near the second half of the fourth century (3500 BCE). Many new villages were established, displaying technical and artistic advances. The use of copper appears in the historical records. Jericho was strengthened, and many other cities were built around defensible rock formations and near a water supply. The peoples spoke a Semitic tongue by this period. Also see Three Lands.

Depth of Bible Words and Places
The Semitic languages

These include Arabic, Hebrew, and Aramaic (including the Moabites and Edomites, the kindred of the Hebrews, along with the Canaanites, and the Phoenicians). Generally speaking, Semitic is used especially of or pertaining to the Jews. The choice of name was derived from Shem, one of the three sons of Noah in the genealogical accounts of the Book of Genesis. In Europe, they have also been known as Oriental languages. In the 19th century, *Semitic* became the conventional name. The Semitic languages covered what are today the modern states and regions of Iraq, Syria, Israel, Jordan, Lebanon, Palestine,

Saudi Arabia, Kuwait, Oman, Yemen, United Arab Emirates and the Sinai Peninsula and Malta. The earliest historic (written) evidences of them are found in the Fertile Crescent (Mesopotamia)   an area encompassing the Akkadian, Babylonian and Assyrian civilizations along the Tigris and Euphrates rivers (modern Iraq).

4. During this period, in Mesopotamia, the Sumerians established their presence.

Depth of Bible Words and Places
The Sumerians

The first people to migrate to Mesopotamia, the "land between the rivers" probably earlier than 4000 BCE. They created a great civilization along the rivers and made many advances in technology. The wheel, plow, and writing (a system that we call cuneiform) are examples of their achievements. The farmers in Sumer created levees to hold back the floods from their fields and cut canals to channel river water to the fields.

There were seven great city-states, each with its own king and a building called a ziggurat, a large pyramid-shaped building with a temple at the top, and having an army to protect itself from its neighbors.

Around 2300 BCE, the independent coalition of Sumer, considered the very beginning of civilization, was conquered by Sargon the Great of Akkad. Sargon was an Akkadian, a Semitic group of desert nomads who eventually settled in Mesopotamia just north of Sumer. Eventually, the Akkadian Empire fell, and was replaced by the Old Babylonian Empire, possibly the first empire in existence.

a. The Sumerians were a non-Semitic people who established the highest standard civilization in existence (see above). They had a form of language, using Pictographs by 3500 BCE. As stated in the above Depth detail, Mesopotamia was invaded from the north by the Akkadians and overrun by Sargon, forming what was perhaps the first empire, including Syria and Palestine. However, only a few years later, the kingdom of Egypt, under pharaoh Pepi (*c.* 2325-2275) invaded Sargon's empire.

b. Recent discoveries of fifteen hundred tablets near Ebla in northern Syria provide us with a rich store of information. Ebla, a town of many three-storied buildings, attained political power over this new empire of Sargon's. Its third king, Ebrum was akin to Eber, one of Abraham's ancestors. The Ebla tablets include references to Sinai, Jerusalem, Hazor, Megiddo, and Lachish. The tablets also include the names of Esau, Ishmael, David, Saul, and Israel. The name Yahweh has also been detected in these documents.

5. During the period of *c.* 2400-2000 BCE, almost every site in Palestine was completely abandoned or reduced to small settlements. Invaders arrived, nomads who destroyed the early way of life. Following was the age of the Amorites. These Semitic speaking groups moved in from the arid Arabian fringes of the Fertile Crescent and by the eighteenth century had conquered upper Mesopotamia, founding Babylon as the capital of a new and powerful dynasty. The lawgiver Hammurabi was its most famous monarch.

    a. In Palestine, development was much slower than in Mesopotamia. Recorded records inform us by pictographs, of the dependence upon Egypt. Egypt wanted access to the timber of Phoenicia (Lebanon) and the coastal highway (the Egyptian Ways of Horus). The land was also indispensable for the safe protection of the valley of the Nile. The leaders in the Palestine lands were Canaanite rulers, mostly independent from one another. By 1800 BCE, these independent city-states were beginning to enlarge their dominions into minor kingdoms, looking after themselves.

    a. Various Dynasties controlled the rule of Egypt. A series of tablets inform us that by the *c.* 1400 BCE, local rulers in Canaan revealed a weakening of Egyptian control, which manifested in revolts. Egypt paid little attention to these actions.

6. Canaan had now established a revival of town life, almost independent from Egypt, and with a newly formed Semitic language. They fortified each city with a new kind of massive rampart, probably brought to Palestine during the Hyksos time of rule in Egypt, and designed to resist attacks against horse-drawn chariots. These cities of included Hazor, Megiddo, Shechem, Gezer, and Jerusalem.

    a. Hazor, located on a small hill close to the Sea of Galilee, had a population of 30,000. The Overlords ruled much of northern Canaan.

b. The Canaanite rulers strengthened their military prowess by the employment of chariots, and reliance on bronze tools and weapons. Much of their copper came by courtesy of the Egyptians and from the island of Cyprus, in exchange of purple dye, oil, wine, ivory, and wood.

c. An alphabet was devised as early as 1800 BCE, a more simple script than the Egyptian pictograph. The Semitic vocabulary developed into twenty-seven Canaanite characters representing consonants. They also had three primary vowel-sounds. This extraordinary feat of dissecting the sounds of human speech into written vocabulary was the crowning contribution of the Canaanites to the world's culture.

d. Documents make it clear that the Canaanites believed in the existence of deity and that a supernatural power could be approached. Their belief included the fact that the history of the ancient Canaanites was divinely guided. However, their religion was polytheistic, which came from Mesopotamia. This is in contrast to the later Israelite strict belief of monotheism. The Canaanite belief in many gods continued to influence Israel throughout the Old Testament period. We would note that El, the Mighty One, existed in most Semitic peoples, however, became blurred by the localizations of cult. They accepted El's son, named Baal, a mighty hero. The Canaanite religion continued well into the Biblical period and as late as the sixth century.

FIVE

The Fall

1   The second event was *THE FALL*.

1.1. Chapter 3 of Genesis is extremely important. It explains thousands of years of heartache, misery, torture, and bloodshed. Without this chapter, life itself as we live, would be incomprehensible. We find *ourselves* in this chapter. We face temptation and falling every day. Guilt is the consequence, perhaps even death.

1.2. Everything was quite pleasant in the garden, *for a time.* Adam and Eve lived in peace, holiness to God, obedience to His commandments, and walked with Him in the garden.

1.3. Man was given total authority; he named all the animals, and was given authority to take care of all God's creation. It was quite evident that Adam was created an intelligent being.

1.4. Imagine that wonderful scene. Envision Adam and Eve, looking over a wonderful animal of creation, perhaps pointing, *"You, lion; you, soaring in the sky, eagle; big guy back there, elephant!"* Wow, was that a great scene or what! Think of what a great mind Adam was given; he had to remember everything he named. Language itself was created with Adam and Eve.

1.5. Moreover, he was to have children, and expand that garden to cover the earth. Earth was a colony of God's Kingdom, which was called Heaven.[1][2]

---

[1] To be a spirit-being, to be the family of God, a fellowship-being in God's Kingdom, it demanded the capacity for choice. There could be no holiness, without the "possibility" of disobedience...of sin; but *NOT* the necessity *OF* it. **CHOICE**

[2] We include a few thoughts concerning God's Kingdom. Far too little has been taught about this topic.

EXPANDED HELP PAPER
God's Kingdom

God's Kingdom of heaven was not complete in itself. He had an expanded plan!

Think with me for a moment. Think first of the original thirteen states, The United States of America. Our country existed, first as those thirteen states and then forty-eight states for a long time. However, there came time when our nation, peacefully added to its territory, to eventually include two more "extensions of America." These two "extensions" were given the same, full rights of the "mother" country, the USA. Same government, benefits, rights, and choices of the nation. Equal representation. States of the United States.

Also, consider England. When they expanded and extended their commonwealth, The British Empire called their extensions, colonies. Let's use this in our comments because most of us understand a colony of a nation.

God extended His Kingdom; He expanded, to include earth as a colony, and extension of His Home, Heaven. However this colony would include something different, beings made like Him.

These beings would have God's authority over the colony; totally in service to God as Father, but with His benefits and rights. Human beings created in the image and likeness of God would walk and talk with Him as His sons and daughters. They would fill the colony with generations of sons and daughters who would fill it and walk together in harmony and love for one another. Every one created with individual gifts to complement every other one.

That plan never changed. Interrupted yes, but never discarded.

1.6. We are told that Eve *walked to*, and then *looked at*, the fruit, which God had been forbidden. She *listened* as the tempter, the father of all lies (John 8:44) came, lied, and deceived her into visualizing the lie. Her mind received a lie. The possibility of choice had to be there. Man's obedience was required for him to complete God's original plan for their fellowship.

   1.6.1.   Satan spotted a weakness and created doubt with the very tone in his question.[1]

---

[1] He used the same method God had used. There is nothing original about Satan. He "created" by first releasing **his** desire, **his** picture, framing it in a container of words. This is the pattern set as a law by God.

1.6.2.	Eve then responded by using the name *Elohim* (which Satan had used), and not the name she knew, *Yahweh*. *Elohim* was power, the Creator— *Yahweh* was her personal Lord.

1.6.3.	Eve *looked*...then *desired*...then *listened* as Satan lied to her and deceived her into visualizing the lie. He said God was only a god of wisdom and power (*Elohim*), not your personal God (*Yahweh*). Eve disregarded her personal Lord and yielded to the god of this world. Then we know, Adam also ate the fruit, and together their act brought conscience to each of them. They hid from God, and today, fallen men still run and hide. *"Where are you?"* is still God's call. And He offers *"come to me."* Adam blamed Eve...Eve blamed Satan...and we continue to blame the system, fate, parents, or others. Blame arrived when sin came.[1]

Depth of Bible Words and Places
Fall
The original sin of Adam and Eve that destroyed the perfect relation-ship between individuals and God the Father.

1.7. We read next, the first of two key verses in Genesis: 3:15.[2] Judgment comes.[3]

1.7.1.	The story does not end without hope. This first prophecy in the Bible is not entirely "doom and gloom." The seed of a woman (a female doesn't produce a seed, a male does). The seed (Christ was born without a physical male's seed), "*shall bruise your head Satan,*" don't you love that? (A bruise to the head is a deathblow); "*and you Satan will only bruise His (Jesus Christ), heal.*" Jesus was only slightly bruised, and His body, the Church is only bruised a little. That "heal," the church, is the foot that is to continually step on Satan.

The AMP version summarizes the law in Hebrews 11:3 *By faith we understand that the worlds were framed (fashioned, put in order, and equipped for their intended purpose) by the word of God, so that what we see was not made out of things which are visible.* (AMP)

[1]Conscience is the voice of your soul; just as your heart is the voice of your spirit and the five senses are the voice of your body. Each voice speaks to the part of you that it is the voice of.

[2]*And I will put enmity* (the Hebrew word is "hostility") *Between you and the woman, And between your seed and her seed; He shall bruise you on the head, And you shall bruise him on the heel.*

[3]The serpent was made to crawl on the ground for all future time. Satan left the serpent's body, ascending to high atmosphere where he is the power. A woman was to suffer multiplied sorrows. And to Adam: thorns, thistles, sweat, and physical death. So they would live, forever banished from the Garden. Two angels were fixed at the entrance with a flaming sword in order to seal the way back in to the garden.

1.7.2.   Then God sheds the blood of an animal to provide a covering for Adam and Eve. An animal slain for a sacrifice; blood shed as a means of redemption.[1]

1.7.3.   Later, Abel would know all about what was an acceptable sacrifice, so would Abraham, and later Jesus. It all is traced back to this shedding of blood.

1.7.4.   Adam and Eve were removed from the garden and two angels placed at the entrance in order to keep man away from the Tree of Life.

1.8. A second generation begins in Genesis chapters 4 and 5, which produces conflict. Conscience was awakened in man, and cps 4 and 5 are the fruit of sin. Eve called her first born, Cain, connecting "I have gotten a man from God" with the promise in 3:15, the seed who would bruise the serpent's head. She would be disappointed, naming Abel, "fading away."

1.8.1.   Cain and Abel present their sacrifices to God. Their lives were a picture of contrasts even though they were brothers.

1.8.2.   Cain a *"tiller of the ground,"* Abel a *"keeper of sheep."*

1.8.3.   Cain brings an offering from the soil, a simple thank offering with no expression of sorrow for sin (he could have brought the offering that God set down—his dad and mom taught him). Abel sheds blood, an offering for sin, the acceptable sacrifice that he too learned from dad, who had learned from God.[2]

1.8.4.   Abel's lamb was the first lamb of sacrifice, Christ would be the last.

1.8.5.   And Cain is angered, the Bible says, *"his countenance fell,"* and God even then shows His love as redeemer and offers Cain a way to turn to the acceptable way and BE accepted.

1.8.6.   But Cain becomes the first murderer and Abel the first martyr for God.

1.8.7.   A mark is placed on Cain (perhaps so that no one would kill him) and he was *"cursed from the earth."* He goes out and

---

[1]Blood begins to run in Genesis, and continues at various times throughout the Old Testament. It's like a scarlet cord of redemption intertwined in every book. From God shedding blood to cover Adam and Eve in the Garden of Eden to the garden in heaven's paradise, the flood of sacrifice is the constant testimony of God's grace. As fallen man was clothed with skins of animals sacrificed by God Himself for such provision, so the blood of the Lamb was shed to clothe the righteousness of God in every member of mankind who will receive His gift. Redemption flowed from Genesis to a cross.

[2]Hebrews 11:4 says *"By faith Abel offered unto God a more excellent sacrifice than Cain, by which he obtained witness that he was righteous, God testifying of his gifts."* Cain did not have the faith of Abel and God didn't accept Cain's' offering as He did Abel's.

dwells in a land SE of Eden called Nor or a "land of wandering." (Note Jude 11).

1.8.8. Then we see later in cp 4 that Cain's line rapidly increased. I looked closely at this first generation of Adam and the genealogies of Cain and Seth (Seth replaced Abel and continued the line to Christ); also refer to the following comments, as well as the footnotes contrasting the character of two ways of life.

1.8.9. Cain's civilization, which was before the flood, is called the "Antediluvian Civilization." Started by Cain—it ended in destruction.

1.8.10. Cain builds the first city, and names it Enoch after his first son, and urban life begins. Interesting to see how civilization develops. From Cain's line comes agriculture, cattle-raising, music develops (one son is Jubal *father of all who handle the harp and the organ*").

1.8.11. Also builders and manufacturers came from Cain. They certainly were not a bunch of ignorant people. In fact, it is said Cain's civilization may have been equal to that of Rome! I have no doubt that much had been learned from Adam and Eve.

1.8.12. Another is Tubal, the father of metal work.

2 Both the Cain and Seth Families are traced in Genesis cp 5 which begins *"This is the book of the generations...."* [1] [2] Both lines gather themselves according to their spiritual tendencies. [3] This introduces the first of ten generations covered in Genesis. The first three generations perished, the fourth being that of Noah; from Noah came interesting generations such as Babylon, Egypt and the Philistines. The sixth generation will cover the life of Abraham, the eighth, Isaac, and the last of the ten is Jacob, which deals mostly with Joseph.

---

[1] *Cain* (six descending groups are listed). Cain the first murderer Lamech, the second murderer and the first polygamist. Not one of the line *"walked with God."* The Cainite line information is sparse, simply mentioning the birth of seven generations and then dropped from historical records. His line had no future. It is noted that the Seth line "called upon the name of God."

[2] How about Seth? The vital place of Abel had to be filled if the mercy plan of God to mankind were to be offered. His name, "appointed" was prophetic. Ten names are listed; this line carries the bloodline to Christ We find in this line, worship is established. Enoch is the first after the fall to be mentioned for his fellowship with God. The Seth line had a much longer life span than CAIN's line. (It was after the flood of Noah, that the tenth name was mentioned; that life was shortened from the effects of sin and disease.) The three sons of Noah became the ancestors of the three great races of mankind.
What a contrast in lives.

[3] This whole story, reminds me of "if you know what is correct to do, then do it. If you don't, it's sin."

3   The third of the four events: *THE FLOOD.* Creation was the first event, The Fall was the second.

3.1. Let's look at the *causes* and the *judgments* of the flood. (6:1-22)

    3.1.1.   After ten generations, a mixing of lines takes place. The two lines of Seth and Cain, are mixed with what the Bible calls *"the sons of God,"* and they produced many giants; mighty men called Nephilim.[1] Mankind reached its highest point of corruption. Sethite faith no longer existed. Literally, "it pained God's heart" that he had made man.

    3.1.2.   The only righteous family left was Noah's. Satan attempted to block any line, which would lead to the *"Seed"* which would bring redemption. But here is Noah. He was told to bring his wife, his three sons, and their wives; eight human beings, not affected by the Nephilim and other mixed lines.[2] Noah was 180 years old when he began construction of the Ark and before any of his sons were born.

    3.1.3.   So judgment is pronounced on the ungodly, and the Ark is built to God's exact specifications.

    3.1.4.   God was taking the first step to separating the righteous from the wicked, the first step toward a chosen nation. [3]

    3.1.5.   Chapter 7 details The Flood, which is an illuminating picture on one's salvation through Christ.[4] This event was only twice referred to in the Old Testament.[5] Brought on the Ark, were one pair of each of the unclean animals, to preserve them, and seven pairs of clean animals, enough for sacrifice or perhaps provide food. Really, no reproduction of animals was needed

---

[1] The Nephilim was an attempt by Satan to destroy the seed line that would lead to his own destruction. Only two Biblical references occur, one before the flood and the second, after. This would indicate Satan used this method two different times. Both times it failed. Even though Jesus said angels do not marry, He did NOT say they were unable to procreate. Jude 6 would indicate they could. The term *"sons of God"* is used elsewhere in the Old Testament and always refers to divine beings, never men. See Angels in the Old Testament, in index. Destroy Noah, and there would be no Shem or Abraham or Israel or Judah or David…or Christ!

[2] Six times in cps 6-8 we are told of those who were on the Ark. The narrative is more centered on those alive, rather than those blotted out.

[3] The Ark was approximately 562 x 94x56 feet, by the old Egyptian measurement. Usually we use 18" to a cubit which would make the Ark 450 feet long. One window was at the top, one door at the side. There was an opening that extended all around the top of the Ark for light and air.

[4] Peter tells us about it in his first letter, 3:18-22. Salvation and the Ark were both planned by God, not invented by any man. There's *one way* to salvation, one door into the Ark. Gen 6:14 is the same word *atonement* used later in the Old Testament, both "held together" by *pitch* or atonement. Those on the outside perish; the inside residents exit to new life.

[5] Ps 29:10, Isa 54:9-10

TRAVEL THROUGH THE OLD TESTAMENT

during that year. There might have been, but it was not necessary.[1]

3.1.6.   Provisions for the twelve months were to be stored in the ark.[2]

3.1.7.   We see Noah was obedient in *"everything just as God commanded"* (Gen 6:22). The rain came and the breaking up of the sea floors erupted (Gen 7:11), as the entire earth was flooded. The flood continued for 150 days. The ark floated upon the waters. In the 7th month, the ark miraculously grounded on one of the mountains of Ararat, in what was later called Armenia.

3.1.8.   After forty days, Noah's wisdom sent out a raven, followed by a raven and doves to see if the water was removed (8:6-8). When the dove returned with the olive leaf, he knew the earth was almost dry however, the dove did not return following the third release.

3.1.9.   Altogether, they spent one year in the ark. Note that Noah and his family were saved from the destruction of the flood by the ark, which was a perfect Old Testament type of Christ, our Ark of Safety.

3.2. In cp 8 we have the *results* of the Flood recorded.

3.2.1.   Even after the earth was dry, Noah waited for the command of the Lord before leaving the Ark. Noah's first act upon leaving was to build an altar to the Lord and offer burnt offerings of every clean beast and fowl...an extensive act of worship, an example of priorities in life. (8:20).[3]

3.2.2.   Then God made His first covenant with man. This was the rainbow, which was to always appear as a symbol of His everlasting mercy. The earth will never be destroyed again by a flood. Prior to this time, apparently the direct rays of the sun did not pierce though the atmosphere in order to scatter in the form of a beautiful rainbow. Nature itself was changed after the flood.

3.3. Let's look at Noah's three sons and what happened to them.

3.3.1.   Who were they? We have insight into each of them from Noah's final benediction upon them. Japheth was to be enlarged and become the ancestor of those nations, which are

---

[1]This was before the Law had been given, and animals were classified as "clean" or "unclean" as proper or improper for sacrifice or for food.

[2]The three floors could accommodate 43,000 tons. Today's ocean liner will carry a maximum of 25,000 tons. There would have been plenty of room in the three decks for Noah, his family, the animals and sufficient food.

[3]An interesting Jewish tradition says Noah built the altar on the exact place where Adam had first built an altar, which was also the same one used by Cain and Abel.

most progressive in government and science. He was to accept the God of Shem, and even dwell in Shem's tents. The curse would be upon Canaan, the son of Ham (thought to be the idolatrous tendencies of the Canaanites, later encountered in the Promised Land). Shem would be the Hebrew hope and received the greatest blessing. He and his posterity were to be the ancestors of Jesus Christ. The "Lord God" of Shem had been the "Lord God" of Adam, and was later to be the "Lord God" of Abraham.

Depth of Bible Words and Places
Canaan, Canaanites

Canaan was a son of Ham and a grandson of Noah. His descendants settled in areas God promised to Abraham. Excavations suggest that there was no middle class in their society. Later the area was known as Palestine and Israel. The cities of Canaan in ancient days of the Bible were each fortified against chariots and ruled by a king. The most powerful city-states included Hazor, Shechem, Gezer, and Jerusalem.

Depth of Bible Words and Places
Semite

The descendants of Shem, one of Noah's three sons. Many groups of people were known as "Semitic" or of a "Semitic Family" of languages. Broadly refers to groups of people from Mesopotamia or South Asia. Some of those were the Canaanites, Hebrews, Arabs, Assyrians, Babylonians, and Ethiopians.

3.3.2.   Where did they settle?

    3.3.2.1.   Japheth had seven sons, and they became the Caucasian peoples of Europe. Greeks, Romans, and Spaniards; the ancestor of what we call the "Gentiles." The Hebrew name meant "to enlarge" and indeed the descendants of Japheth spread out much farther than their relatives.

    3.3.2.2.   The four sons of Ham settled in Egypt and Babylonia. Cush is ancient Ethiopia (not the modern nation), Mizraim is Egypt, and Put may be Libya. His descendants located in areas we know as Egypt, the Sudan, Saudi Arabia, and Yemen. From this line came Canaanites, Philistines, Hittites, Amorites and others.

3.3.2.3.   The five sons of Shem populated Western Mesopotamia and became the line that God chose as the line preserving the seed. Of those five sons, the emphasis is on the family of Arphaxad because he was the grandfather of Eber. From this line came Hebrews, Assyrians, Persians, and others.

3.3.3.   In general we could say Asia was given to Shem, Africa to Ham, and Europe to Japheth. All existing languages have been traced to three original sources.

3.3.4.   A listing of the family lines following the flood is found in cp 9 followed by judgment on all those families in cp 11.

4   The fourth event in the first eleven chapters of Genesis is *JUDGMENT AT BABEL.* The three sons of Noah, and the families that resulted, began to slightly migrate and were all speaking the same language. They continued living in the same general area, the plain of Babylonia; a few of them serving God.[1]

4.1. It is likely that the events in chapter 11 occurred prior to those in chapter 10 since the scattering in chapter 10 was the result of judgment at Babel.

4.2. Much earlier, God had commanded the peoples to be fruitful and scatter across the earth. However they decided to move to Nimrod's city of Babylon and settle (Genesis 11:8-12). This decision was in rebellion against God's command to scatter. Nimrod seemingly wanted the people under his control. They built a tower, known as a "ziggurat."

4.3. When together they reached the area in the lower Tigris-Euphrates valley, they decided to build a capital city with a huge tower, which should *reach into heaven.* Ego and self-will would have prevented them from filling the earth as commanded by God. No remains have been located; we are not told whether the tower was allowed to stand following the dispersal of its builders.

Depth of Bible Words and Places
Hittites

The Hittites are mentioned fifty-four times in the Bible. Many well-known persons are mentioned in connection with Hittites. Abraham and Sarah, Isaac and Rebecca, and Jacob and

---

[1]"Babel" came to mean confusion. The word "babel" sounds like the Hebrew word *balal* which means "confusion." The language was confounded in order to divide and scatter them upon the earth. God wanted a people to fill the earth, so this was what He did to establish nations.

Leah were all buried in the Cave of Machpelah, which Abraham had purchased from Ephron the Hittite (Genesis 49:29-32). Isaac's son Esau married Hittite women (Genesis 26:34; 36:2). Isaac's wife, Rebecca, feared that Esau's twin, Jacob, might marry a Hittite woman. She tells her husband, "I am disgusted with my life because of the Hittite women. If Jacob marries a Hittite woman what good will life be to me?" (Genesis 27:46). There were several references to Hittites during the Kingdoms of Israel and Judah (1 Kings 9:20; 10:29; 11:1; 2 Kings 7:6; 2 Chronicles 1:17; 8:7). Beautiful Bathsheba, whom King David desired when he spied her bathing, was married to a Hittite named Uriah.

Depth of Bible Words and Places
Tower

Many remains of ancient towers have been unearthed in Babylonia. Most cities were built around it with a temple on top to worship a god. The towers were built with many stories, each in a color. The record of the destruction of one of them reads, "The building of this temple offended the gods. In a night, they threw down what had been built. They scattered them abroad and made strange their speech." Many of these towers fell into the hands of later peoples and became forerunners of the Mohammedan mosque.

Depth of Bible Words and Places
Babel

The Tower of Babel was built on the plain of Shinar, a site probably in ancient Babylonia in southern Mesopotamia, after the flood of Noah's time. The structure was built to satisfy the people's vanity: "Let us make a name" (Gen 11:4). The pyramid-like tower was expected to reach heaven. These people were trying to approach God on their own self-serving terms. This tower was probably built of bricks and mortar since no stones were available in the flat plain of southern Mesopotamia. An example of one such tower, built in Ur, in southern Mesopotamia, about 2100 BCE, was a pyramid consisting of three terraces of diminishing size.

4.4. God judges this activity with confusion of tongues and scatters them. He judges their unity of language so that they no longer understood each other and caused dispersion throughout the earth. Actually it is those three boys of Noah who went three directions in order to fill the earth.

4.5. A transition now begins in our travels. Adam's line (Genesis 5) was traced to Noah and his three sons. Shem's line was traced as far as Abraham, where they reach a culmination in history. Now the history of mankind is centered on the Hebrew history as the patriarchal era begins. Sin marred God's plan for man; we now see the first steps toward the redemption of the race through a chosen people.

S E C T I O N 3
The Patriarchs-Four Great Men

Genesis 12-50; Job. The period from 2100 to 1630 BCE

Theme Statement: *"...by faith Abraham, when he was called, obeyed"* (Heb 11:8)

THE KEYS IN SECTION THREE

Section 3: The Patriarchs-Four Great Men

SEE **Keys to Genesis** at the beginning of **Section Two**

Approximate DATES OF KEY EVENTS in Section 3	
1997	Abraham is born in Ur of the Chaldeans
1921	Abraham is called to set out for Canaan
	Life of Job
1896	Isaac is born to Abraham and Sarah
1837	Jacob is born to Isaac and Rebekah
1821	Abraham dies in Canaan
1745	Joseph is born to Jacob and Rachel
1728	Joseph is sold into slavery
1716	Isaac dies in Canaan
1706	Jacob and his family move to Egypt
1689	Jacob dies in Egypt
1635	Joseph dies in Egypt

Keys to Job—

A Key Word: *Affliction*

The Key Verses (13:15; 37:23–24)

13:15 Though He slay me, I will hope in Him. Nevertheless I will argue my ways before Him.

37:23 "The Almighty — we cannot find Him; He is exalted in power And He will not do violence to justice and abundant righteousne ss. 24 "Therefore men fear Him; He does not regard any who are wise of heart."

Key Chapter (42)

The Key People in Job

Job—suffered much loss; faith was tested by God; Job never blamed God; restoration (1:1–42:16)

Eliphaz the Temanite—a friend of Job; believed Job was suffering because of his sin (2:11; 4:1–5:27; 15:1–35; 22:1–30; 42:7–9)

Bildad the Shuhite—a second friend of Job; believed Job had not repented of his sin and therefore suffered (2:11; 8:1–22; 18:1–21; 25:1–6; 42:9)

Zophar the Naamathite—a third friend of Job; believed Job deserved to suffer more for his sins (2:11; 11:1–20; 20:1–29; 42:9)

Elihu the Buzite—a younger "advisor," stood up against Job's three friends; believed God was using suffering to mold Job's character (32:1–37:24)

NOTE: The Book of Job, if placed chronologically, would probably follow Genesis or more specifically, close to chapters 11-12. It is generally grouped with the WISDOM books.

SIX

Abraham

1   The second division of Genesis is Section 3 of our study.

2   The first division was *THE BEGINNING OF HISTORY, Four Great Events* in the first eleven cps which covered the first 1,800 years of history. We continue in the Scriptures to the period of *THE PATRIARCHS,* which is outlined by *Four Great Men* in cps 12 thru 50 and cover the next 250 years.[1]

2.1. When these *Four Great Men* came on the scene, two powerful cultures, Mesopotamia and Egypt, already had a history of a thousand years. So with Canaan at the center of biblical studies, we note the strong, interrelated relationship of Abram (the first of Four Great Men) with Mesopotamia and Joseph (the last of the four men) with Egypt. We detail these *three geographical areas* which are the lands of the Bible.

2.1.1.   What do we know about the area called Mesopotamia ?

2.1.1.1.   The Sumerians[2] were a non-Semitic[3] people who controlled the lower Euphrates Area, or Sumer. Sumer is thought to have been "ground zero" for that First Great event, Creation. We identify Sumer during a

---

[1] A reminder of the theme to keep in mind as we cover this period from 2100 to 1850 BCE. It is found in Hebrews 11:8 *"by faith Abraham, when he was called, obeyed."* What a theme to have of one's life!

[2] Sumerians. The non-Semitic people were inhabitants of the ancient land of Sumer, located in the fertile plain between the Tigris and Euphrates Rivers. Referred to as Shinar (Gen. 10:10; Is. 11:11; Zech 5:11). The Tower of Babel was built "in the land of Shinar" (Gen. 11: 2). One of its main cities was Ur of the Chaldees (Gen. 11:28,31). It was the first high civilization in the history of humanity. Today, this is the southern portion of Iraq.

[3] Semitic. A member of an ancient Semitic people claiming descent from Abraham, Isaac, and Jacob; an Israelite. A descendant of this people, a Jew.

period called *Early Dynastic* period, (or the earliest of Dynasties), 2800-2400 BCE. These Sumerians gave us the first literature in Asia. The Sumerian language became the classical language and flourished in writing throughout Babylonian and Assyrian cultures until about the first century of the Common Era, CE. This Sumerian culture of the *First Dynasty,* during the City of Ur phase, is known to us because of an uncovered cemetery. Wooden coffins of the common people in which food, drink, weapons, tools, necklaces, vanity cases, and bracelets were found; all suggesting these people anticipated a life after death.

2.1.1.2.   Also discovered, was that the Sumerians were well advanced in the field of metallurgy, as well as in the crafts of goldsmiths and gem cutters. Quite advanced for that period in world history; in fact we know they were second to none during that period.

2.1.1.3.   We have some preserved clay tablets, which reveal a detailed analysis of their economic life. Archeologists found a wooden panel (22" x 9") in one of the tombs which reveals for us scenes from both peace and war. It is amazing, but we know chariots were already in use, carrying javelin throwers into battle. Alexander the Great used the Sumerians' battle formations hundreds of years later.

2.1.1.4.   We know they utilized basic principles of construction, which are used in our day by the modern architect. They were successful in agriculture and prosperous in extensive trade, reaching their most advanced stage of culture around 2400 BCE. Their last great king had extended Sumerian power as far west as the Mediterranean. So this early civilization was well advanced.

2.1.1.5.   Then, during this period, three other "masses" of people worked their way into the Mesopotamia land, eventually destroying the Sumerian culture. This was under Hammurabi, consolidating various peoples and establishing a great commercial center called Babylon around 1700 BCE. Very little remains in our day, however, it *will* flourish again one day

2.1.1.6.   King Hammurabi's great achievement, was his Code of Law, discovered by an Egyptian archeologist in 1901 CE, written on a stone slab, located in Iran, and containing 282 laws. So, Babylon reached its early prominence in what we refer to as The First Dynasty of Babylon during the period of 1800-1500 BCE. Babylon was conquered the first time in 1500.

2.1.2.   The *second geographical area* in the Scriptures was Egypt, an amazing, unique, land. (Also refer to additional information on Egypt in this volume).

2.1.2.1.   Most of us are familiar with this land. The Peace Accords, signed a few years ago, established what was to be a permanent peace between these lands. However, terrible unrest with riots and upheaval of the government later destroyed that relationship, even though the agreement is still in effect. Refer to the following list of Egyptian Dynasties, which we will refer to in various sections of this volume.

The Thirty Dynasties in Ancient Egyptian History

Period	Date (All BCE)	Dynasty
	3150 - 3050	0
Early Dynastic Period	3050 - 2813	1
	2813 - 2663	2
	2663 - 2597	3
	2597 - 2471	4
Old Kingdom	2471 - 2355	5
	2355 - 2195	6
	2195 - 2160	7 & 8
First Intermediate Period	2160 - 2040	9 & 10
Middle Kingdom	2160 - 1994	11
	1994 - 1781	12
Second Intermediate Period	1781 - 1650	13 & 14
	1650 - 1535	15 & 16
	1650 - 1549	17
	1549 - 1298	18
New Kingdom	1298 - 1187	19
	1187 - 1069	20
	1064 - 940	21
	948 - 743	22
Third Intermediate Period	743 - 715	23
	731 - 717	24
	752 - 656	25

	664-525	26
	525 - 405	27
Late Period	405 - 399	28
	399-380	29
	380-343	30
During the three Intermediate Periods, a foreign power controlled Egypt		
Greco-Roman Period	332 BCE-30	

The above dates have been established and are accepted in most reference books. However, Radiocarbon dating suggests that the 18th Dynasty may have started a few years earlier than the conventional date of 1550 BCE. The radiocarbon date range for its beginning is 1570−1544 BCE. Thus, the above dates may be approximately twenty years later. The author of this volume uses the earlier dates in his Pharaohs of the 18th and 19th dynasties, later detailed in this volume.

2.1.2.2.　　When Abraham came to Egypt from Canaan, Egypt could boast of a culture already more than a thousand years old. The beginning of history in Egypt is usually traced to King Menes (*c.* 3000 BCE). He united two kingdoms, one in the Northern Delta, along the Mediterranean (called the Lower Kingdom), and another in the Nile Valley (the Upper Kingdom). Each period of a continuous rule was called a Dynasty, and when referring to Egypt, historians usually refer to the particular Dynasty. In all, there were thirty dynasties, the final one ruling into the intertestament period.

2.1.2.3.　　The rulers of the first two dynasties had their capital near Thebes located South just at the bottom of the crook in the Nile River. It was a large city with 40,000 inhabitants. Thebes lasted until about 664 BCE when the Assyrians invaded Egypt. The royal tombs excavated there, have yielded stone vases, jewelry, and copper vessels. All objects buried with the kings, reflect a high level of civilization during this early period. This was the first era of international commerce in historical times.

2.1.2.4.　　The classical age of Egyptian civilization, known as the Old Kingdom period (*c.* 2663-2195) and comprising Dynasties IV-VIII witnessed a number of notable achievements. Huge pyramids, the wonders of centuries to follow, provide ample testimony to the advanced culture of rulers.

2.1.2.5.   The Step Pyramid, the earliest large structure made of stone, was built as a royal mausoleum by Imhotep, an architect who also gained renown as a priest, author of proverbs, and magician. The Great Pyramid at Giza towered 481 feet from a thirteen-acre base. The gigantic Sphinx of the Fourth Dynasty is another work which has never been duplicated. The "Pyramid Texts," inscribed during the Fifth and Sixth Dynasties on the walls of chambers and halls, indicate that the Egyptians, in their sun worship, anticipated a hereafter.

2.1.2.6.   The next five dynasties that ruled Egypt, (c. 2195-1994 BCE), arose during a period of corruption. Centralized government ended. Literature from this period gives us a picture of a weak government, one in a constant state of change. Then, toward the end of this period, the eleventh dynasty, built a strong state at Thebes.

2.1.2.7.   That ushered in a revival of sorts for Egypt. The Middle Kingdom (c. 2000-1650 BCE) marks the reappearance of a powerful centralized government. The Twelfth Dynasty established its capital near Memphis, farther north in what was known as Lower Egypt. Memphis was just below the Delta Area, where all the rivers came together.

2.1.2.8.   The great wealth of Egypt was enhanced by an irrigation project, which opened the fertile valley area for agriculture. New building activities went on near Thebes and elsewhere in the land. Besides promoting copper mining operations, the rulers also built a canal connecting the Red Sea and the Nile River. This enabled them to maintain better trade relations with the coast of eastern Africa. They expanded to the south annexing land along the Nile. A fortified trading colony was maintained there. Some Egyptian objects were found by archaeologists in Syria and Palestine areas attest to the vigorous trading activities of Egyptians in the eastern Mediterranean lands.

2.1.2.9.   While the Old Kingdom of 2700-2200 BCE was remembered for its originality and genius in art, the Middle Kingdom from 2000-1650 made its contribution in classical literature. Palace schools trained officials in reading and writing during the prosperous reigns of the Twelfth Dynasty. Although the masses were in poverty, it was possible for the average individual in that age to enter government service by means of education, training, and special ability. Texts of instruction inscribed in the coffins of others than royalty indicate that many more people now enjoyed the prospect of an afterlife.

2.1.2.10.   Then the weak Thirteenth and Fourteenth dynasties gave way to the Hyksos people. These bold intruders probably came from Asia Minor and overpowered the Egyptians by means of horse-drawn chariots and the composite bow, both of which were unknown to the Egyptian troops. However, they allowed (in retrospect, a mistake) the Egyptians to maintain some authority at Thebes, and in 1600 BCE the Thebans (Thebes) who had grown powerful on their own, and centralized, expelled the Hyksos and established the Eighteenth Dynasty, introducing the New Kingdom.

Depth of Bible Words and Places
Hyksos

A multiracial people, infiltrated Canaan in the late eighteenth century on their way to Lower (Northern) Egypt, taking over and ending the 13th Dynasty in Egypt. They brought to Egypt music instruments and new breeds of animals. Their mighty chariots, drawn by horses were also brought to, and introduced to, Egypt. They remained in power from *c.* 1720 BCE until *c.* 1567, driven out by Ahmose, founder of the eighteenth Dynasty.

2.1.3.   The *third geographical land* is what I refer to as the "center of the world." Canaan is the all-important land bridge between the first two areas we reviewed. It also is a land bridge connecting the continents of Asia and Africa. Indeed, we may think of this land as the crossroads of the ancient world. Compressed between the Mediterranean Sea to the west and the barren desert to the east, the land of Israel provided an important corridor with trade routes connecting Egypt with Mesopotamia. Whoever controlled the land bridge controlled the world economy in ancient days. The land of the "bridge," is divided into four zones, beginning with the Mediterranean Sea and moving east: (1) coastal plain (2) central hill country (3) Rift Valley (all three west of the Jordan River) (4) Transjordan (east of the Jordan

River). The "heart" of the land was the central hill country. There were six sub regions: (1) Galilee (2) Samaria (3) Benjamin (4) Judah (5) wilderness of Judah (6) Negev. We are certainly more familiar with this land than any other. We think of it, and rightly so, as the land of the Bible.

2.1.3.1.   The name "Canaan" applies to the land lying between Gaza in the south and Hamath in the north along the eastern coast of the Mediterranean (Gen 10:15-19). The Greeks in their trade with Canaan referred to the inhabitants as Phoenicians, a name which probably had its origin in the Greek word for "purple." There seemed to be a color of a textile dye developed in Canaan. Some of the earliest manuscripts had a purple color, still seen today on a few of them.

2.1.3.2.   As early as fifteen century BCE the name "Canaan" was applied in general to the Egyptian province in Syria or at least to the Phoenician coast, the center of the purple dye industry. The words "Canaanite" and "Phoenician" have the same cultural, geographical, and historical origin. Later this area came to be known as Syria and Palestine. The name "Palestine" had its origin in the name "Philistia."

2.1.3.3.   With the migration of Abraham into Canaan, this land becomes the focal point of interest in the historical and geographical developments of Bible times. Being strategically located between the two great centers that cradled the earliest civilizations, Mesopotamia and Egypt, Canaan served as a natural bridge linking Egypt and Mesopotamia. Because of that, it is not surprising to find a mixed population in the land. Some of the cities in Canaan, such as Jericho and others were occupied centuries before this patriarchal time of the Four Great Men.

2.1.3.4.   With the first great Semitic (Jewish) movement into Mesopotamia, it seems probable that the Amorites extended settlements down through Palestine and mixed with the people already there. Other invaders such as the Hittites penetrated Canaan from the north and appeared as well established citizens by the time Abraham purchased the cave of (Gen 23). Verses 17-18 read:

So *Ephron's field, which was in Hachpelah, which faced Hamre, the field and cave which was in it, and all the trees which were in the field, that were within all the confines of its border, were deeded over* 18 *to Abraham for a possession.* Over that cave, Herod the Great built a building over 2000 yrs ago. Today it is the 2nd most holy place of the Jewish people.

2.1.3.5.   As a result, the designation "Canaanite" very likely embraced the composite mixture of people occupying the land in the patriarchal era.

Depth of Bible Words and Places
(History of the word) Israel

The word "Israel" has undergone quite a change in its meaning over the years, so demands some detail. It makes for an interesting and educational study. I will trace the appearance of the word *Israel* in the Bible because the meaning has shifted over time.

1. The word begins in the book of Genesis, where we find the famous story of Jacob wrestling with an angel. We will review his life in Four Great Men. In this story for now, we find Jacob, the founding ancestor of ancient Israel, made his journey across the Fertile Crescent moving back from an area called Aram-Naharim to his homeland in Canaan.

As he reaches the eastern side of the Jordan River, near Penuel and Succoth the Bible describes his confrontation with a man who wrestles with him throughout the night. In the end, the man could not prevail over Jacob; you can see from this, the great determination of Jacob, not his power, the angel even knocked Jacob's hip out of joint. As the day begins to break, Jacob holds on to the man and says: "I will not let you go unless you bless me." The man blesses him with a name. He says: "Your name shall no more be called Jacob, but Israel, for you have striven with God and with men and have prevailed." So we find that the name Israel is first used as *the name of a man.*

We learn that Jacob's opponent throughout the night was not a man, but God. In Jacob's struggle with his God, he receives a blessing, a new name, and an injury. Therefore, in our first encounter with the word Israel, we are talking about a person, a founding ancestor who is said to see God face to face, although we know God's face cannot be fully looked upon; it was shielded in some way.

2. Then, the patriarch, Jacob, had twelve sons whose descendents became the nation of Israel. This story is told to us in the books of Joshua and Judges. The book of Joshua

opens with a promise that the twelve tribes of Israel, the descendents of Jacob, will together conquer the land of Canaan. It then narrates this divinely granted conquest with Joshua leading the twelve tribes of Israel to victory after victory. The book of Joshua closes with his call to all the tribes of Israel to gather at a place called Shechem and swear loyalty to their God. So, in our second encounter with the word Israel it designates *a people:* the twelve tribes of Israel.

So first a man, second a people. Later in the books of 1 and 2 Samuel, Israel is the name of **a** *monarchy* headed by King David and his son Solomon. This united monarchy unites and leads the twelve tribes of Israel so the word Israel then designated a kingdom made up of 12 tribes. However, after 75 years, the united monarchy divides and a rebellion within the twelve tribes' results in division, and Israel becomes the designation for the northern 10 tribes, under Jereboam. Judah is the designation for the tribes of Judah and Benjamin in the south under Rehoboam. (One tribe, Levi, is a priestly tribe that is not territorially bound). So Israel, during **this time** of the divided monarchy is still a kingdom, however, much smaller.

The northern kingdom, which has this name of Israel, falls to Assyria in 722 BCE. The southern kingdom of Judah falls to Babylonia in 586. Judah alone continues to exist as a people in exile from their land. As the sole remnant of the original twelve tribes of Israel, Judah becomes *the memory holder* for all Israel. By surviving as a people, Judah wins the right to tell the story of Israel. In that story, Judah sees itself as a remnant of Israel, the only remnant of Israel. In fact, when the Judean exiles return from Babylonia to their homeland in Judah, beginning in 538 BCE, this one remaining remnant tribe returns under the mantle of Israel.

It is interesting, as I was reviewing this history in my mind; David's rule started with only one tribe, Judah, and now again the nation of Israel consists mostly of one tribe, Judah, back in their homeland. Once there, the returning exiles from Babylonia find other Judeans living in the land. These Judeans had not gone into exile. In addition, conflicts immediately erupt between those who had experienced exile and those who had not. THE important factor here is that those Judeans who had experienced exile in Babylonia returned to Judah with a book, some form of the Torah.

It seems that their experience of conquest, deportation, and exile had led them to preserve their stories and their laws and to pass them down to their children in writing. In this written Torah, they preserved the story and the memory of their ancestor, Jacob. Jacob, they remembered, had also experienced exile in Mesopotamia and he had also returned to his homeland. As he returned he was met by God, wrestled with him throughout the night, and received the name Israel. So, the returning exiles who preserved this story saw themselves as the *new Israel*, the house of Jacob; the tribe who would bring the "Lion of Judah" the Messiah. Like their ancestor, they felt that in exile they *also* had wrestled with their God and come away both permanently marked with a limp, but also blessed, and with the name of Israel.

Through the centuries of history, the word Israel has changed. However, one aspect of the term remains consistent during each biblical period. In every period described in the Bible, Israel is of central importance. It is the chosen *person*, the chosen *nation*, the chosen *kingdom* and *remnant* of the Israelite God, and finally *a new-born Israel*. This remains a central theme today.

A man—A people—A kingdom—10 tribes—1 tribe, a memory holder—a captive remnant—a new Israel.

Depth of Bible Words and Places
Israelite

A descendant of Jacob (Israel).

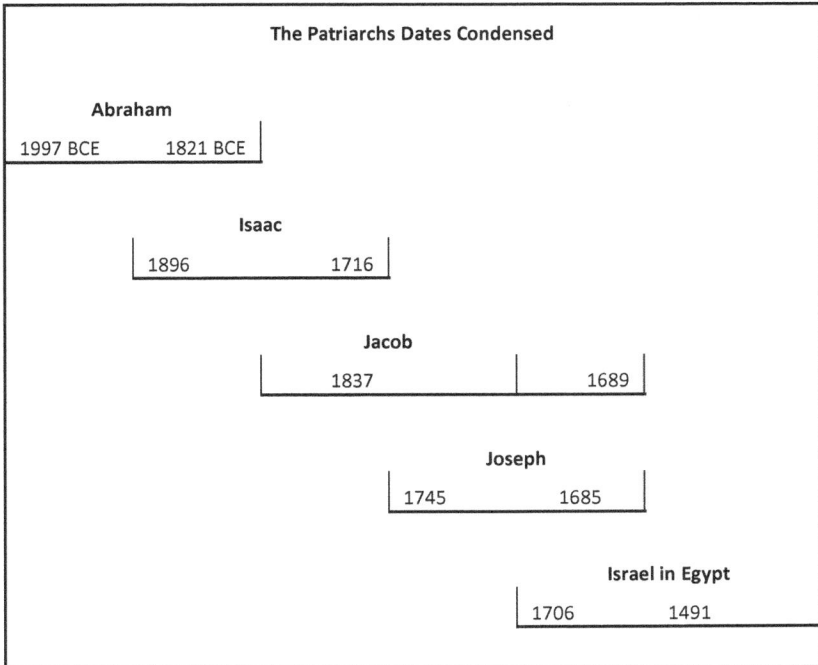

The Patriarchs Dates Condensed				
Abraham				
1997 BCE — 1821 BCE				
	Isaac			
	1896 — 1716			
		Jacob		
		1837 — 1689		
			Joseph	
			1745 — 1685	
				Israel in Egypt
				1706 — 1491

3   Now we begin the *FOUR GREAT MEN*. The first of these men, or leaders, begins in cp 11:10[1] and takes us through the beginning of cp 25. For chronological purposes, we will insert Job, because of the best estimates as to his time of life. It is thought that Job lived in the period between Gen chapters 11 and 12. For clarity in our study, Job will be reviewed following the book of Genesis.

Depth of Bible Words and Places
Patriarchs
The term Patriarchs is assigned to the period before Sinai. From Adam, Seth, Enoch, Methuselah, and Noah before the flood, to Shem, Terah and the four "major" patriarchs of Abraham, Isaac, Jacob, and Joseph, following the flood. Notice a genealogy of Patriarchs in 1 Chron 1:1-2:2. Many times we refer to only the Four Great Men of Abraham, Isaac, Jacob, and Joseph as the Patriarchs; however many men prior to Mt. Sinai are Patriarchs "the founders of a family."

3.1. *ABRAHAM "The Faithful Man."* Fittingly, Abram (his birth name), was the first person to be called a Hebrew. We begin, perhaps surprisingly, with a New Testament verse, Matt 1:1 *The record of the genealogy of Jesus the Messiah, the son of David, the son of Abraham.* Matthew, being a Jew, writing to Jews to prove the lineage of the Messiah, traces Jesus back to Abraham, the first Jew.

3.1.1.   A new era in Bible history begins in "Ur of the Chaldees." Twenty-one centuries before Christ, God began the unfolding of His divine purpose. Ur may be located on Map 2, just NW of the Persian Gulf (however, see two possible locations mentioned below). A great city of its time, the very center of paganism and nature worship. Its religion demanded the worship of many gods, in particular the sun and moon. God knew he had to "cut off" Abram from all that was behind, in order for him to move on and obtain the plan.

Depth of Bible Words and Places
Ur

---

[1] *These are the records of the generations of Shem*

We ask the question "Where is this place of Abraham, called Ur?" It was the place in which Abraham lived before moving to Canaan (Gen 11:28, 31; 15:7; Ne 9:7).

Scholars have suggested two sites. One is in southern Mesopotamia, a second in northern Mesopotamia. We do not know with absolute certainty, which is the city mentioned in the Biblical account (Gen 11:31).

The southern city was located one hundred miles southeast of Babylon near the Euphrates River, in what is now known as Iraq. It was a Sumerian city, a major metropolis in the early world. The Sumerians were the first literate people in Mesopotamia and probably the first literate people in the world. They created a great civilization with major, metropolitan centers, urban centers, of which Ur is probably the most famous.

The city was not known until an archeologist discovered it in the early part of the 20th century. Sir Leonard Woolley found many pieces of gold along with remarkable architecture. Also uncovered were thousands of cuneiform documents telling us about the history, culture, and economics of the city. His 1920 book, *Ur of Chaldees,* was published, however, contained little evidence that this was indeed the birthplace of Abraham. His idea and discovery led to many accepting the southern location of Abraham's Ur.

Today, this southern location is a railway station near the Persian Gulf. Copies of mathematical tables discovered, including square and cube roots, were in their society.

A second possible site, this one in northern Mesopotamia is the city of Urfa, still called that to this day, and located in southern Turkey. As you drive into the city of Urfa, there is a sign "Welcome to Urfa, birthplace of Abraham." There is a lot of biblical evidence for this location. The author accepts the location of Ur in northern Mesopotamia.

Joshua chapter 24, states that Abraham came from *beyond* the Euphrates. Actually, the southern city of Ur is on the Euphrates River, on the western shore. When following God's instructions to travel from Ur to Canaan, using the southern route would not cross the Euphrates. The northern route (from Ur in the south) would not travel from *beyond* the Euphrates. Urfa would be in agreement with Joshua 24. Every time I taught on this journey of Abraham, I questioned the conclusion that Abraham, listening to God's instructions, travelled from a southern Ur, many miles north, when his destination was directly west. A statement in Genesis 11 informs us that when Terah, Abram, Sarai, and Lot set off on their journey from Ur to Canaan, they stopped in the city of Haran where Terah died. Abraham continued onward from

Haran towards the land of Canaan. Again, I ask, why did Abraham travelling from (southern) Ur to Canaan, journey north to Haran, when Canaan was west. The northern location of Ur makes more sense, as it is directly east of Haran.

This would also allow a more clear understanding of Gen chapters 24 and 29. When Abraham's grandson Jacob and others returned to the *family homeland*, they went to the region of Aram in northern Mesopotamia, not to southern Mesopotamia. After the Chaldeans came into Babylonia, Ur was placed under their control and called "Ur of the Chaldeans."

3.1.2.   This area of Ur is where the family of one of those three sons of Noah, the "sons of Shem" settled under their father Terah. Shem lived for five hundred years after the flood, so was a contemporary with Abraham for at least seventy-five years. It is quite possible, even probable that Shem is the one who brought knowledge about the One true God, Yahweh, to Abram. Shem's line led a man named Eber from which the name Hebrew evolved from.[1] Later in Gen 39:14, *some* invading tribes, called the Israelites, Hebrews; also the Israelites called themselves Hebrews in Gen 40:15. The Hebrew word *eber* means "beyond" possibly designating a people who came from beyond the Euphrates, referring to Abraham and his people.

3.1.3.   We know from Jewish writings that Abram's family were idol worshippers. They seemed to have an idol-making business, both in Ur and Haran. I'm confident that Abram's revelation of Yahweh was obvious. His family made idols out of wood, stone, silver, even gold, and some studded with precious stones. Beautiful, but not one of them *talked* with Abram. When Yahweh *spoke* with him, no wonder he walked by faith in the One True God.

3.1.4.   The Scriptures indicate that Terah moved the family to Haran. I believe there was family honor here as Terah was the leader of his family. Later, Joshua records the reason Terah was to have been left behind.[2]

Depth of Bible Words and Places
Haran

---

[1] Gen 10:21 *Also to Shem, the father of all the children of Eber*

[2] Josh 24:2-3 Thus says the Lord, the God of Israel, "From ancient times your fathers lived beyond the River, namely, Terah, the father of Abraham and the father of Nahor, and they served gods."

City in Mesopotamia known for its worship of the moon god, Sin. Abram lived there to care for his ailing father, Terah, after leaving Ur in route to Canaan. He left for Canaan following his father's death. Haran flourished for the next 1,000 years based on its trade with other nations. Assyrian forces captured it in 763 BCE, made it its capital, and then saw it captured by the Babylonians in 609 BCE. Jacob also lived there for a short time. A son of Terah, one of the brothers of Abraham also had this name.

3.1.5.   Keep in mind this line that we call the "seed line." This line would "one day" produce a seed who would *"bruise you on your head."* (Genesis 3:15).[1]

   3.1.5.1.   It seems that all along the journey of the seed line, Satan always tried to destroy it. We saw this with the Nephilim giants, now we see the attempt again in Ur, which will not be the last attempt. What better place than the center of paganism.

3.1.6.   Terah had three sons, Abram, Nahor, and Haran (who had an early death). Abram was the youngest of the three boys.[2]

   3.1.6.1.   It was Abram who God chose from the "seed line" to become the Father of the Hebrew people, and in turn to bless all the nations of the earth. He was born into an idolatress family and environment; it was thought that his father might have worshipped the moon.

   3.1.6.2.   Abraham stands in the unique position of being the father of a nation *and* the father of all believers. He was the origination of the Hebrew nation as well as several Arabic peoples. We point out that the Hebrews look back to Moses perhaps even more than Abraham does; at least they are considered equals.

   3.1.6.3.   God appears to Abram, after his family moved away from the idolatry, and settled in Haran. He places a call upon Abram that certainly could not be mistaken. We refer to this as the Abrahamic Covenant.[3] We detail this

---

[1] Refer to "The Seed Line" chart in index

[2] Gen 11:25 *and Nahor lived one hundred and nineteen years after he became the father of Terah, and he had other sons and daughters. 26 Terah lived seventy years, and became the father of Abram, Nahor and Haran. 27 Now these are the records of the generations of Terah. Terah became the father of Abram...*

[3] The covenant with Abraham in chapter 12 *Now the LORD said to Abram, " Go forth from your country, And from your relatives And from your father's house, To the land which I will show you; 2*

covenant below. In addition, three other covenants are listed later in this volume. Notice, God's five *I Will* statements in vv 2-3. God will do all that He promises. These verses are the "hub" of all Scripture. Compare these to Lucifer's five *I will* statements in this volume.

3.1.7. Examine the six distinct promises in the covenant

3.1.7.1. *And I will make you a great nation.* This has been fulfilled numerically; there were 17 million Jews when Hitler tried to stop the seed; after falling to 11 million, today there are some 21 million worldwide Jews. It's also been fulfilled in economic and political affairs of the world. Actually, God's people have been the longest lasting nation of any people on earth. They continue under persecution, which has never stopped, but rather are increasing.

3.1.7.2. *And I will bless you.* Abraham was blessed in cattle, silver, gold; it seems he always had physical belongings. These blessings have been shared by his descendants, particularly when they have kept their eyes on the Lord.

3.1.7.3. V2c *And make your name great.* Abraham is revered even today by Jew, Arab, and Christian alike. To the child of God Abraham is the "Father of the faithful."

3.1.7.4. V2d *And so you shall be a blessing.* This is a correct translation; most versions have it right. It is understood as *"Be a blessing"* for the verb is a continuous action. It's a missionary purpose for Israel.

3.1.7.5. V3 *And I will bless those who bless you.* And the one who curses you I will curse. Both in Abraham's life, and in later years, it has been apparent that those countries that have treated the Jews favorably have prospered. And the opposite holds true.

3.1.7.6. *And in you all the families of the earth will be blessed.* This is messianic. From Abraham came the line that culminated in the human body of Christ. And through Christ, true blessing has come to all believers. So again, all the promises are centered on the 3-fold covenant; a land; a nation, and a worldwide blessing made available to all.

And I will make you a great nation, And I will bless you, And make your name great; And so you shall be a blessing; 3 And I will bless those who bless you, And the one who curses you I will curse. And in you all the families of the earth will be blessed."

THE ABRAHAMIC COVENANT[1]

Genesis 12:1–3	God initiated His covenant with Abram when he was living in Ur of the Chaldeans, promising a land, descendants, and blessing.
Genesis 12:4, 5	Abram went with his family to Haran, lived there for a time, and left at the age of seventy-five.
Genesis 13:14–17	After Lot separated from Abram, God again promised the land to him and his descendants.
Genesis 15:1–21	This covenant was ratified when God passed between the sacrificial animals Abram laid before God.
Genesis 17:1–27	When Abram was ninety-nine God renewed His covenant, changing Abram's name to Abraham ("the father of a multitude"). Sign of the covenant: circumcision.
Genesis 22:15–18	Confirmation of the covenant because of Abraham's obedience.
This covenant was foundational to other covenants:	Land: Palestinian covenant (Deuteronomy 30)
	Descendants: Davidic covenant (2 Samuel 7)
	Blessing: "old" (Exodus 19) and "new" covenants (Jeremiah 31)

3.1.8.   Would you agree that Abram's detailed calling, which we read in Genesis 12:1-3, was an unmistakable calling? Previously, God had already told Abram to leave everything behind. And it wasn't an easy decision for Abram —it would be difficult to leave everything and almost everyone, behind. However, Hebrews 11:8 informs us: *"and he went out not knowing where he was going."* Isn't that great? He obeyed God. May each of us have it said of us *"he went"* in faith. I love what is referred to in Heb 11.Three statements of faith.

　　3.1.8.1.   Abram did not know WHERE. V8 *he went out, not knowing where he was going. God said "Go"* and Abram *"went out."* Took a step. Do not be afraid to take the first step in response to God's direction. Then take a second. In one of the steps, God's voice inside will say "That's it, walk this way."

　　3.1.8.2.   Abram/Sarah did not know HOW. V11 *By faith even Sarah herself received ability to conceive, even beyond the proper time of life.* "How could this be, how could this come about from me and Sarah. Impossible." However,   with   God   the   impossibilities   become

---

[1] *Visual Survey of the Bible* . Nashville : Thomas Nelson, 1997

possibilities. Abram did not know WHY. V19 *He considered that God is able to raise people even from the dead.* He just "went" in faith. And notice wherever he went he built an altar to God (i.e. Noah stepped off the Ark and the first thing he did was build an altar before moving on). No wonder Abraham is called "God's friend" in the New Testament (James 2:23).[1]

3.1.8.3.   Genesis 12 tells us of the great wealth and respect of Abraham.

3.1.8.4.   Three hundred servants

3.1.8.5.   Thousands of sheep and cattle

3.1.8.6.   Hundreds of camels

3.1.8.7.   Called a prince

3.1.8.8.   Indeed, a man of his era. All because of being a man of faith.

3.1.8.9.   Abram, at the age of seventy-five, left and followed the highway southward from Haran (his father died at Haran), into Canaan stopping at Shechem, thirty miles north of the later site of Jerusalem. Abraham moved further south and made a sacrifice at Bethel (unearthed by archeologists) where God had again talked to him. This location is revered yet to-day.[2]

3.1.8.10.   Abram left Bethel after a severe drought and famine devastated the land.[3] It was a real test of faith to Abraham as he questioned if this dry, parched land was indeed to be the Promised Land. He failed to consult God for guidance and left for Egypt.

3.1.8.11.   Ancient monuments in Egypt confirm how a Pharaoh took a man's wife by force and intended to

---

[1] And we have to note one of the most important verses in the entire Bible. Important to each of us.

Romans 4:3 For *what does the Scripture say?* (And the writer, probably Paul, quotes Gen 15:6) *"ABRAHAM BELIEVED GOD, AND IT WAS CREDITED TO HIM AS RIGHTEOUSNESS."* You and I were given, we received the gift of righteousness, our account was *credited* (I was an accountant, and when it's credited, it's a done deal!). It happened when we believed! It was credited to Abraham, it was credited to you, when you made Jesus Lord. The word "believed" is a Hebrew word meaning to stand fast. Fixed without moving. "Reckoned" means to "weave into" or "fabricate," to become a part with. "Righteousness" means to make right.

[2] A quick picture of Abram's travels thus far: Ur—Haran—Shechem—Bethel—Egypt— Bethel—Hebron

[3] *There was a famine in the land, so Abram went down to Egypt to live there for a while because the famine in the land was severe.* (NET)

murder her husband. It seems that immigration of many families was common at this time.

3.1.9. Following a short stay, he returned to Bethel where he and his nephew Lot parted ways because of a shortage of pastureland. It was here that God again talked with Abram.[1] God enlarged the promise of land to include *all the land which you see*. This promise never ceased throughout the following decades. It was given to *your descendants forever*.

    3.1.9.1. They stood on a high mountain top and viewed the land. Lot spotted a beautiful and fruitful area, as the Garden must have been, near the Sea of Galilee. The land was selected by Lot, not asking God what He wanted him to do. Lot's choice was based on his flesh, and he separated from Abram.

    3.1.9.2. After several years, Lot was captured in the first war recorded in Scripture, near the Dead Sea. From Hebron, Abraham took 318 of his servants and recaptured Lot. Abram had been notified by one who had escaped the battle. Abram attacked the enemy at night, defeating them and capturing Lot. They returned to the area, which later became Jerusalem, with all their goods. At this time, Melchizedek (see below), king of Salem is introduced and blesses Abram. In return Abram gives tithes to Melchizedek. Melchizedek appears suddenly, and disappears suddenly. His name means "King of Righteousness" and points toward the ultimate King of Righteousness, Christ. Hebrews 6:20 names Christ *high priest forever according to the order of Melchizedek*.

Depth of Bible Words and Places
Hebron

A city located twenty miles southwest of Jerusalem. Abraham lived there for a short period. David made this city his capital for the seven and one-half years he was king of the Southern Kingdom, Judah.

---

[1] Genesis 13:14-17 *Now lift up your eyes and look from the place where you are, northward and southward and eastward and westward; 15 for all the land which you see, I will give it to you and to your descendants forever. 16 "I will make your descendants as the dust of the earth, so that if anyone can number the dust of the earth, then your descendants can also be numbered. 17 "Arise, walk about the land through its length and breadth; for I will give it to you..."*

3.1.10.   The Scriptures next record the wonderful story in cps 15-16, that of a promise of a specific child to be born, the questioning, the laughter, and finally, just as God promised — Isaac arrives in cp 21.

> 3.1.10.1.   It followed that God came to him in a vision, assuring him of God's defense against any enemy, and His blessing upon Abram's child. Abram concluded, in error, that his servant Eliezer was the only hope remaining. "But God" confirmed the blessing would be otherwise, and Abram's seed would be numberless. [1]
>
> 3.1.10.2.   However, before the birth of the promised son, Abram fathered a son, Ishmael (his line led to the Arabs) with Hagar (his wife Sarai's maid). Abram knew only that he would father a child and did not know the son of promise would be by Sarai. Sarai made a sacrifice by putting another into her place. Her love of Abram and her despair of having a child of her own, combined to make the proposal on behalf of Hagar. This seemed to be the answer for Abram. Because of eventual strife between Sarai and her servant, God later sends Hagar and Ishmael out of the house (Gen 21:12-14).
>
> 3.1.10.3.   God changes Abram's name to Abraham and tells him that Sarai (renamed Sarah), would be the mother of the promised son, Isaac. Laughter follows, and the LORD said *is anything too difficult for the Lord?*[2]
>
> 3.1.10.4.   Cps 18 and 19 relates the story concerning the location that Lot chose to live, Sodom and Gomorrah. The Scriptures state plainly their sin is exceedingly grave, so justice was demanded by God. Abraham's prayer of pleading and intercession contained several key elements.

3.1.10.4.1.   His prayer was extended. *Abraham was still standing before the Lord.*

3.1.10.4.2.   His prayer was humble. Now *behold, I have ventured to speak to the Lord, although I am but dust and ashes.*

---

[1] Gen 15:4 Then behold, the word of the Lord came to him, saying, "This man will not be your heir; but one who will come forth from your own body, he shall be your heir." 5 And He took him outside and said, "Now look toward the heavens, and count the stars, if you are able to count them." And He said to him, "So shall your descendants be."

[2] Sarah died in Hebron at the age of 127 years. She is the only woman in Scripture whose age is recorded. Abraham's only piece of ground in the Promise Land which he owned was a small cave he purchased for a burial place. Sarah was the first to be buried in it. Abraham died at age 175 and was buried in the same cave by his two sons, Isaac and Ishmael.

3.1.10.4.3.　His prayer was persistent. Abraham made the plea six times, each time accepted by God. Repeatedly he stated his plea; repeatedly God granted the request.

    3.1.10.5.　We would note that a nation was destroyed because it was rotten to the core; not ten were found righteous.

3.1.11.　Abraham's greatest test of faith comes after Isaac's birth. *God tested Abraham.*[1] God asks him to sacrifice his only son; Abraham believes God can raise Isaac from the dead, and steps out in faith. God did not want Isaac's life, He wanted Abraham's heart. Satan tempts each of us that he may bring out the evil that is in our hearts: God tests us that He may bring out all the good. F. B. Meyer said, "Trials are therefore, God's vote of confidence in us."[2]

    3.1.11.1.　Abraham's states his faith by his comment to his servant *I and the lad will go over there; and we will worship and return to you* (22:5)[3]. And of course, God provides a ram, on the future site of Solomon's Temple. Later He will provide His own beloved Son.[4] And don't miss v 4 "on the third day" Isaac would be raised off the altar of wood (prophecy of a Cross?) v 6 *Abraham took the wood.*

Depth of Bible Words and Places
Moriah

Actually, a range of mountains going out from Jerusalem. Mt Moriah in cp 22 is where eventually the Temple would be built. Abraham took his son here, to offer him as a sacrifice (Gen 22:2).

3.1.12.　Abraham, this faithful man, prays a blessing on his sons in cp 27. One of those sons, Ishmael eventually fathers the Arabs. The other is our Second Great Man, Isaac.

---

[1] Most translations are correct using *test*. The older KJV uses *tempt*.

[2] *Abraham*, AMG Publishers, 2001, p. 150

[3] NIV reads *we will come back to you*. Amp reads *come again to you*.

[4] Many times I have paraphrased this Scripture (22:8) to read as "God will provide Himself....a lamb"; (this is how the KJV reads). I see this as God planting a Word-seed to allow Him later to send a part of Himself, His Son, to earth. God provides Himself, a ram; later He provides Himself, His only Son. (I realize this is not the accepted translation, but it is truth, and encouraging once you see it).

SEVEN

Four Great Men: Isaac/Jacob

1   The Scriptures turn to the *second* Great Man *ISAAC* "The Humble Man."

1.1. We see in the Scriptures that the life of Isaac is one of excellence. He was patient, yet powerful when needed. He loved his older son Esau, and wants to bless him, even though God says that the older son will serve the younger, Jacob.

Depth of Bible Words and Places

Bethel

Bethel was named by Jacob, meaning "House of God." It was directly north of Jerusalem in the area now called the West Bank, and played an important role in the lives of Abraham and Jacob (Israel). Abraham built an altar between Bethel and Ai (Genesis 12:8). During Israel's monarchy, it was transformed into a center of idolatrous worship. For example, Jeroboam I set up a shrine to serve as an alternative to Solomon's temple. Hosea later called it "house of wickedness."

1.1.1.   The story of the adult life of Isaac begins in chapter 25 (25:19-26:35) and traces his family in the later verses of cp 25.[1]

1.1.2.   The abbreviated story of Isaac serves as a "connecting link" between his father Abraham, and his own son Jacob. Our second Great Man doesn't fill nearly as much Scripture as the other three. A few earlier verses present to us the record of his brother, Ishmael and a list of his sons. Isaac's father is very interested that he marries a proper girl; the story is related in cp 24.

---

[1]25:19 *Now these are the records of the generations of Isaac, Abraham's son.*

1.1.3.　　　　He marries Rebekah (cp 24) and is happy and full of joy. He inherits his dad's estate, and more importantly, the covenant—a good time of life.

1.1.4.　　　　God's covenant demanded that Isaac & Rebekah have a son to carry the seed line, but they have to wait for many years. Similar to his parents who waited for Isaac.[1] Nineteen years later, twins are born, Jacob and Esau. Isaac's life after his marriage centers on Isaac becoming the father of twins.[2]

1.1.5.　　　　Isaac and Rebekah make the mistake of many parents — playing favorites. It usually created problems as it did with them.

1.1.6.　　　　Esau taunts Jacob, and later Jacob tricks his father and takes the birth right of the first-born and receives Isaac's blessing of Abraham's covenant. The oral blessing in that day was legal and binding, even though Isaac realized he had been tricked by Jacob. That incident caused a persistent hatred in Esau, destined to divide the two families of Edom and Israel.

Depth of Bible Words and Places
Birthright

The birthright was not something taken "lightly." Rather it was taken "highly." It is interesting to realize the ancient birthright concerned mostly the material inheritance. The inheritance was divided into the number of sons, plus one. The eldest son received a double share. So the "stew" or soup bought from Esau the extra share, not the entire inheritance.

1.2. The Old Testament's purpose of redemption continues through *JACOB,* "The Transformed Man," our *third* Person. His story begins in Gen cp 27 and continues twenty-three chapters. We read his death in chapter 49.

1.2.1.　　　　The Seed line ran from Abraham through his son Isaac, and then Jacob. Jacob plays a major part in God's plan of redemption. His story is a little "choppy" which makes it hard to follow at times.

1.2.2.　　　　Jacob and Esau had a battle from the start—seems they pushed each other around, even before momma gave birth.

---

[1] *Isaac prayed to the Lord on behalf of his wife* (25:21); Rebekah prays also in v 22 *So she went to inquire of the Lord.*

[2] Gen 25:21 *Two nations are in your womb; And two peoples will be separated from your body; And one people shall be stronger than the other; And the older shall serve the younger.*

1.2.3.   Chapter 25 records that Jacob and Esau fought for territory in Rebecca's womb.

1.2.4.   Esau's descendants, the people of Edom, seemed to always battle the descendants of Jacob, the Israelites. Obadiah records that the nature of Edom was the same as Esau's.[1] Also in the final Old Testament book, God begins the book mentioning Esau and Edom.[2]

Depth of Bible Words and Places

Edomites

The people from Edom, southeast of the Dead Sea. Edom descended from Esau, the twin brother of Jacob. Their early rulers were called dukes (Gen 36:15-19), and kings (Gen 36:31-43). Many times Edom took advantage of a hatred relationship with Israel, even assisting other nations in attacking Israel and Judah. Because the Edomites were descendants of Abraham, the Israelites were not permitted to war against them.

1.2.5.   Jacob is living in the city where he was born, Beersheba.[3] He flees to Haran in cp 28 where he ponders what he had done. Not entitled to the birthright blessing or inheritance, he received them both due to God's goodness and ultimate plan. Where was the covenant God of Abraham and Isaac? Would He also be the God of Jacob?

1.2.6.   Jacob was running from Esau; he stole the important blessing of a firstborn. So he was fleeing from an angry brother and facing an unknown future. We can read what Esau was thinking in 27:41 *So Esau bore a grudge against Jacob; I will kill my brother Jacob.* Jacob flees!

1.2.7.   Jacob pauses at the end of the first day of travel, (having covered sixty miles), at Luz (Bethel). He had no idea that God was going to meet him there; he just wanted to stay ahead of Esau who was perhaps out to kill him. He was not seriously following God and serving Him.

1.2.8.   Here, during the night, he experiences the "ladder to heaven" with angels going up and down. The Lord Jehovah was standing above and assured Jacob that he was the covenant God Abraham and Isaac, and that the same covenant would be extended to him. It is no wonder this location would always be a

---

[1] Obad 1, 6 *Thus says the Lord God concerning Edom 6 "O how Esau will be ransacked..."*

[2] Mal 1:3, 4 *but I have hated Esau 4 "They (Edom) may build, but I will tear down..."*

[3] Gen 28:10 *Then Jacob departed from Beersheba and went toward Haran.*

special place to Jacob. Much later we read that God tells him to "go back."[1]

Depth of Bible Words and Places
Luz

Luz no longer appears on most maps; in fact, very few antiquity maps will have the name. Refer to these Scriptures: Gen 28:19 *He called the name of that place Bethel; however, previously the name of the city had been Luz*; Gen 35:5-6 6 *So Jacob came to Luz (that is, Bethel), which is in the land of Canaan;* Josh 18:13 *From there the border continued to Luz, to the side of Luz (that is, Bethel) southward; and the border went down to Ataroth-addar, near the hill which lies on the south of lower Beth-horon.* Luz was an important location North of Jerusalem on the cross roads of major traffic. Archeologists have shown that two distinct areas were populated together, sort of a main city and a suburb.

1.2.9.   That first night, at Luz, he has a vision, and experiences a ladder to heaven with angels going up and down. This experience showed Jacob that grandpa's (Abraham's) God, and daddy's (Isaac's) God, was watching over him. These angels were in communication with heaven. God encourages Jacob, who builds an altar, not for sacrifice, rather for worship. After the experience, he renames the location Bethel. Bethel is mentioned in the Old Testament seventy-two times, more that any city other than Jerusalem. Bethel means "house of God" and is where remnants of the twelve tribes returned from their captivity in Babylonia. Bethel disappeared sometime late in the BCE era, and its exact location is unknown today. There is a guess concerning the location, which archeologists in 1924 CE uncovered, near the modern city called Beitin.

Depth of Bible Words and Places
Ladder

This *ladder* in Hebrew is a word describing the passing from one realm to another; a "passageway" from earth through the first heaven and second heaven, to God's heaven, the third heaven. The Lord doesn't have to use a stairway. He is pictured here as standing at the top; actually, the Hebrew has Him beside the ladder.

---

[1] Gen 35:1, 2 *"Arise, go up to Bethel and live there, and make an altar there to God, who appeared to you when you fled from your brother Esau."*

1.2.10.   Angels are indeed quite real. Refer to the Expanded Help Paper "Angels in the Old Testament" in volume two.

1.2.11.   Then Jacob, retracing the path which Abraham traveled from Haran into Canaan.[1] He finds Rachel and has to "really work" to win her. But he loves her, and works fourteen years.[2] Jacob completed a total of twenty years of servitude: fourteen years for Rachel, followed by six years for his herds.

    1.2.11.1.   Interesting description of Laban's daughters; Leah is "weak eyes," that's it! How would you like to have one describe you as "weak eyes?" Rachel is pictured for us as *a lovely figure and beautiful* (NET). The NIV has it *lovely in form, and beautiful*. AMP reads *beautiful and attractive*. The Jewish Bible translates it *good-looking, with beautiful features*. Pretty clear! So Jacob is willing to work for her.

1.2.12.   He marries both of the sisters immediately, and they are quite fruitful during the following years. Ten of his sons are born from two wives and their two handmaids. Interesting to note that Jacob's firstborn, Reuben is not the one who continues the seed line to Christ. We have to wait for the eleventh son to continue that line.

1.2.13.   Note that God does not approve of everything that is recorded in Scripture. We saw that with Abraham and Sarah with the birth of Ishmael. We see this again with Jacob's two wives, and two other mothers of his children. We do however conclude that societal customs seemed to allow for what they did—God never sanctioned them, but man did.

    1.2.13.1.   Being in the Bible, does not mean it had God's approval.

    1.2.13.2.   God didn't approve of Satan's lie in the garden

    1.2.13.3.   He did not approve of David's sins; he did judge him for them. However, the record of these are inspired Scripture.

1.2.14.   An eleventh son is born in cp 30. This boy will travel down into the land of Egypt. We will follow this remarkable person in our next story, the story of Joseph. Jacob, after being successful with those cattle and goats in the latter part of chapter

---

[1] Gen 29:1 *Then Jacob went on his journey, and came to the land of the sons of the east,* referring to his relatives located in Northern Macedonia, Haran, grandpa's home, where great-grandpa Terah died. Relatives lived off to the East of Bethel.

[2] Another personal note: I've often thought about this. I concluded, I would work 14...24... or 44 years, to marry my wife.

30, turns toward Canaan and begins his journey back home. It was time to get away from Laban and the climate they were living in. By now Jacob's eleven boys are learning the ways of idolatry, still prevalent in Haran (sounds similar to Abram leaving Haran years before).

1.2.15.　　　He continues toward Canaan with his father-in-law behind him in pursuit, and Esau with 400 soldiers, before him! What should he do? He stopped, along the Jabbok River, and throughout the night, he was in a wrestling match with an Angel. He certainly experienced angels in his life. The ladder in Cp 28, angels in cp 32 which encouraged him, and now this angel The Angel, who changes his name to Israel, The Prince.

　　　1.2.15.1.　　　Jacob showed great determination with This Angel

　　　1.2.15.2.　　　He came away with (1) a blessing (2) a new name and (3) an awful limp.

1.2.16.　　　From this time forward, Jacob (now Israel) never deceived anyone again. From Israel were to arise the twelve tribes, descendants of the twelve sons who were to bear his name.

1.2.17.　　　Jacob met with Esau who came from the south with his warriors. Jacob was greatly concerned about this "reunion" with the brother he so wronged.[1] What's about to happen? Jacob had stolen Esau's rights as firstborn. So Jacob protects his family by separating them in case they had to escape. However, Jacob was shocked as Esau ran to meet him, embraced, and kissed him, and they wept together. Jacob had starting bowing (seven times in all) to Esau before Esau could even see him. However, they meet and it turns out, we are informed, that Esau needs no gifts from brother Jacob, for he too is rich in goods.

　　　1.2.17.1.　　　These twin boys separated once more. Rachel died as Jacob neared Bethlehem during the continued journey, leaving a newborn son, Benjamin. Jacob erected a pillar over her grave, and the memorial today is called Rachel's Tomb. Jacob had been transformed.[2]

---

[1] Gen 33:1 *Then Jacob lifted his eyes and looked, and behold, Esau was coming, and four hundred men with him.*

[2] Gen 35:1 *then God said to Jacob, "Arise, go up to Bethel and live there, and make an altar there to God, who appeared to you when you fled from your brother Esau. 2Jacob said to his household and to all who were with him, "Put away the foreign gods which are among you, and purify yourselves and change your garments."* A transformed man.

1.2.18.   His journey to return to Canaan is about to end; he tells his family several things when they were near Shechem.

    1.2.18.1.   "Put away" the strange gods. He takes spiritual charge of his family for the first time. A family grows as its leader says, "put away that which is wrong."

    1.2.18.2.   Jacob says "get clean," and confess everything that is wrong.

    1.2.18.3.   Finally, Jacob says, "change your garments." In Scripture, garments speak of habits. Change your clothes. The day that Jacob went back to Bethel, back to worship of God, is the day he put on the garments of God and committed to Him.

1.2.19.   Jacob, now a transformed man, collects everything that is not worship of God, and buries it at Shechem. He goes home to Bethel. Sometime later he moves further south where his beloved Rachel died and was buried. Following a short time after that, Isaac, at the age of 180, dies at Hebron.[1] Jacob and Esau met one last time; Esau's genealogy is listed in cp 36.

JACOB'S LIFE INDEXED[2]

Recorded Events	Place	Reference
Birth of Jacob and Esau, sons ot Isaac and Rebekah.	Beer-sheba	Ge 25:22-26
Jacob the favorite of his mother. Esau the favorite of his father.	Beer-sheba	Ge 25:27-28
Jacob purchases the birthright from Esau.	Beer-sheba	Ge 25:29-34
Jacob deceives Isaac by impersonating Esau and receives his blessing.	Beer-sheba	Ge 27:1-29
Jacob is sent by his father and mother to Padan-aram to secure a wife.	Beer-sheba	Ge 28:1-7
He spends the night at Bethel where he has the vision of the ladder and the angels, and the Lord renews the promise made to Abraham.	Bethel	Ge 28:10-15
Jacob builds a memorial and makes a vow to the Lord.	Bethel	Ge 28 16-22
He comes to Padan-aram, to the home of Laban, his mother's brother, and stipulates to serve Laban for seven years to make his daughter, Rachel his wife.	Padan-aram	Ge 29:1-20
Laban deceives him and requires him to marry Leah, and	Padan-aram	Ge 29 21-30

---

[1] Gen 35:28 *Isaac breathed his last and died and was gathered to his people, an old man of ripe age; and his sons Esau and Jacob buried him.*

[2] Table utilized from *Nelson's Foundational Bible Dictionary*, Katharine Harris, World Publishing, Nashville TN, 2004, pp 352-353

bargains tor another seven years' service for which Jacob should obtain Rachel.

Eleven of his sons are born to Jacob by his two wives and their maids The sons of Leah: Reuben. Simeon, Levi, Judah, Issa-char, Zebulun. Sons of Zilpah. Leah's maid Gad, Asher Son of Rachel Joseph. Sons of Bilhah. Rachel's maid Dan, Naphtali	Padan-aram	Ge 29:31-30:24
Jacob by cunning gains an advantage and loses the favor of Laban.	Padan-aram	Ge 30:25-43; 31:1-2
The Lord directs Jacob to return to Canaan and assures him of His presence with his family and property he steals away from Laban.	Padan-aram	Ge 31:3-21
Laban pursues and overtakes Jacob, and the Mizpah covenant is made between them	Mt. Gilead	Ge 31:22-55
Fearing his brother Esau, he arranges a gift of cattle to be sent to him. He spends the night alone wrestling with the angel His name is changed to Israel. This marks the great change in Jacob's life.	Peniel	Ge 32
The affectionate meeting of Jacob and Esau; Jacob settles in Shechem.	Shechem	Ge 33
The incident regarding Jacob's daughter. The slaying of Hamor and his family by Jacob's sons.	Shechem	Ge 34
Jacob is divinity directed to move to Bethel Here he builds an altar and the Lord talks with him	Bethel	Ge 35:1-15
Leaving Bethel. Rachel dies in giving birth to Benjamin, the twelfth son, and is buried near Bethlehem	Ephrath	Ge 35:16-20
He comes to Beer-sheba and he and Esau bury Isaac	Beer-sheba	Ge 35:21-29
Jacob's special love for Joseph; Joseph's dreams incur the enmity of his brothers.	Beer-sheba	Ge 37:1-11
Jacob sends Joseph to his brothers who are with their flocks. They sell him to some Midianites on their way to Egypt, and tell Jacob he has been killed by a wild beast	Dothan	Ge 37:12-35
A famine in the land compels Jacob to send his sons to Egypt for corn They are recognized by Joseph who treats them kindly and arranges for them to move to Egypt	Beer-sheba	Ge 42-45
Jacob and his people, seventy souls, settle in Goshen where they become prosperous After 17 years in Egypt, Jacob dies and is carried back to Canaan by his sons and buried beside his people in the cave of Machpelah	Goshen	Ge 46:1-50

EIGHT

Four Great Men: Joseph

1   The *fourth* man of Genesis: *JOSEPH, "The Truthful Man."*[1] This is the tenth and last genealogy of Genesis. His life presents to us many lessons for our own life, and nowhere do we find in the Scriptures, that he complained.

1.1. The story of Joseph begins in cp 30, with the story of Jacob,[2] and continues through the remainder of Genesis. It's a story that illustrates the promises God made to Abraham, even though he is the only Patriarch to whom God did not make an appearance. And yet there is no other person in the Old Testament, whose life reflects the purpose of God any clearer.

1.1.1.   A favored son of a father.

1.1.2.   The resentment and sins of Joseph's brothers, including hatred.

1.1.3.   Thrown into a pit.

1.1.4.   Taken away into Egypt, never to return to live in his homeland.

1.2. Joseph is a roller coaster of emotions, in which we ask the question "Does God have a purpose in difficulties, troubles, and suffering?" Is God involved in the troubles in our life? The Psalmist cries out in Psalms 34.[3] I remind you as we begin his story: When everything seemed to fall apart in Joseph's life, it is recorded *"the LORD was with Joseph."* At key times in his life, the same encouragement is offered.[4] No question or doubt, God's presence protected Joseph IN

---

[1] A reminder: We saw Abraham *"The Faithful,"* Isaac *"The Humble,"* and Jacob *"The Transformed."* Next we look at Joseph *"The True."*

[2] Gen 30:23 *then God remembered Rachel, He listened to her; she became pregnant and gave birth to a son; 24 She named him Joseph..."*

[3] *6 This poor man cried, and the Lord heard him And saved him out of all his troubles. 7 The angel of the Lord encamps around those who fear Him, And rescues them.*

[4] Gen 39:2; 39:21; 41:38

the suffering, IN the troubles, allowing him to fulfill His promise to Abraham, the promise in Gen 12:1-3.

1.3. There are more cps devoted to Joseph than the other three of the Four Great Men we reviewed; more on Joseph than the two great men, Abraham an Isaac, combined. I suggest three levels of reading Joseph's story. Read his story three times, each time using a different level.

    1.3.1.   First, understand the story as Fascinating Literature.

        1.3.1.1.   Perhaps you read the story in Sunday School and love that "brightly colored coat." Read the story, enjoying it as you flow through the events: A loving father and a pampered son, jealous brothers, a conniving wife in a foreign land, an international food crisis; the heart wrenching reunion of a family. For centuries, artists have turned to this story of literature, as their inspiration. The German novelist Thomas Mann wrote four novels based on the life of Joseph. In our own recent times we had a rock cantata "Joseph and the Amazing Technicolor Dreamcoat." Read the story as Great Literature.

    1.3.2.   A 2nd level that may be of interest. Read the story watching for Profound Theological Implications. The hand of God is evident in every scene. His attributes are displayed during every step of the story.

        1.3.2.1.   We see God ruling and overruling the decisions people make, and in the end, God builds a hero, saves a family, and creates a nation that will bring blessing to the whole world.

        1.3.2.2.   Behind the story is the heart of the "covenant making" God, who always keeps His promises. Read the story watching for the actions of God. Look for His involvement in lives of His people. The story is theological.

    1.3.3.   A 3rd level in particular, is for the Christian reader and the one we will view. Joseph is one of the richest illustrations of Jesus Christ found in the Old Testament.

        1.3.3.1.   Joseph is like Jesus in these fourteen chapters. Watch for Joseph as a type for Christ. Jesus was loved by His Father, obedient to His will, hated and rejected by his own brethren, sold as a slave, falsely accused, unjustly punished, and finally, elevated from the place of suffering to a powerful throne saving his people from death.

1.3.4.   Before we continue the story of Joseph, observe the following comparison with Jesus.

Joseph in Genesis	Happening	Jesus
37:3	Their fathers loved them dearly	Matt 3:17
37:2	Shepherds of their father's sheep	John 10:11, 27
37:13-14	Sent by father to brothers	Heb 2:11
37:4	Hated by brothers	John 7:5
37:20	Others plotted to harm them	John 11:53
39:7	Tempted	Matt 4:1
37:25, 28	Taken to Egypt	Matt 2:14-15
37:23	Robes taken from them	John 19:23
37:28	Sold for the price of a slave	Matt 26:15
39:20	Bound in chains	Matt 27:2
39:16-18	Falsely accused	Matt 26:59-60
40:2-3	Placed with two other prisoners, one who was saved and the other lost	Luke 23:32
41:41	Exalted after suffering	Phil 2:9-11
45:1-15	Forgave those who wronged them	Luke 23:34
45:7	Saved their nation	Matt 1:21
50:20	What people did to hurt them God turned to good	1 Cor 2:7-8

1.4. Now the story. Chapter 37 introduces this genealogy by its most outstanding person, Joseph, one of the twelve sons of Jacob. He was born in Haran, the first son of Rachel.

1.4.1.   He possessed the faith and patience of Abraham,

1.4.2.   The meekness of Isaac,

1.4.3.   The foresight of Jacob,

1.4.4.   And showed a patient and lovable nature.

1.4.5.   The story of Joseph offers at the beginning, the unfolding and destructive dynamics of a family that knew the true and living God and yet sinned against Him. I offer *Four Dynamics of a Family*, which bring about trouble. Lessons for a family

1.4.6.   The home which Joseph was raised in, was a family filled with angry, jealous people. For seventeen years, the older sons of Jacob had watched as their father favored the younger son. Vv 2-4 of chapter 37 pictures the destructive dynamics:

Joseph, when seventeen years of age, was pasturing the flock with his brothers while he was still a youth, along with the sons

of Bilhah and the sons of Zilpah, his father's wives. And Joseph brought back a bad report about them to their father. 3 Now Israel loved Joseph more than all his sons, because he was the son of his old age; and he made him a varicolored tunic. 4 His brothers saw that their father loved him more than all his brothers; and so they hated him and could not speak to him on friendly terms.

> 1.4.6.1. Here we find *HATRED*. Don't miss the final words in v 4. The NIV translates it *they hated him, and could not speak a kind word to him.* Joseph was the favorite son, and his brothers knew it. Joseph received what we generally read as the "coat of many colors," even though we don't know what it really looked like. Both the NAS and NIV translate the coat as *richly ornamented robe, which* I agree with.

Depth of Bible Words and Places
Coat of Many Colors
The Hebrew word carries a meaning of "wrists" or "ankles." One scholar describes this coat as being sleeved and extending to the ankles.[1] Only one other place in the Scriptures do we find such a garment, that which describes the rich garment of David's daughter.

1.4.6.1.1. So the type of garment, along with brightness of color, set it apart and certainly was not what a shepherd needed out in a field. Jacob intentionally set this favorite son apart from the others.

> 1.4.6.2. A 2nd dynamic is in vv 5-11, notice v 11 *His brothers were jealous of him.* The dynamic of *ENVY*, a sister of MALICE. Read about those two siblings in Titus 3:3[2] Also consider 1 Peter 2:1[3]

1.4.6.2.1. Envy causes an inward pain when we see others succeed. Malice produces an inward satisfaction when we see others fail. They just work side-by-side.

1.4.6.2.2. Joseph eventually shares, both of his dreams and following them, his family couldn't help but increase in irritation

---

[1] V 31 *Then they took Joseph's (distinctive) long garment* (AMP)
[2] Titus 3:3 *For we also once were foolish ourselves, disobedient, deceived, enslaved to various lusts and pleasures, spending our life in malice and envy*
[3] *putting aside all malice and all deceit and hypocrisy and envy and all slander, 2 like newborn babies, long for the pure milk of the word, so that by it you may grow in respect to salvation*

and make things worse for him. V 5 ends *they hated him all the more.* The brothers hated him and also envied him in their hearts. When he reported the 2nd dream, even his father, Jacob, became upset.

    1.4.6.3.   Vv 12-20 offer a 3rd dynamic in the family troubles, *VIOLENCE.* The combination of hatred and envy is lethal; bound to lead to some kind of violence. It simmers in the heart and waits for a spark that will set off the explosion. The brothers didn't have to wait long to explode.

1.4.6.3.1.   Interesting to notice the location where the boys led the sheep to pasture; the same location where they had murdered the men of Shechem, concerning their sister Dinah (cp 34). This is probably what caused Jacob to send Joseph to them and check of their well fare. *See whether everything is all right with your brothers* he says in v 14.

1.4.6.3.2.   Then the revealing v 19, *Here comes that dreamer!* I would offer a good translation "here comes the dream expert!" According to Jesus, the ENVY is one of the works of the flesh that comes out of the sinful heart of man *All these evil things proceed from within and defile the man* (Mark 7:22). Paul included this in his long list of weaknesses of the flesh (Gal 5).[1] The brothers shout *let us kill him* in v 20.

EXPANDED HELP PAPER
Dead or Alive

An excerpt from chapter seven of the author's book *Travel Through Ephesians* explains Paul's "Old Man." Before knowing Him personally, from Chapter two of Ephesians

#1 *You were dead.* Paul says the people (before accepting Christ) were spiritually dead in sin. They were lifeless towards God. One might have looked alive, but inside were cut off from life. Verse 1 *(you were dead) by [your] trespasses and sins* (AMP). In the Scriptures, death always means *separation.* That was a horrible place to be in...like a graveyard. The unbeliever isn't sick, he's dead; no appetite for food or drink. He doesn't have any pain; can't talk and complain. Dead. Every person (before accepting Christ) was dead.

#2 *You were defiant.* Notice as Paul continues, he uses next the words *you walked [habitually].* Nicely translated in the AMP Bible because the

---

[1] Gal 5:19 *Now the deeds of the flesh are evident 20 strife, jealousy, outbursts of anger, disputes, dissensions...*

Greek's compound of words means, "to walk around in one area all the time." This was the beginning of spiritual death, walking against the will of God. Three forces are at work to act as a magnet to attract the human being. The world-system, the devil, and his hierarchy of angels, and the human flesh with its desires for self-fulfillments.

#3 *You were degenerated.* V3 _obeying_ *the impulses of the flesh and the thoughts of the mind [our cravings* _dictated_ *by our senses and our dark imaginings]* (AMP, underlines added for emphasis). This unsaved person not *only* does evil (by defying God), but now has grown and is worse. So we add the word *degenerated.* The lost person lives to please the desires of the flesh and the mind. He is incapable of doing good. He is incapable of doing anything to be saved. However, always know the Spirit of God can break in to this degenerate person; however, it will take the constant prayers by others to do so.

#4 *You were damned.* The unsaved person has been condemned. The God-judge already passed the sentence, however in His mercy, is staying the execution. God loves a human because He sees *in* that person, the image He created. He loves that image. In fact, if we removed the results of sin from him, it would be hard to over-praise him. God's image, that man...would be perfect. So understand this—God will always welcome one back. There is this place of darkness; the one involved has no urging towards God; His love is available, just withdrawn from action in the life. Deuteronomy 31:17 *Then My anger will be kindled against them in that day, and I will forsake them and hide My face from them. 18 And I will surely hide My face in that day because of all the evil which they have done in turning to other gods.* Sin is like a cancer *in* every man, eating all it can get away with. God still reaches out to that sinner.

Every person alive should keep in mind; God will accept anyone into His Kingdom. God will never stop drawing him; patience, long suffering, not ever wanting a man to perish.

    1.4.6.3.3.   In the family we are detailing, the dynamics reveal, because of ENVY Joseph's brothers first threw him into a pit.[1] Then they sat down and ate lunch![2]

    1.4.6.3.4.   Judah has an idea when he spots the travelling merchants; pull him from the pit and sell him to a group of traders on their way to Egypt. "We'll never hear from him again;

---

[1] Archeologists have found several deep, dry pits with bones of people in them. Not a common method, but certainly one used during Old Testament times.

[2] V24 *Then they took him and cast him into the (well-like) pit which was empty' there was no water in it. 25 then they sat down to eat their lunch!*

we won't ever have to explain what happened." Violence followed envy.

1.4.6.4. One final (the fourth) family dynamic in vv 29-39. *DECEPTION.*[1]

1.4.6.4.1. Reuben, the firstborn of Jacob, and oldest son, supposedly leader of the brothers, is absent when his brothers sold Joseph. When he visited the cistern, possibly to rescue him, he was shocked to find that Joseph was gone. So he hurried back to the camp to find out what had happened. His brothers knew right away that his sympathies were with Joseph, for Reuben tore his clothes like a man in mourning.

1.4.6.4.2. Among Jacob's sons, one sin led to another as the men fabricated the evidence with deception and lies, which would deceive their father into thinking that Joseph was killed by an animal.

1.4.6.4.3. Dad accepts that his favorite son is dead and went into deep mourning. This was the son of his beloved wife Rachel; a favorite child, a chosen child, special. We read in 42:36 —twenty years later, he was still grieving over the death of Joseph.[2]

1.4.7. Allow me to offer three lessons from our family story.

1.4.7.1. *No enemy is more subtle than passivity.* Passivity waits and waits until finally, when it can wait no longer, it comes down with both feet. Unfair to the child, usually resulting in revolting. Proper discipline is not a suggestion; it should be a mandated action. Any parent, who stands on the sideline of discipline, falls short of parenting.[3]

1.4.7.2. Lesson number two which we find in the life of this teenager, Joseph. *No response is more cruel than jealousy.* Solomon wrote *Jealousy is cruel as the grave.*[4] If jealousy rages in a family, at some point, it will strike in some terrible way.

1.4.7.3. The third lesson is a positive one. We can learn from the family of Joseph. Hope. *No action is more powerful than prayer.* The Bible does not record where

---

[1] HATRED, ENVY, VIOLENCE; now DECEPTION

[2] *Their father Jacob said to them, "You have bereaved me of my children: Joseph is no more.."*

[3] According to public school teachers, fifty years ago "talking out of turn" was the big problem, today it's drug abuse. Chewing gum was a no-no, today it's not drinking before class. Years ago is was cutting into line, today it's assault. I'm not sure if parents even know what a real disciplinary action would be.

[4] SS 8:6

Joseph prayed, however he surely did. Years earlier, another shepherd boy, David, out in a field with his sheep, prayed. I can't but think that Joseph was a pray-er. How else could he have gone on in life? Where else could a teenager in the midst of such a difficult life, turn?

1.4.8. The events in chapter 38 seem to interrupt Joseph's story. Think of it an interlude. One unknown writer said "Cp 38 seems to be about as necessary as a fifth leg on a cow." The ugly events do take place during the time of Joseph's story. However, we continue with Chapters 39, 40, and 41. [1]

1.4.9. Joseph has been taken to Egypt where he finds great favor in cp 39, (reminds me of that saying, "it's hard to keep a good man down").

    1.4.9.1. Easy to follow the journey along the major road into Egypt. We will see this road later, as a possible way of the Exodus. This major trade route was called the Great Trunk Road, starting in Memphis, eventually extending to Mesopotamia.

    1.4.9.2. God saw to it that the young man Joseph was sold to one of Pharaoh's chief officers, Potiphar, a high official, probably Pharaoh's bodyguard.

Depth of Bible Words and Places
Captain of the Guard

The NIV translates this as *captain of the guard.* This *guard* was an elite, courageous band of rugged men. The Jewish historian Alfred Edersheim describes that group by telling that Potiphar was the "chief of the executioners." Potiphar was nobody to fool around with; he was a man of seasoned military experience with power over life and death.

    1.4.9.3. For a seventeen-year-old boy, it had all the markings of a dreary life; surrounded by words he did not understand, thrown into a culture he was not familiar with, and sold as a slave.

    1.4.9.4. Very little, if any, natural hope. But we immediately read the words in v2 *that the Lord was with Joseph, so he became a successful man.*

    1.4.9.5. Joseph is appointed by God to be a blessing to Egypt; when he was in his home in Hebron, Joseph's brothers considered him "a trouble-maker"—the

---

[1] Gen 39:1 *AND JOSEPH was brought down to Egypt.*

difference was those words we read, *God was with him.* And this happened even though Egypt recognized at least two thousand gods, including Pharaoh himself.

1.4.9.6.   As we consider this story, we remind ourselves of the first Psalm.[1] Also Joshua 1: 8 comes to mind *everything this righteous young man did, prospered.* I offer another lesson in our story. Joseph is a good example of a believer who trusted God *and made* the best of his difficult circumstances. He never read what Peter wrote to the Christians in the Roman Empire in 1 Peter 2:13 *Submit yourselves for the Lord's sake to every humane situation, whether to a king as the one in authority, or to governors;* Peter wrote all the way through v20. However, Joseph did not have those New Testament words; he certainly put the instructions into practice. Joseph would rather have been at home, but made the best of his circumstances in Egypt, and was blessed by God.

1.4.9.7.   This blessing of the Lord was evident to the people in Potiphar's household; they knew that Joseph was the cause. V 5 of cp 39 tells us that everything in the house was blessed by the Lord because of Joseph. Here was a young Hebrew managing the entire household of a Pharaoh.[2]

1.4.10.   We read in the latter part of v 6, the physical description of Joseph, which prepares the way for this episode involving Potiphar's wife.[3] Remember the Holy Spirit hovered over the writing of the text and wisely chose the words. These words to describe Joseph's appearance are only found four times in Scripture.[4]

1.4.10.1.   Joseph was Godly, dependable, efficient and handsome-well favored. These were qualities he inherited from his mother who was described in 29:17 as lovely in form and beautiful.

1.4.10.2.   Potiphar's wife was forward and persistent. Recorded in v 10, she spoke to Joseph day after day—

---

[1] Ps 1 *Blessed is the man, who walks the right path and delights in the Word of God. For whatever he does prospers.*

[2] Gen 39:5 *It came about that from the time he made him overseer in his house and over all that he owned, the Lord blessed the Egyptian's house on account of Joseph.*

[3] *Now Joseph was handsome in form and appearance.* The AMP reads *fine looking;* Holman and the NET Bibles have Joseph *well-built.*

[4] Joseph, Saul, David, and Absalom.

quite a temptation for a young man. Then one day... v 12 *and she caught him by his garment, saying, "Lie with me!"*

1.4.10.3.   A couple of thoughts here, #1 Joseph respected the man he worked for, and #2 he served God and wasn't about to ruin that relationship with moral failure.

1.4.10.4.   Joseph, even though he suffered in a pit because of the hatred of his brothers, now faces an even greater danger. Prov 23:27 says it clearly[1]

1.4.10.5.   It is reasonable to conclude that Potophar's wife did some reasoning such as "After all, isn't he a Jew and a slave? Doesn't he work for my husband and therefore work for me? Since my husband isn't here, I'm in charge, and Joseph is my employee. It's his job to take orders." But when her advances were rejected, she turned against him. Never forget the challenging words here. Both v 12 and v 13 command men in similar situations *he fled and got out; he fled away.* For a second time, Joseph loses a garment, and we are offered another lesson from Joseph's life.

1.4.10.5.1.   It took a great deal of courage and determination, day after day, for him to fight this temptation day; however, he succeeded. Joseph, long before Paul's day, followed the same advice Paul gave to Timothy.[2]

1.4.10.6.   The episode closes with Joseph back in prison. Many individuals would be discouraged; this is where he began, in prison, but sure enough, God was with him. Joseph cannot get away from God's favor, (as if he would want to). I do not find any other account of a man's life that is so favored by God.

1.4.10.7.   And we discern another lesson! Wait on the Lord until it is His time to act. Joseph had time to think about, pray concerning, and ponder upon, what had happened. He would learn that God's delays are not God's denials. Somehow in the midst of unfair situations you will sense that God's hand is upon you. He will tell you "I'm in charge, relax, I'll take care of it." Again, we

---

[1] *For a harlot is a deep pit And an adulterous woman is a narrow well. Surely she lurks as a robber, And increase the faithless among men.*

[2] 2 Tim 2:22 *Now flee from youthful lusts and pursue righteousness, faith, love and peace, with those who call on the Lord from a pure heart.*

read v 21 *but the Lord was with Joseph, and showed him mercy and loving-kindness and gave him favor.*

1.4.11.   The writer of Scripture continues in chapter 40. Pharaoh's chief butler (cupbearer) and the royal baker each have a dream and God gives the meaning through Joseph.

Depth of Bible Words and Places
Cupbearer

The cupbearer was quite high in rank, Pharaoh's inner circle. We see the similar position of Nehemiah. Nehemiah said, *"now I was the cupbearer to the King"* (1:11b). He had the King's "ear." As a result, he King of Persia, Artaxerxes, heard Nehemiah and granted him his request to return and rebuild his home city. Without that action of a cupbearer, we possibly would not know of a restored Jerusalem.

1.4.11.1.   The cupbearer is restored to his position in front of Pharaoh. This cupbearer was a trusted servant who tasted all the food, beverages, and delicacies before Pharaoh consumed them. Following his release, nothing was said to Pharaoh concerning Joseph—the cupbearer seems to have forgotten Joseph completely.[1]

1.4.11.2.   *Two years* pass and we find Joseph still working in the prison house. Joseph has lived a life of disappointments,

1.4.11.2.1.   Favored son, but mistreated

1.4.11.2.2.   Rejected

1.4.11.2.3.   Life of fear and false accusations

1.4.11.2.4.   Slavery

1.4.11.2.5.   Prison

1.4.11.3.   Perhaps you relate to Joseph and need encouragement; God is with you, He will keep you if you trust Him.

1.4.12.   Pharaoh has *two* dreams to confirm exactly what would happen.

1.4.12.1.   Both dreams occurred in the same night, with no one able to figure them out. At that time, there were actual organized groups of magicians whose tasks were to interpret signs and dreams and come up with remedies.

---

[1] Gen 40:23 *Yet the chief cupbearer did not remember Joseph, but forgot him.*

1.4.12.2.   The time had come for Joseph to be delivered from prison and given a throne! Month after month he had waited to be released, but seemingly, nothing happened.

1.4.12.3.   However, while Joseph sees nothing, God is seeing something. God is at work behind the scenes. We do not know what happened during the two years, but we do know Joseph was being shaped for greatness. You will notice during the eighty additional years of Joseph's life, never once do we find one word of resentment. I offer two lessons from for the captivity of any Christian.

1.4.12.3.1.   #1 During the season of trial and waiting, trust God and do not panic; #2 When deliverance comes, Give God all the credit, without any pride.

1.4.12.4.   Joseph is released, freedom came. Interesting in v 14 of chapter 41, Joseph shaves, probably both face and head, to be presentable to Pharaoh. Again God gives him the meaning of the two dreams of Pharaoh. As a result, God moved upon Pharaoh to free and elevate Joseph.[1]

1.4.12.5.   Thirteen years after his brothers had stripped him of his special robe, now at the age of thirty; Pharaoh gave him a robe of far greater significance. The signet ring and the gold chain were symbols of Joseph's authority as second in command in Egypt.

Depth of Bible Words and Places
Signet
The word verifies royalty. It would contain the name of the ruler, so one using it was acting for the "top man."

1.4.12.6.   Joseph was given his own chariot, with men going before him to command the people to bow down just as they did to Pharaoh. I suspect that Joseph was embarrassed and humiliated by the attention. However, it came with the position. It is known from ancient writings that Egypt occasionally had a position called Overseer of the Royal Estates. Such a position is carved

---

[1] Gen 41:38 *Then Pharaoh said to his servants, "Can we find a man like this, in whom is a divine spirit?" 39 So Pharaoh said to Joseph, "Since God has informed you of all this, there is no one so discerning and wise as you are. 40 You shall be over my house, and according to your command all my people shall do homage; only in the throne I will be greater than you."*

on Egyptian tombs and reflected long flowing robes and rings of distinction.

1.4.12.7.   Another lesson, we learn from Joseph: disappointing situations, pain of discouragement, can shape a life for greatness. Usually, suffering and struggles bring eventual benefits. Perhaps the toughest of all the lessons Joseph offers.[1]

1.4.13.   We learn this similar lesson from Job. He was searching for God's answer. Listen to Job's conclusion following all he experienced:

Job 23:3-10
"Oh that I knew where I might find Him,
That I might come to His seat!
"I would present my case before Him
And fill my mouth with arguments.
"I would learn the words which He would answer,
And perceive what He would say to me.
"Would He contend with me by the greatness of His power?
No, surely He would pay attention to me.
"There the upright would reason with Him;
And I would be delivered forever from my Judge.
"Behold, I go forward but He is not there,
And backward, but I cannot perceive Him;
When He acts on the left, I cannot behold Him;
He turns on the right, I cannot see Him.

1.4.14.   Job said, "I want to find God. If only I could set down with Him and talk openly with him. Why am I going through these things? I want to have all my 'Why?' questions answered. I want to have all my 'How long?' problems solved." Ever felt like that?

1.4.15.   Here is what is so encouraging to us. Despite everything, Job had been through, Job still believed that God is there; sort of like those angels ascending and descending on that ladder confirming to Jacob that he is not alone. You may ask along with Job "Will God slap me across the face and say, 'Be quiet, Job, and just sit there?'" No, He is with you; He will pay attention to you.

1.4.16.   Even though Job now believes this, he still questions why: "What's God doing, I don't know. Where is He, I cannot find

---

[1] A.W. Tozar said "It is doubtful whether God can bless a man greatly until He has hurt him deeply."

Him. *But* I know this ... I *know* this Job says." I love Job's statement of faith as he continues in v10:

> But He knows the way I take; When He has tried me, I shall
> come forth as gold. 11 My foot has held fast to His path; I have
> kept His way and not turned aside. 12 I have not departed
> from the command of His lips; I have treasured the words of
> His mouth more than my necessary food.

1.4.17.　　　I draw your attention to the key to all of this. It is in Job's few words, *When He has tried me.* What a lesson. Our Fourth Man, Joseph had some trials. He came forth as gold.

1.5. Therefore, Egypt enjoyed seven years of bumper crops, and Joseph put 20% into storage. A wise plan for OUR life, 20% to savings? Following seven years of "fat," famine came exactly as the dreams had forecasted. Nations were coming to Egypt for food, and Joseph knew that one day his brothers would come. All in God's plan. According to his earliest dreams when he was home; *all* of his brothers would bow down before him.

1.5.1.　　　So in cp 42 we see reconciliation. For a reconciliation to take place, God had to bring Joseph's brothers to where they admitted the terrible deception and the selling a brother to strangers.

1.5.2.　　　The Scriptures return to Canaan; and during the first two years of famine, we visit briefly again, with Jacob. Jacob of course is the leader of a large clan of people, leader of his family; he makes the decision to send ten of the eleven brothers, to Egypt to purchase food. I think after what had happened earlier to Joseph, Jacob was going to keep his only living link with his beloved Rachel, Benjamin, at home.

1.5.2.1.　　　We read in v 38 *My son will not go down there with you, for his brother is dead* (after all these years, his heart still ponders after that 11th born son) *and he alone* (Benjamin) *is left.* (Quite a statement, ten other sons, but it's as though he really only has this one remaining boy). He says *If an accident happens to him on the journey you have to make, then you will bring down my gray hair in sorrow to the grave.* (The NET Bible) He had never forgotten his first born of Rachel, his favored son; and now thinks of him.

1.5.2.2.　　　Of course what Jacob and his sons didn't know was that God was at work making sure *all* the brothers went to Egypt and bowed down before Joseph.

1.5.3.   Another lesson, God can use anything in accomplishing His plan. You don't know how He will accomplish His plan in YOUR life. Ps 115:3 *Our God is in heaven; he does whatever pleases him.* Acknowledge Him, trust Him, and let Him work.

1.5.4.   In Egypt, Joseph knew that someone from his family would come for food. He did not know who or even when. Seven years of famine were going to happen next. So look at how God works in vv 6-14. Joseph as second ruler in Egypt certainly did not participate in each individual grain transaction. Many nations came at various times of need. And also the food supply was stored in several cities (41:46–49). But by the direction of God, Joseph was on hand at the place and at the time when his ten brothers arrived to buy grain—and he recognized them.

    1.5.4.1.   As for Joseph, he was no longer a 17 year old with a Hebrew beard and shepherd's clothing, or brightly colored robe. He certainly would have changed in appearance far more than his older brothers. Now he was clean-shaven like an Egyptian, no long hair of the Israelite. Now dressed like an Egyptian, no shepherd's clothing; and he spoke to them in the Egyptian language through an interpreter. Of course, the boys certainly had no idea that the young brother even survived. The might have surmised he lived as a slave. They did not recognize him.

    1.5.4.2.   So the ten men bowed before him, and Joseph knew that His God was beginning to fulfill the promises He had revealed in the two older dreams (37:7, 9). All his brothers would bow before him. Notice I said "all." Not all his brothers were before him...yet.

    1.5.4.3.   Undoubtedly difficult for Joseph to control his emotions; I think he intentionally forced harsh words to his brothers, to overcome the emotions. His natural desire would have been to speak to them in Hebrew and reveal who he was. However, Joseph knew that all eleven brothers would bow before him.

    1.5.4.4.   Benjamin would have to come with them on a future trip. He must have rejoiced to hear that his father and younger brother were both alive and well.

    1.5.4.5.   Joseph is not ready to reveal God's plan. So four times he accused them of being in Egypt under false pretense (42:9, 12, 14, 16), and puts all ten of them in confinement for three days, just to teach them what it was like to be prisoners.

1.5.4.6.   I like how the Scriptures are explicit. The Holy Spirit always directs the correct word to use. He could have used various words to identify the location. The KJV translates the Hebrew word as "prison" in verse 17, but the AMP has it closer to the original, "in custody." The word is the same used for "house" in other places. However, the word translated "prison" in Genesis 39-40, describing Joseph's experiences, means a *dungeon* and not just being under guard or house arrest. Joseph suffered as a prisoner in a real prison, while his brothers were only confined under guard. Mercy.

1.5.4.7.   He gave them an order, and then changed it. He would keep only one brother, Simeon as security while all the others returned home and bring Benjamin to Egypt. Joseph knew that eventually they again would need food and have to return to Egypt and would be forced to bring Benjamin with them or else.

1.5.4.8.   At this point, Joseph's emotions simply had to come out, so he left the room and wept. Six times, he weeps in this story.[1] We need to weep at times. The reason behind weeping is the mark of character.

1.5.5.   The boys returned home, to tell Jacob of their experience. They carried with them food, but strangely enough, they also returned with all the money they started with. Brother Joseph was kind to them.

1.5.5.1.   In Canaan (43:1–10), Jacob was expressing his concern for the son left in a foreign land. When the supplies were again running low, Jacob told his sons to return to Egypt and "buy a little food."[2] Tensions were high in the family. Jacob seems to have hidden suspicions about his sons, food is gone, all combined to make him a man difficult to deal with. Judah reminded his father that they could not return to Egypt without taking Benjamin. They also took twice the amount of money so they could return what they found in their sacks and also purchase more food.

---

[1] 42:24; 43:29; 45:2; 46:29; 50:1, 7
[2] Gen 43:2 *they had finished eating the grain which they had brought from Egypt, that their father said to them, "Go back, buy us a little food."*

1.5.6.　　　　Joseph was informed concerning the brothers return. It undoubtedly was met with great joy. And what does he do? He plans a banquet for them at his house.

1.5.6.1.　　　　They did not know what to expect, perhaps thinking they were in trouble because of the money placed in their sacks from the first visit. However, Joseph's steward knew about the money, for he was responsible for the surprise. He assured them that they had nothing to fear.[1]

1.5.6.2.　　　　Simeon is released,[2] and to his own surprise, finds that Benjamin was with the other brothers. Joseph comes before them, receives the gifts, followed by the bowing of brothers. *All* eleven brothers bowed before him, fulfilling the earlier two dreams of a youthful Joseph.

1.5.6.3.　　　　Soon after seeing that his little brother, Benjamin was present, Joseph left them, again to weep[3]. After what he has been through, Joseph's sensitive heart was a miracle of God's grace. We can imagine the he could have been extremely upset with his brothers for what they had done to him. However, this man of truth and godly character proved his own nature to forgive, when he names his own two sons.[4]

1.5.6.4.　　　　What happened at the banquet was quite a surprise to the eleven brothers. As they were showed to each one's seat, they were directed according to their order of birth. Only Joseph could have known that. In addition, the food was great! Benjamin was given five times more than his brothers were. Joy must have filled these boys, rather than the punishment, which they anticipated.

1.5.6.5.　　　　However, we must keep in mind; their sins had not yet been dealt with. They continued to harbor the past mistreatment of their brother and their deception of their father.

---

[1] Gen 43:23 *Fear not, be at ease your God...the God of your father gave you treasure in your sacks.*

[2] Gen 23b *Then he brought Simeon out to them.*

[3] Gen 43:30 *he was deeply stirred over his brother, and he sought a place to weep; and he entered his chamber and wept there.*

[4] Gen 41:51-52 *Joseph named the firstborn Manasseh, "For," he said, "God has made me forget all my trouble and all my father's household." 52 He named the second Ephraim, "For," he said, "God has made me fruitful in the land of my affliction."*

1.5.7.　　　We are reminded from Scripture, *Be sure your sin will find you out* (Num32:23). Something must occur to bring about repentance followed by forgiveness. However, why would they confess those mistakes? There seemed to be no reason or no person to unveil the truth.[1]

　　1.5.7.1.　　　Then the words of cp 45:1-2

Then Joseph could not control himself before all those who stood by him, and he cried, "Have everyone go out from me." So there was no man with him when Joseph made himself known to his brothers. 2 He wept so loudly that the Egyptians heard it, and the household of Pharaoh heard of it. 3 Then Joseph said to his brothers, "I am Joseph!"

　　1.5.7.2.　　　Time for family privacy, and quickly the simple statement in v 3 *"I am Joseph!"* What joy must have burst forth. Words that must have exploded into his brother's ears, like a lightning bolt of terror. *"Is my father still alive?"* A shock with such force that no response could be immediately given. However, Joseph was weeping again—the secrete was out! He invites them to come *closer*[2] and encourages them.[3] (Quite unusual for a Pharaoh to invite any one to come closer).

　　1.5.7.3.　　　Joseph had on his mind, his father (who was now quite elderly)[4] and a reunion with him. Pharaoh had heard concerning the brothers of Joseph and encouraged the relocation of entire family, offering them the best location.[5]

1.5.8.　　　How excited Jacob must have been when the boys, including Simeon and Benjamin returned home. I think at this time, the boys confessed to Jacob, telling him of the deceit from years before.

　　1.5.8.1.　　　Chapter 46 begins with Jacob and his family leaving their home. Jacob experiences some fear; he was leaving his home and was quite elderly. There were many unknowns before him. He did not know of the blessings

---

[1] Gen 44:20 *We said to my lord, We have an old father and a little child of his old age. Now his brother is dead*

[2] Gen 45:4 *"Please come closer to me."*

[3] Gen 45:5 *do not be grieved or angry with yourselves,*

[4] Gen 45:9 *"Hurry and go up to my father, and say to him, 'Thus says your son Joseph, "God has made me lord of all Egypt; come down to me, do not delay.*

[5] Gen 45:18b *I will give you the best of the land of Egypt and you will eat the fat of the land.*

he would experience during the next/last seventeen years of his life. I love the encouragement, which Jacob received.[1] God's voice calling *Jacob, Jacob* must have filled Jacob with such peace. He would no longer experience any fear. Interesting, I found in Gen 22:11 *Abraham, Abraham.* Something special in hearing God say a name twice. Again I find in 1 Sam 3:10 *Samuel, Samuel*, and Luke 10:41 *Martha, Martha*, and then in Acts 9:4 *Saul, Saul.*

    1.5.8.2.   It is encouraging to know that the Lord knows our name. He's the Lord of all. He knows your name in America, Europe, Africa, or wherever you live.

1.5.9.   Some of Joseph's family was presented to Pharaoh, and Jacob blessed him.[2] We realize now, how important this entire story is. Jacob's move to Egypt, the multiplication of his family,[3] the position of Joseph, all contributed to God's plan to bring blessing to the entire world.

    1.5.9.1.   Joseph's family settled in the best section of land, and five years later, following the famine, began to establish farming of the ground. They increased in goods, and greatly multiplied in number over the years.[4]

    1.5.9.2.   Jacob lived in Egypt for seventeen years before his passing. We read of his failing sight in 48:8.[5] However, when Joseph walked into the room, Jacob sat up to utter final words to him. There were no words of sadness or pity, only how he had been blessed by God.

Gen 48:3-4 *God Almighty appeared to me at Luz in the land of Canaan and blessed me, 4 and He said to me, 'Behold, I will make you fruitful and numerous...."*

Gen 48:15 *God who has been my shepherd all my life to this day*

Gen 48:21 *Behold, I am about to die, but God will be with you, and bring you back to the land of your fathers*

---

[1] Gen 46:2 *God spoke to Israel in visions*

[2] Gen 47:2-3 *He took five men from among his brothers and presented them to Pharaoh. V 10 And Jacob blessed Pharaoh, and went out from his presence.*

[3] Gen 46:8 *Now these are the names of the sons of Israel, Jacob and his sons, who went to Egypt...*

[4] Ex 1:7 *But the sons of Israel were fruitful and increased greatly, and multiplied, and became exceedingly mighty, so that the land was filled with them.*

[5] Gen 48:10 *Now the eyes of Israel were so dim from age that he could not see.*

1.5.10.   He gathers the strength to review some of the experiences of his walk with God.

      1.5.10.1.   The promises God had given to him at Bethel

      1.5.10.2.   The death of his beloved Rachel, Joseph's mother

      1.5.10.3.   Jacob assured Joseph that God would multiply their number and one day take them out of Egypt into their inheritance in the land of Canaan.

1.5.11.   Jacob calls for his sons.[1] We read that Jacob blessed each one of them with a unique blessing, and each according to the order of birth. Each blessing was prophetic, telling of the character and eventual purpose. Chapter 49 details the blessing placed upon each son.

      1.5.11.1.   The six sons of Leah

1.5.11.1.1.   Reuben, vv 3-4

1.5.11.1.2.   Simeon and Levi, vv 5-7

1.5.11.1.3.   Judah, vv 8-12

1.5.11.1.4.   Zebulun, v 13

1.5.11.1.5.   Issachar, vv 14-15

      1.5.11.2.   The two sons of Bilhah, vv 16-18,21

1.5.11.2.1.   Dan, vv 16-18

1.5.11.2.2.   Naphtali, v 21

      1.5.11.3.   The two sons of Zilpah, vv 19-20

1.5.11.3.1.   Gad, v 19

1.5.11.3.2.   Asher, v 20

      1.5.11.4.   The two sons of Rachel, vv 22-27

1.5.11.4.1.   Joseph, vv 22-26

1.5.11.4.2.   Benjamin, v 27

      1.5.11.5.   All the sons blessed, vv 28-33

1.5.12.   Jacob said nothing more, and died with his sons standing by his bed.[2] Joseph weeps loudly and hugged his father.[3]

      1.5.12.1.   Joseph knew what his father wanted concerning his burial.[4] Joseph stands before Pharaoh and asks for permission to bury him in Canaan.

---

[1] Gen 49:1 *Then Jacob summoned his sons and said, "Assemble yourselves that I may tell you what will befall you in the days to come."*

[2] Gen 49:33 *When Jacob finished charging his sons, he drew his feet into the bed and breathed his* last, *and was gathered to his people.*

[3] Gen 50:1 *Then Joseph fell on his father's face, and wept over him and kissed him.*

[4] Gen 47:29-30 *Please do not bury me in Egypt, 30 but when I lie down with my fathers, you shall carry me out of Egypt and bury me in their burial place." And he said, "I will do as you have said."*

1.5.12.2.   The return to Canaan for a funeral included a large entourage of family, Egyptian leaders, and *a very great company*. The sons were all present; Joseph comforted them and assured them of his continued kindness.

1.5.12.3.   Finally, vv 22-26 record the end of Joseph's life at the age of one hundred and ten years. His entire adult life was lived in Egypt where he was embalmed and buried.

Depth of Bible Words and Places
Embalming

Found in our story 50:1.[1] The Egyptian's extensive art of embalming became well known in other nations. Their idea was that the preservation of the body was essential to the life of the soul. As far as we know, it was not often practiced by Hebrews, with the exception of Jacob and Joseph. Jacob's sons carried his body back to Canaan at the close of Genesis.

JOSEPH'S LIFE INDEXED[2]

Recorded Events	Place	Reference
Jacob's eleventh son by his favorite wife, Rachel	Padan-aram	Ge 30:22-24
Jacob loves Joseph more than all his children, and makes him a coat of many colors. For this, his brothers hate him.	Beer-sheba	Ge 37:1-4
He relates two dreams, which indicate his future superior position, and they hate him the more.	Beer-sheba	Ge 37:5-11
Sent by Jacob to his brothers at Dothan they conspire to slay him. Judah proposes that they sell him to some Midianites on their way to Egypt. Dipping his coat in the blood of a kid, they tell Jacob he was slain by a wild beast. The Midianites sell him to Potiphar, Pharaoh's officer.	Dothan	Ge 37:12-36
Joseph's efficiency wins Potiphar's favor, which makes him overseer of his house.	Egypt. House of Potiphar	Ge 39:1-6
Failing in her attempt to entice Joseph to sin, Potiphar's wife makes a false charge against him and prison. Potiphar has him confined in prison. He is	Egypt. In prison.	Ge 39:7-23

---

[1] Gen 50:2-3 *Joseph commanded his servants the physicians to embalm his father. So the physicians embalmed Israel. 3 Now forty days were required for it, for such is the period required for embalming.*

[2] Table information utilized from *Nelson's Foundational Bible Dictionary*, Katharine Harris, World Publishing, Nashville TN, 2004, p. 402

placed in charge of the prisoners.		
He interprets the dreams of two prisoners, the king's butler, and baker. They are fulfilled.	Egypt. Prison	Ge 40
Two years afterward, Pharaoh has two dreams that trouble him. Joseph interprets them. There will be seven years of plenty and seven years of famine, and he counsels Pharaoh how to deal with the situation.	Pharaoh's Court	Ge 41:1-36
Pharaoh makes Joseph his prime minister. He acts wisely and the storehouses of Egypt are filled.	Pharaoh's Court	Ge 41:37-57
The famine in Palestine compels Jacob to send his sons to Egypt to buy corn. Joseph recognizes his brothers, but does not reveal his identity. He sends them back with corn and hides their money in the bags	Pharaoh's Court	Ge 42
He requires them to return with Benjamin. He reveals himself to his brothers, treats them with great kindness and offers them a home in Egypt.	Egypt	Ge 43-45
Jacob and his people, seventy souls, are placed by Joseph in Goshen, where they greatly prosper. Jacob blesses Ephraim and Manasseh, sons of Joseph, gives a prophetic statement of the tribes and dies. Joseph and his brothers bury him beside his people in the cave of Machpelah in Hebron.	Egypt. Israel in Goshen	Ge 46:1-50:13
After Jacob's death, Joseph deals kindly with his brethren, assures them that God will restore them to their own land and receives from them a pledge that they will carry back with them his remains. He dies at the age of 110 years.	Egypt	Ge 50:14-26

1.5.13.　　　　Ask yourself the following questions to summarize your knowledge of Genesis.

　　　　1.5.13.1.　　　What were the Four Great Events of cps 1-11?[1]

　　　　1.5.13.2.　　　Who were the Four Great Men in cps 12-50?[2]

　　　　1.5.13.3.　　　What was the approximate period of time covered in Genesis?[3]

---

[1] Creation, Fall, Flood, Babel
[2] Abraham, Isaac, Jacob, Joseph
[3] 4000-1630 BCE

NINE

Job

1   There are two main thoughts as to when the story of Job took place. This author places the book at 2000-1500 BCE, most likely during Abraham's time. Others have suggested Moses as the author (*c.* 1450 BCE), or place Job during the period of Solomon (Hebrew Poetry, 900 BCE). My commentary of Job is quite brief and will not be detailed verse by verse.

2   Let's proceed with The Book of Job.

Depth of Bible Words and Places
Job Key Word: *Affliction*

The Key Word in Job is found in 10:15; 30:16, 27; 36:8. *Affliction* comes from a root word which means "misery." It pictures someone bowed down under the weight of a heavy burden. We can relate sometimes to this.

The Bible says our Father sees the afflictions of His kids, He urges us to cast every burden upon HIM. He knows everyone of them. This is the setting of Job.

A Basic Outline of Job

1.   Job's Dilemma, Cps 1-2
2.   Job's Debate, Cps 3-37
3.   Job's Deliverance, Cps 38-42

> *Jesus in Job...*He's our *everlasting Redeemer. Job eventually cries out to Christ, His Mediator.*

2.1. Think of some of the great literature of past years; Lord Alfred Tennyson (mentioned in this section), the English poet, (many still admire his poetry).[1] Another man who knew great literature, called Job "the greatest poem ever written."

2.2. Thomas Carlyle, the Scottish historian and essayist and strict Calvinist, said Job was *"one of the grandest things ever written with the pen ...nothing in the Bible or out of it of equal merit."*

2.3. Most scholars agree it's greater than the greatest of writings such as Dante's' *"Divine Comedy"* and Milton's *"Paradise Lost,"* great long lasting works that most of us are familiar with.

3   The Bible book of Job is the oldest book in the Bible, taking place around Gen. 11-12 near 2000 BCE; Reece in his Chronological Bible, places it in Genesis 12. Smith's unusual Chronological Narrated Bible places Job with Jeremiah, using a "flash back" to an earlier time. However, many scholars place it sometime during the period of Abraham. In my reading of James Ussher's "The Annals of the World," first published in 1658, two years after his death, I located his dating of Job, 1635 BC (BCE).

3.1. From a Christian writer known for his chronicle of sacred history, a history of the world in two books, Sulpicius Severus, (*c.* 363-*c.* 425) noted lawyer, orator and scholar, we note his following account of Job:

> "At this time lived Job, a man embracing the law of nature, and the knowledge of the true God and very righteous and rich in goods. He was renowned for the fact that neither the enjoyment of those riches corrupted him, nor the loss of them depraved him in any way. When he was plundered of all his goods by Satan, bereft of his children and at last tormented with grievous botches and sores in his body, he did not sin. Having first been commended by God, he was later restored to his former health and had double of what he possessed before."[2]

3.2. The book itself does not give us the author.

   3.2.1.   Perhaps it was Job himself

   3.2.2.   Some think Moses wrote it

   3.2.3.   Others suggest an unknown writer during Solomon's time.

3.3. The book of Job is sort of a "play" with "acts" and "scenes" taking place.

---

[1] Tennyson gave us "The Charge of the Light Brigade." Who could forget those words : *Into the valley of Death Rode the six hundred. Forward the Light Brigade* . He gave us other works such as "Sir Lancelot and Queen Guinevere"; and of course "Ulysses."

[2] Sacred History, 1.1.c.13.11:76}

3.4. In order to really understand as much as we are able to, we have to understand first the prevailing thought about suffering, before and during this period of Job.

3.5. It was believed that suffering was not from some spiritual-being hostile to God—Satan was not even in their thinking. Suffering was solely a result of man's disobedience. That was the very foundation of thinking in that day.

3.6. Wickedness and evil resulted in punishment. Therefore, if there was punishment, there had to have been evil. That was the prevailing thought that wise men dealt with in that day.

3.7. I would suggest in reading Job, that you do not try to "think and reason" your way through it. Rather, feel it, "play the role on stage."

    3.7.1. Put yourself in the prosperity and happiness of a wealthy farmer. The book opens with a beautiful country scene in which the respected Job is enjoying the fruits of his labor (1:1-5). Read of his wealth:[1]

    3.7.2. Shake in front of God as Satan stands there (he has access to God), and states that Job is a materialist. Take away his possessions and he will curse you God to your face. (1:6-12).

    3.7.3. Shudder with Job during the attacks of calamity after calamity as his possessions are stolen or destroyed. (1:13-2:10).

    3.7.4. Sit with Job at a gate and agonize with him, feel his loss. Feel the sores running over his entire body and his banishment outside the city gate.

    3.7.5. Endure his frustration with friends, as they do not even recognize him. His friends, it is suggested, represent religious arguments. (2:11-37:24)

        3.7.5.1. Eliphaz the oldest, is intelligence; calm, dignified, something of a Puritan, cold in heart.

        3.7.5.2. Bildad is tradition. Wisdom of the past with an answer for everything in neat formulas.

        3.7.5.3. Zophar is common sense. Deep convictions and demands that things be done within those convictions.

    3.7.6. Next, come close to defying God!

    3.7.7. Then hear with your inner ear the voice of a gracious and loving God, and realize He has never changed. Hear God answering out of a whirlwind as darkness settles on earth.

    3.7.8. Then bow to Him in surrender after being asked question after question. Oh, Job! God is so much greater than any

---

[1] 7,000 sheep, 3,000 camels, 500 yoke of oxen, 500 mares, 7 sons, 3 daughters

man can understand. What does Job know about the mighty works of creation and the mighty mysteries of nature? Job shrinks as he realizes, if he cannot answer questions about nature, how can he answer the greater questions related to man?

3.7.9.　　　And finally, envision the restoring to happiness and prosperity. Job ends his spiritual journey in victory. He is restored.

3.8. Allow me to offer some statements to help understand this book and what we learn from wise men.

3.8.1.　　　First, know some things about "the accuser" who stood before God and brought about these experiences in Job's life. This next Expanded Paper is from the author's printed manuscript ***Help From the Bible When You Need It!***

EXPANDED HELP PAPER
Satan

#1, He's not some imp with a red body and a pitchfork sitting on your shoulder whispering ugly thoughts in your ear.

#2 He is the most attractive, brilliant, powerful archangel that God ever created; not a popular thought, but one you should not forget.

#3 Job never knew what was going on in heaven. Satan still loves to work in the background; however being invisible—does not mean he is unreal. Not heard doesn't mean he is silent. Not being flashy does not indicate he's asleep.

#4, As I read through the first 2 cps of Job, I found some interesting things about our enemy that I wrote down. You may be surprised to realize:

- He is alive
- Has access to heaven
- Accuser of believers
- Goes from place to place
- Associates with angels
- Appears before God
- Roams the earth
- Carries on conversations with God
- Singles out individuals hoping to destroy them
- Hates good men
- Envies the blessing of God upon others
- Seeks to destroy fellowship between God and His children
- Seeks to cause men to curse God
- Limited by God in touching His children
- Can destroy riches of men
- Has agents on earth who do his bidding

- Can send fire from heaven
- Would like to destroy good men
- Propagator of sickness and disease in the bodies of men.

3.8.2.　　　Next we can learn three lessons for one who is going through a dark place....a deep pit....or a dreary prison. These lessons are summarized from Charles Swindoll's book on Job [1]:

    3.8.2.1.　　　#1 you will have a day or two that are so dark, you won't see any light. It might happen...yes to a believer.

    3.8.2.2.　　　#2 you might have difficult experiences so extreme you don't have any hope...peace is gone...unrest is deep. It could happen.

    3.8.2.3.　　　#3 there might be deep places you are in, which you have no apparent hope of finding relief; at that point you may wonder how to go on. [2]

3.8.3.　　　However, know this: None of those three statements is true! There is no pit so deep but that our Father is not deeper still!

3.8.4.　　　There is HOPE in Christ, He will NEVER leave you or forsake you, and don't EVER let the devil cause despair. Live on IN Christ, your hope. Do not quit, do not give up, and do not stay down. [3]

3.8.5.　　　Then these lessons (again summarized from Charles Swindoll) [4] which Job learned, are a help for us:

    3.8.5.1.　　　*#1 Resist the temptation to explain everything: GOD KNOWS*...He is aware of it all;

    3.8.5.2.　　　*#2 Focus on the future benefits, not the present pain: GOD LEADS*...Acknowledge Him in all you do, and

---

[1] Used in part from Swindoll, Charles, *Job*, Charles Swindoll, Inc., The W Publishing Group, Nashville, 2004

[2] I worked with a man who served God, taught Bible studies...a happy life; then he lost his job. He couldn't keep up with his hojme, strife set in affecting his wife and three children he was trying to provide for. His words to me were "Sometimes I feel like getting in my broken-down car, driving off and never stopping." I hope I encouraged him enough to carry on until it gets better.

[3] Encourage yourself with these scriptures:

Philippians 4:12 *I can do all things through Him who strengthens me.*

Philippians 4:19 *And my God will supply all your needs according to His riches in glory in Christ Jesus.*

Psalm 91:1-2 *He who dwells in the shelter of the Most High Will abide in the shadow of the Almighty. 2 I will say to the Lord, "My refuge and my fortress, My God, in whom I trust!"*

Deuteronomy 31:6 *He will not fail you or forsake you.*

[4] ibid

you can be sure He will direct your path. His word is a lamp to every step you take.

3.8.5.3.　　　And #3, *Embrace the sovereignty of the Almighty: GOD CONTROLS*—His omnipresence and omnipotence are sufficient for you.

Depth of Bible Words and Locations
OMNIPRESENCE

The ability of God to be everywhere at all times. God was present as Lord in all creation (Psalm 139:7–12), and there is no escaping Him. He is present in our innermost thoughts. Even as we are formed in the womb, He knows all the days of our future. He looks not only on outward actions, but also especially on the inner attitudes of a person's heart (Matthew. 6:1–18).

Matthew 18:20 *"For where two or three are gathered together in My name, I am there in the midst of them."*

Matthew 28:20 *"teaching them to observe all things that I have commanded you; and lo, I am with you always, even to the end of the age."*

Hebrews 13:5 *He Himself has said, "I WILL NEVER DESERT YOU, NOR WILL I EVER FORSAKE YOU."*

OMNIPOTENCE

God is all-powerful. His power is all-encompassing. He has created all things and sustains them by the Word of His power (Genesis 1:1–3; Hebrews 1:3). Before Him "the nations are as a drop in a bucket, and are counted as the small dust on the balance" (Isaiah 40:15). He is the ruler of nature and history. Yet He has so fashioned humankind that He graciously appeals to every person to return to Him.

3.8.6.　　　Then from cp 27 of Job, let's conclude with five priorities for our life:

3.8.6.1.　　　#1 Think like God. His thoughts must always be the foundation for our own thinking

3.8.6.2.　　　#2 Travel through life by walking in integrity in all you do

3.8.6.3.　　　#3 Realize that problems do occur, difficulties do arise in every person's life----they will not triumph if you stand strong in Christ!

3.8.6.4.　　　#4 It is time lost, if you seek answers without direction coming from His Word.

　　　#5 Wisdom and understanding come to you as you develop a holy fear of God.

SECTION 4
Moses, Deliverance, and Law

Exodus, Leviticus, Numbers, Deuteronomy. The period from 1570 to 1451 BCE

Theme Statement: *"Did not Moses give you the Law…?"* (John 7:19)

THE KEYS IN SECTION FOUR

Section 4: Moses, Deliverance, and Law

Keys to Exodus—

A Key Word: *Delivered*

The Key Verses (6:6; 19:5–6)

6:6 Say, therefore, to the sons of Israel, 'I am the Lord, and I will bring you out from under the burdens of the Egyptians, and I will deliver you from their bondage. I will also redeem you with an outstretched arm and with great judgments.

19:5 'Now then, if you will indeed obey My voice and keep My covenant, then you shall be My own possession among all the peoples, for all the earth is Mine; 6 and you shall be to Me a kingdom of priests and a holy nation.' These are the words that you shall speak to the sons of Israel.

The Key Chapters (12–14)

The Key People in Exodus

Moses-author of the Pentateuch and deliverer of Israel from Egyptian slavery (24:4)

Miriam-prophetess and older sister of Moses (2:7; 15:20, 21)

Pharaoh's daughter-the princess who rescued baby Moses from the water and adopted him (2:5-10)

Jethro-Midian shepherd who became Moses' father-in-law (3:1; 4:18; 18:1-12)

Joshua-assistant to Moses and military leader who led Israel into the Promised Land (17:9-14; 24:13; 32:17; 33:11)

Keys to Leviticus—

A Key Word: *Blood*

The Key Verses (17:11; 20:7–8)

17:11 For the life of the flesh is in the blood, and I have given it to you on the altar to make atonement for your souls; for it is the blood by reason of the life that makes atonement.

20:7 You shall consecrate yourselves therefore and be holy, for I am the Lord your God. 8 'You shall keep My statutes and practice them; I am the Lord who sanctifies you.

A Key Chapter (16)

The Key People in Leviticus

Moses-prophet and leader who acted as God's mouthpiece to explain His law to Israel (1:1; 4:1; 5:14; 6:1-27:34)

Aaron-Moses' brother and first high priest of Israel (1:7; 2:3; 10; 3:5, 8, 13; 6:9-24:9)

Nadab-son of Aaron, in training to become a priest, died because of disobedience to the Lord's commands (8:36; 10:1, 2)

Eleazar-son of Aaron who succeeded him as high priest of Israel (10:6-20)

Ithamar-son of Aaron who also became a priest (10:6-20)

Keys to Numbers—

Two Key Words: *Wilderness, Anointed*

The Key Verses (14:22–23; 20:12)

14:22 "Surely all the men who have seen My glory and My signs which I performed in Egypt and in the wilderness, yet have put Me to the test these ten times and have not listened to My voice, 23 shall by no means see the land which I swore to their fathers, nor shall any of those who spurned Me see it

20:12 But the Lord said to Moses and Aaron, "Because you have not believed Me, to treat Me as holy in the sight of the sons of Israel, therefore you shall not bring this assembly into the land which I have given them."

The Key Chapter (14)

The Key People in Numbers

Moses-great prophet and leader who acted as God's mouthpiece to explain His Law to Israel (1:1, 19, 48; 5:1, 4, 5, 11, and over two hundred other references)

Aaron-Moses' brother and first high priest of Israel (1:3, 17, 44; 2:1; 3:1-10; 12:1-5; 20:23-29)

Miriam-sister to Moses and Aaron, also songwriter and prophetess; stricken with leprosy because of jealousy toward Moses (12; 20:1; 26:59)

Joshua-Moses' successor as leader of Israel; one of the only two people to see both the Exodus from Egypt and the Promised Land (11:28; 13; 14; 26:65; 27:15-23; 32:11, 12, 28; 34:17)

Caleb-one of the men sent to scout Canaan; faithful to God in his desire to conquer the land; one of the only two people to see both the Exodus from Egypt and the Promised Land (13-14; 26:65; 32:12; 34:19)

Korah-Levite who assisted in the Tabernacle; killed because of his rebellion against the Lord (16:1-40; 26:9)

Balaam-prophet and sorcerer who halfheartedly obeyed God; attempted to lead Israel into idol worship (22:1-24:25; 31:7, 8, 16)

Keys to Deuteronomy—

A Key Word: *Covenant*

The Key Verses (10:12–13; 30:19–20)

10:12 "Now, Israel, what does the Lord your God require from you, but to fear the Lord your God, to walk in all His ways and love Him, and to serve the Lord your God with all your heart and with all your soul, 13 and to keep the Lord's commandments and His statutes which I am commanding you today for your good?

30:19 "I call heaven and earth to witness against you today, that I have set before you life and death, the blessing and the curse. So choose life in order that you may live, you and your descendants, 20 by loving the Lord your God, by obeying His voice, and by holding fast to Him; for this is your life and the length of your days, that you may live in the land which the Lord swore to your fathers, to Abraham, Isaac, and Jacob, to give them

The Key Chapter (27)

The Key People in Deuteronomy

Moses-leader of Israel; instructed the people on the law of God but was not allowed to enter the Promised Land (1-5; 27; 29; 31-34)

Approximate Dates of Key Events in Section 4	
1571	Moses is born
1531	Moses flees Egypt for Midian
1491	Moses leads the Israelites out of Egypt; The Israelites cross the Red Sea
1491	The Law is given on Mount Sinai
1491-1451	Events in Numbers Wilderness wandering
1451	Moses Dies Israel enters the Promised Land

TEN

Moses

1   Section 4 details the period of Moses, *MOSES, DELIVERANCE, AND LAW.*

2   The next four books, Exodus, Leviticus, Numbers and Deuteronomy comprise the life of Moses.[1] Even today, the Jewish people understand their vocation in the light of the events of these books.

3   Exodus introduces us to Moses and marks a second beginning in the Bible's account of the history of Israel. The patriarchs recorded the first of their history. Moses is chosen by God to bring His people to Him at Sinai.

3.1. We are not aware of the names of for Old Testament books that were inspired. For example, each of the next four books was referred to by the Jews, using the beginning words. They *highlight* the words in order to point to that book. We might *italicize* them.

3.1.1. Exodus *"and now these are"*

3.1.2. Leviticus *"and He called"*

3.1.3. Numbers *"in the wilderness"*

3.1.4. Deuteronomy referred to, as *"these are the words."*

3.2. The titles of the books, which we refer to, were not assigned until the Bible was translated from Hebrew into Greek *c.* 250 BCE, called the Septuagint. We will refer to this Greek translation of the Hebrew several more times. Refer to the Expanded Help Paper, "Septuagint" in this volume. Also, see the following *History of the Written Word*.

---

[1] According to accepted tradition, and many recognized scholars, the author of the first five books was Moses; at the least he was its subject and oral contributor (see JEDP). God told him in Exodus 17:14 *Then the Lord said to Moses "Write this in a book as a memorial and recite it to Joshua...."*

Exodus 24:4 records *Moses wrote down all the words of the Lord.*

Sometime during the last 40 years of his life, and following the Exodus from Egypt, in approx. 1450 BCE, Moses was inspired to pen down and pass on the Torah (Pentateuch).

Refer to the following, showing *A Partial History of the Written Word of God* which lists many Bible versions/ translations.[1]

2600 BCE	Papyrus and parchment first used as writing materials	
2500	First known use of ink	Egypt and China
1400	The first written Word of God	The Ten Commandments
500	All original Hebrew Autographs completed	All 39 O.T. books included
250 BCE	Septuagint	All 39 O.T. books into Greek
200	Dead Sea Scrolls	All O.T. books except Esther
100 CE	All original Greek Manuscripts completed	All 27 books of the N.T.
200	The Jewish Mishnah, the Oral Torah recorded	
200	The first portion of a Latin version originated among Latin-speaking Jews. Later versions emerged in the late fourth century.	This eventually led to Jerome's complete Hebrew to Latin version in approximately 400 CE.
Early to mid 4th century CE	Gothic Bible	
315 CE	Recognition of the New Testament	27 books in the N.T.
330	Codex Sinaiticus	Found in 1844 CE near Mt. Sinai. Many pages had been used as kindling for fires. Written with brown ink in beautiful script on the finest vellum. Entire NT and 199 leaves of OT. In British Museum today.
340	Codex Vaticanus	A priceless treasure in the Vatican Museum, written in Alexandria, found in 1481. Only a few pages missing of a complete Bible.
c. 400	Jerome translated the entire Bible into the best Latin form. The first printed edition of his work was the Gutenberg Bible, also known as "Bible with 42 lines," because it had 42 lines per page.	The Vulgate, the first book of importance ever printed with movable type, 1456 CE.
425	Codex Alexandrinus	Originally contained the entire Bible plus four books of the Maccabees and several other writings. Many of its pages have been lost. In the British Museum today.
382	Latin Vulgate completed by Jerome	39 O.T., 27 N.T. and the 14 Apocrypha books,
433	Armenian Bible Monasteries helped preserve the written Word beginning in the 3rd century; they were immersed in the Bible and its guidelines	

---

[1] Compiled by author from various source

476-1000	Civilization had "sunk" to a new low in Europe; few writers with literary "light"; papal power ruled; dogmas of councils controlled. Some pockets of light from Spain to India. Challenges to the Roman Church; the Bible fell into general disuse. A few translations were made in others areas.	The Dark Ages
3rd -4th century	Middle Persian Bible	
4th century	Georgian Bible	
6th century	Ethiopian Bible (called Abyssinia)	
7th century	Arabic Bible; Anglo-Saxon Bible	
8th century	Oldest copy of the Latin Vulgate Bible	Codex Amiatinus
8th century	Nubian Bible	
9th century	Slavonic Bible	
10th century	Oldest copy of the Hebrew Tanakh	
1384	Wycliffe produces a complete hand written manuscript. Advocated the people's right to read the Bible in their own language. Scriptures had been "locked" within the Latin, which few people knew. Sent out preachers to the common people to translate into English. Hostility against him, body was exhumed and burned in 1415	All 80 books; from the Latin Vulgate
1450	Gutenberg invented the printing press	Printed a Latin Bible in Mainz, Germany
1462	First dated Bible to have the name of the printer and place of printing	Fust & Schoeffer
1466	First German Bible printed	
1471	First Bible printed in Rome	Second Bible with a printed date
1475	Thomas Aquinas Gospels	
1477	First Old Testament in Dutch	
1478	First French Bible	
1482	First printing of the Pentateuch in Hebrew	
1486	First Bible with a title page	
1488	First Bible into Czech	From the Vulgate
1516	Erasmus produces a Greek/Latin New Testament	A parallel translation
1518	First separate complete Greek Bible	Printed in Venice
1522	Martin Luther's New Testament	
1526	William Tyndale, a brilliant Greek and Hebrew scholar was burdened to make the Bible available to the common people. Beginning his translation in 1524 and then moving from place to place because of his belief, finally fleeing to Worms where 6000 copies of his Bible were printed in English. Fleeing again, he was tried eventually for heresy, strangled, and his body burned. See Expanded Paper on Tyndale in this volume.	Today there are only two remaining copies of the original 1525-1526 First Edition.
1530	First Pentateuch in English	
1530	First Bible in French	

1534	Martin Luther completes a German Bible	
1535	Coverdale's Complete Bible in English resulted from Wycliffe's influence.	The first complete Bible in English print
1537	Matthew's Bible; a revision of Tyndale and Coverdale Bibles	Second complete Bible in English; all 80 books.
1539	The first Bible printed for public use, The "Great Bible." So named because of its size and exclusive use in the church. The only Bible that could be lawfully used in England. Fundamentally the Coverdale Bible; known essentially as the Cranmer Bible because of Thomas Cranmer's fundamental preface.	Included all 80 books; sponsored by Thomas Cromwell.
1541	First complete Swedish Bible	
1551	First New Testament with Verses	
1555	First Latin Bible in Verses	
1560	The Geneva Bible printed. First Bible to have numbered verses and include notes with strong Protestant implications. The Bible of the common people, used by Shakespeare, Puritans of England, and John Bunyan in his *Pilgrim's Progress*.	Included all 80 books
1568	The Bishops Bible printed. The King James became a revision of this translation	Included all 80 books
1569	Spanish Bible	From original language
1576	First Bible printed in Scotland	
1582	Douay-Rheims Bible, approved by the Roman Catholic Church	From the Latin version. New Testament, 1582; OT, 1610
1590	First Bible into Hungarian	
1597	First Bible into Polish	
1609	The Douay O.T. is added to the Douay N.T. of 1582, making the first complete English Catholic Bible	Included all 80 books and translated from the Latin Vulgate of 382 A.D.
1611	The King James Bible printed as approved state version, stating that none of the existing translations was accurate enough for a national Bible. Most scholars agreed that the KJV contains the most beautiful form of English the world has ever known. The writers did not question the integrity and authenticity of the Bible.	From the original Hebrew and Greek. Originally included all 80 books; The Apocrypha was removed in 1885 leaving the 66 books.
1629	First Revised King James Bible	Printed at Cambridge
1637	First Bible into Dutch	From original Hebrew and Greek
1642	First Completed Finnish Bible	
1661	Indian New Testament	John Eliot
1678	First Old Testament in Yiddish	
1690	First Complete Irish Bible	
1752	Challoner's revision of the Douay-Rheims Bible of 1609	
1764	Quaker Bible	Masoretic Text[1]

---

[1] The Masoretic Text is the authoritative Hebrew and Aramaic text of the Tanakh

Year	Description	Notes
1782	Robert Aitken's Bible. First Bible printed in America (KJV)	
1790	First Catholic Bible printed in the US; first New Testament published in New York	
1791	The First Family Bible and first Illustrated Bible printed in America.	Included all 80 books
1804	Book of John translated into the Mohawk Indian language	
1808	Robert Aitken's daughter, Jane, was the first woman to print a Bible	
1808	Charles Thomson's Translation, first Septuagint in English in the world	Septuagint, excluding the Apocrypha and the New Testament
1809	The first book printed in America in Hebrew; New York Bible Society founded	
1814	First Hebrew Bible printed in U.S.	Philadelphia
1816	American Bible Society founded, produces its first Bible	
1830	Joseph Smith Translation of the Bible	
1833	Noah Webster's Bible, a revision of the King James	
1841	English Hexapla N.T.	Comparing the Greek and six English Translations
1841	ABS publishes the complete Bible for the blind	
1846	The Illuminated Bible; the most lavishly Illustrated Bible printed in America	
1847	First Gutenberg Bible brought to the North American continent	James Lenox
1853	Ferrar Fenton Bible	Masoretic Text
1855	The English Revised Version; major revision of the King James	
1860	The New Testament in Cherokee	
1862	Young's Literal Translation (YLT)	Masoretic Text
1876	Julia E Smith Parker Translation	
1878	Rotherham Emphasized Bible	
1885	Revised Version of the King James Bible	N.T. printed 1881; O.T. in 1885; entire Bible in 1898. From the Masoretic Text
1890	Darby Bible (DBY)	
1890	Weymouth New Testament	
1895	The Woman's Bible	
1899	Gideon Bible Society founded	Boscobel, Wisconsin
1901	The American Standard Version, major American revision of the King James. Used the mistranslation *Jehovah* (Yahweh), *Holy Spirit* for Holy Ghost, and *love* for charity.	The American scholars had contributed to the Revised Version; agreed not to publish their "revisions" for fourteen years.
1902	Rotherham's Emphasized Bible	
1903	Ferrar Fenton Bible	
1904	Canadian Bible Society founded	
1904	Worrell New Testament	
1917	Jewish Publication Society (JPS)	Masoretic Text

1924	James Moffatt Translation; a quite liberal translation; incorporated the JEDP theory of Bible authors.	N.T. only was in 1913; Bible in c. 1924
1924	The Millennium Bible published	
1936	Westminster Bible (WVSS)	
1941	The Douay Bible Published	
c. 1950	The Berkely Version	Contains numerous footnotes of difficult passages.
1950	Jehovah Witnesses New World translation of the N.T.	
1952	Revised Standard Version (RSV)	Masoretic Text
1955	Knox's Translation of the Vulgate	
1956	Wuest Expanded Translation	Gospels; other books followed
1958	Berkeley Version	
1959	New Testament in Modern English	From the original Greek by J.B. Phillips
1961	The Jerusalem Bible in English	
1963	Dake's Annotated Reference Bible	Four equal sized columns on each page; extensive notes
1965	Amplified Bible (AMP)	
1966	Jerusalem Bible (JB)	
1969	Zondervan Topical Bible	
1970	New English Bible (NEB)	
1970	New American Bible (NAB)	
1971	King James II Version (KJ2)	Masoretic Text
1971	The Living Bible (TLB)	
1971	The New American Standard Bible (NASB).	
1971	The Story Bible	
1972	The Bible in Living English	
1973	The New International Version (NIV)	
1976	Good News Translation (GNT)	
1976	Ryrie Study Bible	
1977	The Reese Chronological Bible	King James
1978	New International Version (NIV)	
1982	The New King James Version (NKJV)	Masoretic Text
1984	The Hebrew-Greek Key Word Study Bible	
1985	New Jerusalem Bible (NJB)	
1986	New Life Version (NLV)	
1989	Revised English Bible (REB)	
1989	New Revised Standard Version (NRSV)	
1990	Vietnam Verteran's Bible	Tyndale
1991	New Century Version (NCV)	
1991	Life in the Spirit Study Bible (NIV)	
1994	Clear Word Bible	
1995	Contemporary English Version (CEV)	
1995	God's Word (GW)	
1996	New Living Translation (NLT)	
1998	Complete Jewish Bible by David H. Stern (CJB)	
2001	English Standard Version (ESV)	Revision of the RSV
2002	The Orthodox Jewish Bible (OJB)	

2002	The Message (MSG)	
2002	The English Standard Version (ESV); to bridge the gap between the accuracy of the NASB and the readability of the NIV	
2002	Today's New International Version	Update to NIV
2002	Gutenberg Bible on CD-ROM	Library of Congress
2003	Discovery of first N.T. verse carved into a shrine	Jerusalem
2004	Holman Christian Standard Bible (HCSB)	Masoretic Text
2004	The Sportsman's Bible	HCSB
2004	The Soldier's Bible	Holman
2005	New English Translation (NET)	
2005	User's Guide to Bible Translations	David Dewey
2007	Maxwell Leadership Bible	NKJV
2007	Kindle Editions downloadable	Amazon
2008	The Orthodox Study Bible (OSB)	LXX
2009	The [expanded] Bible	New Testament
2009	The Transformation Study Bible	NLT
2011	The Names of God Bible	God's Word Translation
2011	International Standard Version (ISV)	
2011, 2014	Names of God Bible	
2012	Spiritual Warfare Bible	New King James
2014	Tree of Life Bible	Masoretic Text
2014	Modern English Version (MEV)	Masoretic Text
2016	Tree of Life	TLV
2016	Cultural Backgrounds Study Bible	NIV
2016	Word Study Bible	NKJV
2016	The Modern English Version	MEV

Many Study Bibles and "specialized Bibles" have expanded the available translations with additional study notes. A partial list (there are dozens of additional Bibles).

Apologetics Study Bible	Men's Study Bible
Archaeological Study Bible	Military Bible
Discover God Study Bible	Modern English Study
Duck Commander KJV	NKJV Study Bible
The Essentials Study Bible NIV	NIV Leadership Bible
Fire Bible for Students	New Oxford Annotated
Key Word Study Bibles	NIV Leadership Bible
ESV Study Bibles	NIV Study Bible
Faith In Action Study Bible	Orthodox Study Bible
Green Bible NRSV	Quest Study Bible
Healing Holy Bible ERV	Rainbow Study Bible
Holman Illustrated Study Bible	Reformation Study Bible
Homeschool Mom's Bible NIV	Ryrie Study Bible
Journalizing Bible (in various forms)	Scofield Study Bibles
King James Study Bible	Spirit of The Reformation
Key Word Study Bible	Step Stone Bible CEB
Legacy Study Bible	Streams in the Desert Bible
Life Application Study Bibles	The Story NIV
Life In The Spirit Study Bible	Thompson Chain-Reference Study Bible
The Life Plan Study Bible	Women of Faith Bible
MacArthur Study Bibles	Worship Together Bible

The next Expanded Help Paper is added because of Tyndale's vital place in the history of the English translations of the Bible.

EXPANDED HELP PAPER
William Tyndale

William Tyndale is the greatest figure in the history of translating the Bible into English. His work laid the foundation for what many of us now have for our Bible reading. He studied at Oxford, and then Camb ridge, from the ages of 16 to 21. He was a fabulously skilled linguist, commanding Hebrew, Greek, Latin, Spanish, French, Italian, German, and, yes, English. He wanted to undertake the translation of the Bible in the same year that Luther published his translation of the New Testament into German, 1522. However, he was not given permission by the bishop of London.

So, in 1524, Tyndale, moved to Germany where his Reformation ideas could be more safely expressed. He began his translation working d irectly from the Hebrew and Greek. His New Testament translation w as completed in 1525, and immediately attacked in England.

He printed his translation of the Pentateuch and the Psalms in 1530, and Jonah in 1531. By the time of his death in 1536, Tyndale had also completed Job through 2 Chronicles in manuscript form.

Tyndale was arrested by Henry VIII near Brussels, strangled, and burned at the stake. Tyndale prayed at his death, "Lord, open the King of England's eyes." It was a prayer that was fulfilled in 1537 when Henry VIII allowed the English Bible to be distributed in his kingdom.

Tyndale's translation was the foundation for subsequent translations including the King James Version. About 80 percent of Tyndale is included in the King James Bible. Tyndale had a marvelous cap acity for coining memorable expressions: "Let there be light," "My brother's keeper," "The salt of the earth," "Fight the good fight," and "The spirit is willing, but the flesh is weak." We may easily conclude that Tyndale laid the foundation for our English Bibles we read.

3.3. We return, next to Exodus. The name Exodus is actually a Greek expression for "a going out." It marks the beginning of the history of Israel as a people. Other names have been used to describe this book: "deliverance," "departure," and "out of captivity."

Basic Outlines of Exodus
#1 THREE LOCATIONS

1. Captive in Egypt Cps 1-12

2.   The Journey Towards Sinai Cps 13-18
3.   Maturation At Sinai Cps 19-40

Basic Outlines of Exodus #2
1.   Redemption, God's Power, Cps 1-17
2.   Righteousness, God's Holiness, Cps 18-24
3.   Restoration, God's Grace, cps 25-40

Depth of Bible Words and Places
Exodus Key Word: *Delivered*

Found in 3:8; 5:18; 22:7, 10, 26. Its Hebrew meaning is quite clear and appropriate: "To strip away" or "to snatch away."
And that's what God did; he snatches away His people from Egypt, to move them in to a land He had set aside for them. God is a God who delivers.
We see this word used when God is in action delivering or rescuing His people.
Also consider Ps 18:4 *He delivers me from my enemies;* Ps 34:17 *the righteous cry and The Lord hears and delivers them out of all their troubles;* Job 36:15 *he delivers the afflicted in their affliction.* Your personal God will deliver you.

Jesus in Exodus...The Passover Lamb. The Hebrew word is derived from "that which one brings near to God." He is your perfect lamb, His blood—your passage to God.

3.4. We offered two basic outlines of Exodus. The book of Exodus may also be divided into *five distinct episodes*:
  3.4.1.   The childhood and call of Moses
  3.4.2.   The struggle to free Israel by plagues, climaxing with the Passover
  3.4.3.   The escape and journey into the wilderness of Sinai
  3.4.4.   The giving of the covenant and its laws
  3.4.5.   The instructions for building the ark, the tent of meeting, and the executing of the instructions.
3.5. We note that Exodus begins *and now these are...;* therefore we conclude that Exodus was a continuation of the Genesis record.
  3.5.1.   Exodus is a book of redemption—beginning in gloom, ending in glory.
      3.5.1.1.   150 years passed since the fourth Great Man, Joseph. Exodus continues the story. His death was

recorded in the last verse in Genesis.[1] We find in the closing verses of Genesis, Joseph's people, the Israelites enjoying the favor and bounties of Egypt.

3.5.1.2.   However, those days of bounty were left behind. We find in the opening chapter of Exodus, a different situation.

3.5.2.   In Egypt, Satan again attempts to destroy the seed by killing all the male children. Pharaoh commanded the midwives to destroy all these male children. All newborn boys were to be thrown into the Nile.

3.5.2.1.   We go from a time of favor and bounty in Egypt to a time when the descendants of Joseph, multiplied greatly, the Bible says in v7 of Exodus 1 *"the land was full of them."*

3.5.2.2.   Read vv 8-11 in Exodus 1.[2]

3.5.2.3.   In approximately 1570 BCE, the Scriptures inform us that the Hebrews were in bondage. They are described as toiling under enforced labor. Even their male children were to be destroyed. They went from a time of royal favor, to a time of servitude.[3]

3.5.2.4.   We read about a new king in verse 8, who did not know Joseph, and he feared that some Eastern army might invade Egypt and gather these Hebrews as allies. Who was the new Pharaoh? A question that cannot be answered with absolute certainty. Ahmosis I was the first ruler following the expelled Hyksos people. He probably was the new *king over Egypt who did not know Joseph.* However, also, the Pharaoh who brought oppression to the Hebrews cannot be identified with certainty. See below.

---

[1] Gen 50:26 *So Joseph died at the age of one hundred and ten years; and he was embalmed and placed in a coffin in Egypt.*

[2] Exodus 1:8-11 *Now a new king arose over Egypt, who did not know Joseph. 9 He said to his people, "Behold, the people of the sons of Israel are more and mightier than we. 10 "Come, let us deal wisely with them, or else they will multiply and in the event of war, they will also join themselves to those who hate us, and fight against us and depart from the land." 11 So they appointed taskmasters over them to afflict them with hard labor.*

[3] There's a passage in Deut. which summarizes the Exodus; Deut 26:6-9 *And the Egyptians treated us harshly and afflicted us, and imposed hard labor on us. 7 'Then we cried to the Lord, the god of our fathers, and the Lord heard our voice and saw our affliction and our toil and our oppression; 8 and the Lord brought us out of Egypt with a mighty hand and an outstretched arm and with great terror and with signs and wonders;* Notice the action that God took. He *heard,* He *saw,* He *acted,* and He *brought them out.* God never changes; He takes the same action when one asks Him. He hears, he sees, he acts, he brings out.

EXPANDED HELP PAPER
Two Possible Exodus Pharaohs

Scholars disagree on the time period and kings (pharaohs). The following history of two periods, each of which could have been the oppression and exodus of the Israelites, should be considered. Of course, the question must be asked, "Why did Moses omit the name of the Pharaoh that he faced?" We should note that the Bible is not trying to answer the question, 'Who is the pharaoh of the exodus?' to satisfy the curiosity of modern historians; rather, it was seeking to clarify for Israel who was the God of the exodus."[1] The conclusion seems to be that the exodus-pharaoh's throne-name is absent for one reason alone: a skilled writer named Moses, born in Egypt and trained as a prince in all of the ways of the royal court of Egypt (Acts 7:22), followed the standard practice of his day by leaving unnamed the foreign monarch who assumed the role of a dreaded enemy of his own nation, in this case Israel.[2]

It is this author's opinion that Amenhotep II is the only legitimate candidate for the exodus-pharaoh. However, consider both the following two possible Exodus Pharaohs.

1. Amenhotep II ruled during the period following his father, Thutmose III.

   a. Amenhotep II, meaning "satisfied," was the seventh Pharaoh of the 18th dynasty of Egypt (see list of 18th and 19th dynasties in this volume). Amenhotep, who was not a firstborn son, inherited a vast kingdom from his father Thutmose III, holding it together by several military campaigns. His elder brother, Amenemhat was the intended heir; born of the chief wife, Satiah. However, Amenemhat died shortly after his father became Pharaoh. A Pharaoh generally had a chief wife, a "second favorite" as well as other "lower" wives.

   b. Amenhotep II became Pharaoh at the age of eighteen, according to an inscription from his great Sphinx notation. It is concluded that

---

[1] See 1 Kgs 11:40, 14:25; and 2 Chr 12:2, 5 (twice), 7, and 9. The fact that this new trend of identifying the name of a Pharaoh began during the reign of Shishak (Shoshenq I) should be of no surprise to the student of Biblical history, since Shishak's reign signaled both the beginning of a new ruling dynasty, the 22nd Dynasty of Egypt, and the beginning of foreign rule under pharaohs who hailed from Libya.

ALSO See 2 Kgs 23:29, 33, 34, 35; 2 Chr 35:20, 21, 22; 36:4; and Jer 46:2. Pharaoh Hophra is named once as well, though his name appears only in a prophetic writing, where God calls him, "Pharaoh Hophra, King of Egypt" (Jer 44:30).

[2] ibid

the most accurate dates of his twenty-six year reign are *c.* 1453 to 1426 BCE. However there are questions as to exact dates.

c.   Egyptian records show that Amenemhet was the eldest son of Thutmose III, allowing Amenhotep II to have lived through the tenth plague, since he was not the firstborn.

d.   The oldest son of Amenhotep II would have died during the tenth plague, which must be true of the exodus-pharaoh's son. In fact, none of Amenhotep II's sons claimed to be his firstborn. Even one prominent Egyptologist theorizes that the eldest son died inexplicably during childhood.

2. The 19th Dynasty in Egypt (see list of Pharaohs of the 18th and 19 Dynasties), began with Rameses I. Rameses I was a very old man when he was surprisingly appointed Pharaoh. The reason for his appointment was interesting. Pharaoh Horemheb (the last of the 18th dynasty) had no children, so actually chose his successor. Rameses, an older military man, had several children and grandchildren, who would assure a long succession of family rule. Rameses' son Seti I was followed by Seti II, known as Rameses the Great.

a.   Rameses the Great was groomed to be pharaoh from childhood and he would rule for 67 years, the longest rule in Egyptian history (1304-1237 BCE).

b.   Rameses distinguished himself in two ways: as a military leader and as a builder.

   i.   He completed several halls and temples started by his father. However, Rameses the Great always carved his own name into the buildings. He also built his own structures, one of which was carved out of a mountain, the temple of Abu Simbel, designed to scare any boats sailing north. Four giant 67-foot tall statures of Rameses the Great seated on his throne greeted any visitor.

   ii. He organized the army into skill levels— infantry, archers, and charioteers. His army was 20,000 strong, divided into four divisions, each named after a god—Amun, Ra, Ptah, and Set. The army marched into Syria, where he met strong opposition of 40,000 Hittites. Rameses defeated the enemy almost by himself! "Follow me" was his cry to his 20,000. The fight was a standoff, but depicted as a great victory throughout Egypt.

c.   About the 21st year of his reign, Rameses signed a peace treaty with the hated enemy of Egypt, the Hittites. This was perhaps the first peace treaty in history with the hated enemy of Egypt, the Hittites. Rameses continued to mellow. He married a Hittite woman, heaping many riches upon her. He took a 2nd Hittite bride a few years later, thus cementing the arrangement with the

Hittites. Rameses had abandoned his military campaign and his first-born son died. Incredible but true, Rameses had over 100 children and dozens of wives. Surrounded by death, his attention turned to building tombs. A tomb built for his first and favorite wife, Nefertari, is the most beautiful in all Egypt.

   i.   It has been suggested that Rameses set the Israelites to work as slaves. It is also possible that some of the Israelites were originally hired to work for pharaoh to complete the city of Raamses, although the later Hebrew writers who reported this bondage are unlikely to have referred to "slaves."

d.   It is possible that Rameses the Great was the pharaoh who had begun the oppression of the Israelites. His successor, Merneptah (1224-1211) would then have been the "the pharaoh who did not know Joseph." A large black granite stele, inscribed with a reference to "Israel is laid waste," referring to a people, not a nation.

e.   Many Biblical scholars who affirm the historicity of the exodus now date it to the 13th century BCE, a step that requires a redefinition of concrete numbers in Biblical passages that, if taken literally, would indisputably place the exodus in the 15th century BCE, the period of Amenhotep II.

3.5.2.5.   Fear started the oppression. Fear is always an enemy of God.

3.5.2.6.   We see early in Exodus that God's people are placed under hard labor in an attempt to break their spirit.

3.5.3.   We could easily call Moses "The Deliverer," for that's exactly what he was. His life in these four books is very neatly packaged in three, forty-year periods.

3.5.3.1.   Forty years in Egypt in Pharaoh's home

3.5.3.2.   Forty years in exile in Midian

3.5.3.3.   And forty years from Egypt to the crossing of Jordan.

3.5.3.4.   Stephen in Acts 7, gives a summary of that forty year division.

3.5.4.   D.L. Moody's thoughts here:

3.5.4.1.   "Forty years thinking he was somebody,

3.5.4.2.   "Forty years learning he was nobody,

3.5.4.3.   "Forty years discovering what God can do with a nobody."

Depth of Bible Words and Places
Egypt

(Also see additional information on Egypt in this volume).

Egypt handed down its history like no other country. Back to 3000 BCE, we can trace many details that confirm the Old Testament's writings.

Years of drought are well attested in record; a seven-year famine is detailed on a discovered rock; *"My heart is heavy over the calamitous failure of the Nile floods for the past seven years."* Several paragraphs of writing details the seven years. The story of Joseph in Egypt has astonishing confirmation.

At the time of the Exodus, Egypt was a strong and very advanced society/dynasty, already using papyrus and ink for hundreds of years; certainly a world leader. The pyramids had already been built some 1,500 years before.

The land was settled by Ham—and all nations can be traced back to one of the sons of Noah after the occurrence at Babel.

The Pharaoh during some of the years of oppression was perhaps Thutmose III, called "The Napoleon of Egypt"; he was on a mission to keep expanding Egypt's borders and influence to the Euphrates River. He marched many times through Palestine.

You might also recognize some other Pharaoh's names: Tutankhamen or "Tut." Of course there was Rameses I and II. Also refer to the Land of Egypt in this volume.

Pharaohs of the Eighteen and Nineteenth Dynasties

Egyptian Pharaoh	Egyptian Dynasty	Dates of Rule (all BCE) [1]	Historical Event
Senusret I		1934-1899	Birth of Joseph 1915 BCE
Amunemhet III		1843-1798	Hebrews settle in Egypt
The Hyksos nation ruled Egypt for over 150 years, 1720-1567. The Egyptians expelled the Hyksos and the Eighteenth Dynasty began.			
Ahmosis I	Eighteenth	1570-1545	Hyksos expelled from Egypt. Hebrews greatly oppressed in Egypt
Amenhotep I		1545-1529	
Thutmose I		1529-1517	Moses born 1525; Pharaoh's order to kill male babies; Aaron, three yrs older than Moses was not exposed to the order.
Thutmose II		1517-1504	Moses taught in Egypt; Thutmose was married to

---

[1]Data compiled by Hiegel, Thomas, 2008, Dayton, Ohio

			Hatshepsut; died young due to unknown circumstances; had named his son as heir
Thutmose III, "Napoleon of Egypt"		1504-1453	Hebrew oppression continues. First usage of "Pharaoh" as a person. Named the Pharaoh as a young boy, mother-in-law ruled.
Hatshepsut, female		1503-1483	Moses reared as foster son. Moses Killed an Egyptian 1485, flees
Amenhotep II		1453-1426	Moses return to Egypt. "Let my people go." Deliverance from Egypt 1446, date from 1 Kings 6:1
Thutmose IV		1426-1416	His mummy found; 25 yrs old at death
Amenhotep III		1416-1377	Moses dies 1405; Egypt at its greatest extent and power. Conquest of Canaan by the Israelites
Akhenaten		1377-1360	First Judge Othniel 1350
Smenkhkare		?	
Tutankhamen		1360-1350	Egypt's greatest splendor
Ay		1350-1347	
Horemheb		1347-1218	Assyria rises, conquers Babylon
Rameses I	Nineteenth	1318-1317	
Seti I		1317-1304	
Rameses II, "The Great"		1304-1237	Could not have been the Pharaoh of the Exodus. Deborah and Barak 1250
Merneptah			
Amenmesse			
Seti II			Gideon

Depth of Bible Words and Places
Hyksos People

The Hyksos People were ruling Egypt in 1730 BCE, and the Israelites were pretty much at ease. The Hyksos were foreigners in Egypt and treated other foreigners with dignity and kindness. The Egyptians drove out the Hyksos rulers in about 1570 BCE. This is the period when the Israelites went from royal favor, to reduced servants as a new king came to power.

3.5.4.4.   God hears his people, and He prepares a deliverer. God was always near, in some way, to preserve His line that would lead to the seed that would crush the head of the enemy.

3.5.5.   Moses was born in approximately 1571 BCE to Amram and Jochebed, both of the tribe of Levi. Levi was Josheph's half-brother. His older brother was Aaron, his older sister named Miriam. He was named by Pharaoh's daughter with the name possibly meaning "to draw out," a Hebrew name. She took him out of a   basket in a river. But why would an Egyptian name the boy with a Hebrew name? Another more likely meaning for the naming of Moses is the Egyptian name meaning "birth." There would have been little reason to refer to a Hebrew child. All Hebrew boys were to be eliminated.

3.5.5.1.   This chosen child was placed carefully in the Nile, not thrown in as Pharaoh demanded. Why God picked a baby and preserved him, only He knows. Why not use one of the Hebrews already in slavery, allow him to gain respect, rise to leadership, and become their deliverer? This child, called "a goodly child" or "beautiful in God's site" was placed and protected in a basket. God always had a plan to preserve the line that would eventually crush the head of the enemy. His plan rules.

3.5.5.2.   He was soon rescued by Pharaoh's daughter and raised in Pharaoh's own palace for the first third of his life. We are almost certain this daughter's name was Hatshepsut, the daughter of Thutmose I, the wife of Thutmose II and the stepmother of Thutmose III.

3.5.5.3.   Moses knew who he was, for God allowed his birth mother to raise him. The amazing grace of God. You think momma might have told Moses who he was? Maybe told him how he was saved from Pharaoh's massacre? Oh I think he knew!

3.5.5.4.   What a picture of a much later deliverer. They tried to kill *that* baby too. But God sent *that baby* to a protected place, then "drew" *Him* out, despised and rejected by his own, only to become *THE* Deliverer.

3.5.5.5.   Moses had a valuable forty years, learning much of the knowledge of the Egyptians, along with valuable spiritual knowledge from his own mother.[1] He learned about the various Egyptian gods. Later His God would destroy each of them with a plague.

---

[1] Hebrews 11:24-25 *By faith Moses, when he had grown up, refused to be called the son of Pharaoh's daughter, 25 choosing rather to endure ill-treatment with the people of God than to enjoy the passing pleasures of sin,*

3.5.6.   Moses began to live for the deliverance of his people, and came to the assistance of a fellow Hebrew, killing an Egyptian.

Depth of Bible Words and Places
Hebrew

Exodus 2: 11-15 tells the story of an Egyptian beating a *Hebrew* slave. What is the meaning of the word Hebrew? A name derived from Eber, a descendant of Noah's son Shem, the line of the Hebrew race and used to refer to the people of God's nation. Shem was called *the father of all the children of Eber* (Genesis 10:21), which is perhaps the origin of Hebrew.

Today the term is often used to refer to the Jewish people or to their classical language, Hebrew, but it once had a much wider meaning.

In the Old Testament the term appears most frequently in the Joseph story (Gen. 39: 17; 40: 15; 41: 12), the Exodus story (Ex 1:16; 2:7; 3:18; 5:3; 7:16), and the story of the Philistine wars (1 Sam. 4:6, 13:19; 14:11).

The word is generally used by outsiders in speaking of the Israelites or by Israelites when speaking **to** outsiders. It does not express the sense of solidarity implied by the word "Israel," for there were Hebrews who were not members of the Israelite community.

Abraham is called a Jew for the first and only time in a peculiar tradition found in Genesis 14 about Abraham's wars with the kings of the east (Gen. 14: 13) According to Bible tradition, Abraham the Hebrew *('ihri)* was a descendant of Eber *C'eber)*. In the genealogy found in Genesis 10 26-30, however, Eber was also the ancestor of other peoples. Arabs, Arameans, Moabites, Ammonites, and Edomites could trace their ancestry to him. All of this suggests that the term Hebrew" originally was more inclusive than it is in biblical texts, which refer specifically to the Hebrews who were slaves in Egypt and who eventually became the community known as Israel.

Later the term was restricted to the biblical Hebrews, the Jewish people, as in the Jonah story (Jon 1: 9) The Apostle Paul insisted that he was "a Hebrew born of Hebrews" (Phil. 3: 2).

3.5.6.1.   Recorded in cps 2-4, Moses flees and spends the second forty-year period of his life, in Midian, east of the Red Sea. He became a shepherd, tending the flocks of his new father-in-law, Jethro.[1] He acquired a thorough knowledge of the area where he would later lead God's

---

[1] Ex 3:1 *Now Moses was pasturing the flock of Jethro his father-in-law, the priest of Midian;*

people through. In Midian he married Zipporah the daughter of a priest named Jethro.

Depth of Bible Words and Places
Midian
Descendants of one of the six sons of Abraham born after the death of Sarah, the Midianites (Genesis 25:1-2). Moses settled in the city of Midian after he first fled from Egypt (Exodus 2:15-21). East of Egypt.

3.5.7.　　　　At the age of eighty, and continuing into the third period of his life, the Lord appears to Moses at Horeb in a "burning" bush, but not a "burned" bush. This was a revelation of God's glory, He IS light.

    3.5.7.1.　　　　The call, the instructions, were unmistakable.[1] To assist him, his older brother Aaron was directed to meet Moses in the wilderness. Moses had been concerned that the people would not believe him, and that his speaking was not eloquent. Aaron would help him.[2]

    3.5.7.2.　　　　Notice the threefold significance in the "burning bush."

3.5.7.2.1.　　It revealed God's glory and power. Moses needed to have this revelation of assurance.

3.5.7.2.2.　　It symbolized Israel going through the fire of affliction and not consumed.

3.5.7.2.3.　　It illustrated Moses, who with God's help, would become a fire that could not be put out.

3.5.8.　　　　Moses takes the rod of God, and travels to Egypt. He had to have gone with great confidence; God told him "I place you

---

[1] A voice is heard *I am the God of your father, the God of Abraham, the God of Isaac, and the God of Jacob.* How would like to hear that! And from out of a glowing bush! Little wonder of Moses' hesitation.

[2] Notice the reflection of Moses on many problems that he would face in going back to Egypt:

Moses: "Who am I to face mighty pharaoh?"
God: "I will be with you."
Moses: "By whose authority shall I go to face my own people?"
God: "I AM, the God of Abraham, Isaac, and Jacob sends you."
Moses: "The Israelites will not believe me."
God: "Use the rod in your hand to perform miracles before them."
Moses: "I am not an orator."
God: "I will send Aaron to speak for you."

in the role of God in front of Pharaoh." [1] I know of no one else that God made this type of statement to.

    3.5.8.1.   Following a period of talk with his fellow people in Egypt, he is eventually accepted by all the tribes as the deliverer from God. Then he confronts Pharaoh.

    3.5.8.2.   The Exodus from Egypt is the central moment in Israel's history. Here was Israel's true beginning, the time of its creation as a people.

Depth of Bible Words and Places
Rameses

The location of the Israelites during their time in Egypt. Moses was raised in the palace located nearby. He also held audience with the pharaoh here during the plagues. The location was excavated in the 1990s CE.

3.5.9.   The first request to let the Hebrews go, not only failed...but Pharaoh increases the work load, which already...was "slave-like." [2]

3.5.10.   The ten plagues were initiated by God, and were not *simply* natural events of nature as some have suggested. The frogs and flies were all "pests" well known to the Egyptians.

    3.5.10.1.   However, note that they came and went at the command of Moses, and, most of them came upon the Egyptians not the Jews.

    3.5.10.2.   They were proof of the power of God over Pharaoh and his gods. Note Ex 12:12 *against all the gods of Egypt I will execute judgments.*

    3.5.10.3.   According to a modern Hebrew commentary[3], this verse reads *I will mete our punishments to all the gods of Egypt.* The commentary explains this: "punishments means to destroy the gods to show their ineffectuality." To destroy the Egyptian idols.

3.5.11.   Following Moses' third request to Pharaoh, and Pharaoh's third refusal, the plagues began.

---

[1] Ex 7:1 *Then the Lord said to Moses, "See, I make you as God to Pharaoh..."*
[2] Exodus 5:9 *Let heavier work be laid upon the men that they may labor at it and pay no attention to lying words (*AMP)
New Living Translation: *Load them down with more work. Make them sweat! That will teach them to listen to lies!"* Carved into a rock west of Thebes, is a depiction of the forced labor to manufacture bricks using light-skinned workmen and dark-skinned overseers.
[3] *The Torah, A Modern Commentary*, Union of American Hebrew Congregations, New York, 1981, p. 459

EXPANDED HELP PAPER
The Plagues of Egypt

Following are the ten plagues, as recorded in Ex 7:14-12:30. The timing and severity of the plagues was under the direction and control of God. Some natural occurrences were used by God, at His calling.

1. *The Water of the Nile Turned into Blood* (Ex 7:14-25). This first plague probably was the pollution of the Nile River by large quantities of fine, red earth, brought down from the Sudan and Ethiopia by abnormal flooding. The pollution of the water provided a favorable environment for the growth of microorganisms and parasitic bacteria. Their presence could have led to the death of the fish in the river (Ex 7:21). In addition to depriving Egypt of water and fish-an important part of their diet-the plague also had a religious effect. The Nile River, god of the Egyptians, had been confronted by the power of the Redeemer God of the Hebrew people.

2. *Frogs Cover the Land* (Ex 8:1-15). Seven days after the first plague, frogs came out of the river and infested the land. The frogs would have been driven from the Nile and its canals and pools by the polluted water. When Moses prayed to God, the frogs died in the houses, courtyards, and fields. The frogs were symbols of the Egyptian goddess, Heqt, who was supposed to help women in childbirth. This plague was another demonstration of the superior power of God over the gods of Egypt.

3. *Lice Throughout the Land* (Ex 8:16-19). Insects of various kinds are common in Egypt. It is not easy to identify the exact pests involved in the third and fourth plagues. Various translations have lice (KJV, NKJV), gnats (NASB, RSV, and NIV), maggots (NEB), and sand flies and fleas (RSV).

4. *Swarms of Flies* (Ex 8:20-32). Many kinds of flies are common in Egypt. The mounds of decaying frogs would have provided an ideal breeding ground for these pests. Some scholars suggest that the swarms mentioned here were a species known as the stable-fly, a blood feeder that bites man as well as cattle. This fly is a carrier of skin anthrax, which is probably the disease brought on by the sixth plague.

5. *Pestilence of Livestock* (Ex 9:1-7). Either the frogs or the insects may have been the carriers of this infection. The livestock of the Israelites were miraculously protected (Ex 9:6-7). This was the second time God had made a distinction between the Israelites and the Egyptians in the plagues which He sent (Ex 8:22-23).

6. *Boils on Man and Beast* (Ex 9:8-12). This infection was probably skin anthrax, carried by the flies of the fourth plague. The festering boils broke into blisters and running sores.

7. *Heavy Hail, with Thunder and Lightning* (Ex 9:13-35). Egypt was essentially an agricultural country. By destroying the crops, this plague and the next struck at the heart of Egypt's economy. Moses' warning gave the Egyptians a chance to save their remaining livestock, and some acted upon it (Ex 9:19-20). The severe storm caused great destruction (Ex 9:24-25). The flax and barley were ruined, but not the wheat because it had not yet been planted (Ex 9:31-32). This would suggest early February as the time of this plague. Again the Israelites received special protection. There was no hail in the land of Goshen, where the Hebrews lived (Ex 9:26).

8. *Swarm of Locusts* (Ex 10:1-20). The destruction from the previous plague was fresh in the minds of Pharaoh's advisors (Ex 10:7). The eighth plague must have followed the hail very closely. Heavy rainfall in July-September would have produced conditions favorable for locusts in March. These locusts, swarms of foliage-eating grasshoppers, probably were driven into the Egyptian delta by strong winds. They wiped out the vegetation, which had survived the earlier destruction. Again, as after the seventh plague, Pharaoh confessed, "I have sinned" (Ex 10:16). But again, after the plague was withdrawn, Pharaoh hardened his heart and would not let the children of Israel go (Ex 10:20).

9. *Three Days of Darkness* (Ex 10:21-29). This darkness could have been caused by a severe dust storm. For three days darkness covered the land (Ex 10:23). This storm would have been intensified by fine earth deposited over the land by previous flooding. This plague probably occurred in March. Again, the Israelites were spared the effects (Ex 10:23). By showing God's power over the light of the sun-represented by one of Egypt's chief deities, the sun-god Ra-this plague was a further judgment on the idolatry of the Egyptians.

10. *Death of Egyptian Firstborn* (Ex 11:1-12:30). The tenth plague, although not considered as a "plague," was the most devastating of all—the death of the firstborn in Egyptian families. The Hebrews were spared because they followed God's command to sprinkle the blood of a lamb on the doorposts of their houses. The death angel "passed over" the houses where the blood was sprinkled-hence, the name PASSOVER for this religious observance among the Jewish people. Only a supernatural explanation can account for the selective slaughter of the tenth plague.[1]

3.5.12.   Nine plagues were sent (each one directed at one of the gods of Egypt), however the tenth "plague" was the death-blow. This one was death to the Egyptian's firstborn of both man and animal. Following the first three plagues, the Hebrews were not affected.

> 3.5.12.1.   Pharaoh brought this terrible calamity of firstborn death, as well as the first nine plagues, upon his own people! This Pharaoh will stand one day in front of God and receive his eternal punishment!
>
> 3.5.12.2.   Throughout history, many tried to destroy the seed (some knowingly, others out of pure hatred); King Ahasuerus[2], Pharaoh[3], Hitler, and Ayatollah Khamenei.
>
> 3.5.12.3.   From the beginning of Adam and Eve, Satan has attempted to destroy the coming of a seed who would end his existence. He attempted to corrupt the human race, destroy the chosen people, interfere with the mission of Jesus, and finally has tried to destroy the work of God in the world today.

3.5.13.   Note with me the three triads, each with a consistent pattern.

> 3.5.13.1.   In introducing the first plague of each triad, God tells Moses the main lesson the triad will teach (7.17; 8:18; 9:14).

---

[1] (Some of the above information is consolidated from Nelson's Illustrated Bible Dictionary, Copyright © 1986, Thomas Nelson Publishers)
[2] Esther 3:12-14
[3] In our story of Exodus 1

3.5.13.2.   We read that God warns Pharaoh before the first two plagues of each triad, while the third has no warning.

3.5.13.3.   Before the first plague in each group God sends Moses to Pharaoh in the morning, saying, "Station yourself before (Pharaoh)," and before the second he says, "Go to Pharaoh" without specifying the time of day.

3.5.13.4.   All the plagues in the first triad are brought on by an action of Aaron; in the second triad, the first two are brought about directly by God and the third by Moses; in the third triad, all are brought on by an action of Moses.

3.5.13.5.   These nine plagues resemble calamities known within nature, but their patterns, their timing and rapid succession, and their announcement and removal by Moses show that they are the purposeful workings of divine power.

A Personal "sketch" of the Nine Plagues for Clarification

7:17	Blood
	Frogs
	Vermin
8:18	Insects
	Pestilence
	Boils
9:14	Hail
	Locusts
	Darkness
	First Born of Egypt

3.5.14.   Cp 12 gives the wonderful story of the Passover, a clear picture of an individual salvation through faith in the shed blood of Jesus Christ. A picture of the cross. Jesus is our lamb (1 Corinthians 5:7). The Israelites would have suffered Plague #10 like everyone else, if they had not killed the lamb and sprinkled the blood over, not under, the door. If they had left the blood in a basin, they would have died. Perhaps some failed God's instructions and did die. Blood had to be applied. The shedding of blood on a tree has to be taken and applied, in order to save.

3.5.14.1.   This of course brought the protection and observance of Passover--the very sight of a young lamb's blood indicated a household of Israelites, "covered by the blood of a lamb!" Every home of a Hebrew was under divine protection of blood *if* it was applied. You may have heard someone "pleading the blood" which came from both this Passover, and the cross of Jesus.

3.5.15.　　　The author has calculated from the most Scriptural date for the Exodus, approximately 1491 BCE[1] (alternative date suggested of 1290-1225 BCE)—deliverance was taking place! Seventy people went down to Egypt[2], but it has been estimated that nearly three million left.

3.5.15.1.　　　Complete redemption involved more than getting Israel out of Egypt. It also involved getting "Egypt" out of Israel. Do you see this? (Exodus 16:3). This applies to each of us today.

3.5.15.2.　　　Soon at a seashore, facing a swollen river before them, an enemy behind them, and a mountain which closed them in...Moses stands and commands:

3.5.15.3.　　　*"Do not fear! Stand by and see the salvation of the Lord which He will accomplish for you today; for the Egyptians whom you have seen today, you will never see them again forever. 14 The Lord will fight for you* (Exodus 14:13-14).

3.5.15.4.　　　As a best guess, approximately three million people cross through a river on dry land. The *people* became a *nation* when they passed through the Red Sea together.

3.5.15.5.　　　Although difficult to contemplate, seventy Hebrews could have become three million during the time in Egypt. First, we accept the numbers in the Scriptures as being accurate. Second, if each family had eight children during the forty years, the number could have been reached.

3.5.15.6.　　　When the enemy pursued, the waters engulfed them.[3]

3.5.15.7.　　　Interesting, just a few years ago (2000 CE), pieces of chariots were found deep under the mud of this river. Scientists agree with the method for possible preservation of hundreds of pieces of chariots and armament. One chariot wheel was removed from the many located. It was taken to Egypt and verified to be a wheel from a 1400 BCE, 18th dynasty, identical to the

---

[1] Refer to Old Testament Chronology, Appendix

[2] Ex 1:2 All the offspring of Jacob were seventy persons; Joseph was already in Egypt.

[3] Ex 14:30 *Thus the Lord saved Israel that day from the hand of the Egyptians, and Israel saw the Egyptians dead on the seashore.*

chariot wheel scribed on a Pharaoh's tomb. The additional artifacts located in the Red Sea, have never been allowed to be viewed. However, they were filmed and are available for review. Perhaps, when Israel regains the territory, a full revelation will take place.

3.5.15.8.　　In cp 15 Moses and the Israelites sing "the song of Moses" a wonderful piece of Hebrew poetry called "The Song of Triumph." Miriam, a prophetess responds with her short "Song of Deliverance." Can't you picture this joy! [1]

3.5.16.　　Living like nomads, they made a three-day journey southward to only find bitter water at Marah, where murmurings began. We will see this murmuring several times during their journey. What a lesson for us; murmuring seems to come after a recent victory.

3.5.16.1.　　However, our wonderful, merciful God turned the bitter waters to sweet, so much so that the next visitors found twelve wells of waters and seventy palm trees in what became an oasis! God is not temporary or incomplete. What He does—stands.

EXPANDED HELP PAPER
The Topography of the Sinai

It is difficult to describe 24,000 square miles of nothingness, poised between Africa and Asia. Indeed, it was a land of "wandering." A wilderness where a new nation of people could easily become disoriented and move in circles. Even today, it would be quite easy to get lost. With this in mind, along with the knowledge that the land has had little change over the past 3000 years, we might understand the difficulties of the Israelites' journey.

As mentioned previously, the most probable route the Israelites followed was the southern. The Sinai is divided into three distinct inhospitable regions. **(1)** The northern could be called classical desert, mostly flat, mounds of sand formed by winds, and a few oases. Most of the inhabitants would live in this area, as it remains the most temperate. **(2)** The middle layer of the Sinai is one of sandy hills and multi-colored canyons. This is perhaps the area, which we would identify with the

---

[1] *Exodus 15:20-21 Miriam the prophetess, Aaron's sister, took the timbrel in her hand, and all the women went out after her with timbrels and with dancing. 21 Miriam answered them, "Sing to the Lord, for He is highly exalted; The horse and his rider He has hurled into the sea."*

Israelites' wandering. It is a land of constant change; atmosphere, soil, and color of hills. Little is desired of its lackluster mountains. It could be considered as the least hospitable part of the peninsula. The lack of water can be noticed by the absence of dew in the morning. **(3)** The southern region (which has already been stated, is the most obvious route of the exodus). There are several oases along the Gulf of Suez.

Depth of Bible Words and Places
Oasis
Found in Ex 15:23, 27. The Hebrew word means "the most beautiful place of the desert." Oases are mentioned throughout the Bible as locations where the Israelites camped during the years following the exodus.

The Israelites would have stopped at several of the oases as they escaped. The southern route has more mountains, (mentioned in the Scriptures), in fact quite hilly, and in general, more available water. The soil changes by location, from north to middle to south; from limestone and sand near the Mediterranean, sandstone in the middle with hills two thousand feet in height, and granite in the southern mountains with a height of some seven thousand feet. Also, there seems to be an abundance of acacia trees along the southern route, adding to what we may view as quite beautiful as we reach a southern terrain. Seems to be a "doorway" to enter the grand mountain, Mt. Sinai.

Along the southern route, it is known that Egyptian pharaohs sent expeditions to mine for needed minerals. To this day, carvings can be seen on the entrances into some of the mines. One, discovered in the 1970's, shows the picture of a pharaoh, perhaps the earliest relief ever found. It is also interesting to note that the initial forms of a Semitic alphabet, the oldest letters ever found, are etched in pale white on a terra-cotta stone cave. This is not Egyptian, but the "ancestor" of all alphabets!

It could be said that the biggest problem in the desert is not heat, but rather cold. It is known that the color black absorbs heat, perhaps the reason goats are black along with beetles. Also, the tents are black for this reason. It is noted that heat may be escaped by shade; however, you cannot escape the cold of night. However, we do mention the heat of the Sinai was severe when contrasted with the chill of evening and cold of night. The local people call this the "four seasons of the day."

It may also be noted that the southern Sinai, although mostly colorless, has a few dense forests of green, but surrounded by the terrain of "nothingness." We can understand how the Israelites realized their dire condition of no water, no food, not idea of where they were going. It is certainly no wonder they began to complain, and continued to do so for many years.

Bruce Feiler summarizes this nicely. "The first source of grumbling, described in Exodus 15, was the bitter-tasting water, which God rectified by directing Moses to throw a piece of wood into the water. In Exodus 16, the people complain about the lack of food, which God solves by delivering manna in the mornings and quail in the evenings. In Exodus 17 the people complain about having no water to drink, which God addresses by instructing Moses to strike a stone with his staff. In each case the people receive God's blessing and continue their trek."[1]

3.5.16.2.   As they *travelled* further, God began His provision for His people; the morning manna and evening quail. The bread and meat never failed for those forty years. This provision did not stop until the next generation crossed the Jordan into the Promised Land.

Depth of Bible Words and Places
Manna

A special food, which resembled white seeds or flakes and was sweet to the taste. God provided this to His people for the forty years in the desert. Manna explains who Jesus is.

It was *small*; which speaks of His humility; He became a baby, then a servant.

It was *round*; a circle of His eternality, the Son of God.

It was *white*; purity and sinlessness

It was *sweet*; "taste and see that the Lord is good." The Hebrews asked for onions and garlic of Egypt; we cannot improve on what God brings by His Word.

It was *nourishment*. A nation lived on it for 40 years; all that is needed for us, is to feast on the Bread that will always fill.

Note the place where the manna was found. Each morning, it came from heaven and was on the earth all around them. It was not high on the mountains where each family would have to climb to retrieve. It was not in some deep valley outside the camp where the people would have to search for it. It was not placed on hard rocks or in tree branches. The manna was outside every tent.

Depth of Bible Words and Places

---

[1] Bruce Feiler, *Walking The Bible,* HarperCollins Publishers, 2001, p. 217

Quail

A migrating bird that arrives in droves along the shores of the Mediterranean Sea. They have poor flying skills, but usually fly rapidly for only a short time because of their heavy body weight. They seem to just be exhausted after a flight and can be caught by hand. They give away their presence by a shrill whistle.

So when the Hebrew people longed for meat in the Sinai desert, God just directed thousands of quail to their camp, where they dropped in exhaustion and whistled their presence.

3.5.16.3. Moses' father-in-law came into the wilderness to meet with him in cp 18. He saw the immense task which Moses had undertaken and advised him to delegate authority to leaders. This is the first instance of governmental organization among the Hebrews. [1]

3.5.16.4. So Moses led them to "the Mount of God," Sinai, the actual birthplace of the Hebrew nation. Genesis was a family history, Exodus, a national history. [2]

3.5.16.5. Three months after leaving Egypt, God summons Moses to the peak of Sinai. He's about to make *"a peculiar nation"* with laws and ceremonies for purification, all under the direction of God. Israel had escaped physical bondage in Egypt, but still had much to gain in moral and spiritual discipline. Moses would spend one year in establishing a permanent covenant relationship for the Hebrew nation.

3.5.16.6. Until this time, Israel's history had all been grace and mercy, to which it will return at a future date. Now a change takes place. *The law of the Lord is perfect* (Psalm 19:7). It's God's mirror to show sinfulness and then demand a choice.

---

[1] *Ex 18:17 Moses' father-in-law said to him, "The thing that you are doing is not good. 18 "You will surely wear out, both yourself and these people who are with you, for the task is too heavy for you; you cannot do it alone. 19 "Now listen to me: I will give you counsel, and God be with you. You be the people's representative before God, and you bring the disputes to God,*
Ex 18:21 "Furthermore, you shall select out of all the people able men who fear God, men of truth, those who hate dishonest gain; and you shall place these over them as leaders of thousands, of hundreds, of fifties and of tens.

[2] It took them at least six weeks to reach Sinai. It is quite doubtful a northern route was followed. God explicitly prohibited such a route (Exodus 13:17)

3.5.16.7.　Paul in Galatians 3:24 wrote, *"The Law was our schoolmaster to bring us to Christ."* Can you see how much God loved this people?

3.5.16.8.　God began their training by writing The Ten Commandments; the first four...*relationship to God*, thought to have been on one tablet...then six for *relationship to man* on a second. The two tablets were written by the finger of God.[1] Could this be anything less than what we may think of as a laser beam of light from His hand?[2]

3.5.16.9.　As God's glory filled the top of Mt Sinai, Moses talked with God. God seemed to "uncover" Himself, or reveled Himself for a moment. He is Light.

Expanded Help Paper
Light

The author has done many hours of studying on "light." It's almost impossible to separate "I am light", from His Glory. Where He is, His glory is. It's pure light. Remember God said "I am light?" Don't forget He also said "YOU, are the light of the world." The source of everything is Light. Science is just now accepting this fact. They even measure distance by *light* years.

In studying the Glory of God, there seems to be two distinct divisions. First the actual Glory that God is, which is seldom seem, but many times experienced. This was/is God manifesting Himself in a powerful, and many time, visible form. I have concluded that there is a three stage progression of growth: (1) an absolute surrendering of self in worship (2) the manifesting of healings and miracles (3) a visable Glory of God. We have, to some extent, these today. However, the fullness of this Glory is a future experience.

Consider the following Scriptures:

Psalm 104:1-2
Lord my God, You are very great;
You are clothed with splendor and majesty,
Covering Yourself with light as with a cloak

---

[1] Ex 31:18 *When He had finished speaking with him upon Mount Sinai, He gave Moses the two tablets of the testimony, tablets of stone, written by the finger of God.*

[2] Hab 3:4 His *radiance is like the sunlight; He has rays flashing from His hand, And there is the hiding of His power.*

Ezekiel 3:22-23
The hand of the Lord was on me there, and He said to me, "Get up, go out to the plain, and there I will speak to you." 23 So I got up and went out to the plain; and behold, the glory of the Lord was standing there....

Daniel 7:9
"I kept looking
Until thrones were set up,
And the Ancient of Days took His seat;
His vesture was like white snow
And the hair of His head like pure wool.
His throne was ablaze with flames,
Its wheels were a burning fire.

Matthew 17:2
And He was transfigured before them; and His face shone like the sun, and His garments became as white as light
And serveral other New Testament passages refer to this.
In addition, those tablets given to Moses… You think God just wrote them, or Moses wrote them? Listen to this: Habakkuk 3:4 *His radiance is like the sunlight;*
He has rays flashing from His hand, And there is the hiding of His power.

So it's no wonder Moses' face shown as he came down to the people. The reflection of God remained upon him for a long time.

3.5.16.10.   The code of life to live by is this same two-fold command: To love God and to love others. No other moral code has ever surpassed that code. Jesus came to "seal" that code, (Matt 5:17). Also, Matthew 22:37 and John 15:12 sum up the entire Ten Commandments. ALL of the Law and ALL the Prophets "hang" on this two-fold code according to Jesus.

3.5.16.10.1. Love God with all your heart
3.5.16.10.2. Love your neighbor as yourself.
3.5.17.   The Book of the Covenant (Ex 24:7) follows The Ten Commandments (called Decalogue). These were judicial statues growing out of the moral requirements. Moses reads them to the people.[1]

---

[1] Exodus 24:7-8 *Then he took the book of the covenant and read it in the hearing of the people; and they said, "All that the Lord has spoken we will do, and we will be obedient!" 8*

3.5.18.　　　Never take the Ten Commandments lightly! No matter what a country or a courthouse does with them, do not ever allow them to slip away or be removed from your life.

The Ten Commandments

	Commandment	Subject	OT Statement	NT Reference
1st	You shall have no other gods before Me.	Polytheism	Ex 20:3	Ac 14:15
2nd	You shall not make for yourself an idol, or any likeness of what is in heaven above or on the earth beneath or in the water under the earth.	Graven Images	Ex 20:4	1Jn 5:21
3rd	You shall not take the name of the Lord your God in vain, for the Lord will not leave him unpunished who takes His name in vain.	Swearing	Ex 20:7	Jas 5:12
4th	Remember the Sabbath day, to keep it holy. 9 Six days you shall labor and do all your work, 10 but the seventh day is a Sabbath of the Lord your God; in it you shall not do any work, you or your son or your daughter, your male or your female servant or your cattle or your sojourner who stays with you. 11 For in six days the Lord made the heavens and the earth, the sea and all that is in them, and rested on the seventh day; therefore the Lord blessed the Sabbath day and made it holy.	Sabbath	Ex 20:8-11	Col 2:16
5th	Honor your father and your mother, that your days may be prolonged in the land which the Lord your God	Obedience to parents	Ex 20:12	Eph 6:1

So Moses took the blood and sprinkled it on the people, and said, "Behold the blood of the covenant, which the Lord has made with you in accordance with all these words."

gives you.

6th	You shall not murder.	Murder	Ex 20:13	1Jn 3:15
7th	You shall not commit adultery.	Adultery	Ex 20:14	1Co 6:9, 10
8th	You shall not steal.	Theft	Ex 20:15	Eph 4:28
9th	You shall not bear false witness against your neighbor.	False Witness	Ex 20:16	Col 3:9, 10
10th	You shall not covet your neighbor's house; you shall not covet your neighbor's wife or his male servant or his female servant or his ox or his donkey or anything that belongs to your neighbor.	Coveting	Ex 20:17	Eph 5:3

3.6. A place of worship was needed; they were not to travel alone without knowing the real reason for existence...God desired for them to learn true worship and make it the center of their encampment, the center of their life. Other nations they encountered did not know true individual or corporate worship.

   3.6.1.   The tabernacle was under the supervision of two construction supervisors, Bezalel and Aholiab, who were filled with the Spirit of God and given ability and intelligence to supervise. (Ex 31:1-11)

   3.6.2.   The great importance attached to the Tabernacle is shown by the extraordinary care in describing it. Seven chapters of details are recorded in Ex 25-31, given to Moses; five additional chapters, 35-39 are recorded, devoted to the execution of the temple work and inventory; chapter 40 records God's glory.

EXPANDED HELP PAPER
The Tabernacle

This is an *"extended,* expanded paper," for it cannot be treated lightly. It is a separate study for the serious student.

The design of this portable tent was given directly to Moses by God. We read the details in cps 25-40 of Exodus (cps 32-34 comprise a parenthesis, not a part of the directions). Moses was not merely given a design, but in fact, an entire plan to follow. What is amazing about this and what we make note of are the details, specifically the materials used. Every single part of the Tabernacle speaks of Christ, as we will note in this

170

brief sketch. We note that it was all of God and none of man, for as in salvation all is God's doing, none is man's.

The coverings of the Tabernacle, the way it was set up, and its sacred vessels, without exception speak of Christ in either His role in atonement, in mediation, or His role in intercession. So as you read this EXPANDED HELP PAPER, it is my deepest prayer that you develop a greater understanding of the Lord Jesus Christ.

The longest section in Exodus (cps 25-40) is the Holy Spirit's description of the tabernacle. It took but two chapters to portray the record of God's work in creating earth, however twelve were needed to tell us about the Tabernacle. How could we not respect its vital importance to us? The truths contained in describing the details must be relative, or the space in the Holy Scriptures would not have been allotted.

The twelve chapters in Exodus describing the structure, furnishings, and priesthood, begin with the Ark, the innermost item, in the innermost place and work outward. I believe this is significant.

In this paper, we will look at the measurements of the overall structure as well as various sections of the tent. Consider the following.

3 inches.....................................Make 1 handbreadth
9 inches.....................................Make 1 span
18 inches or two spans.............Make 1 cubit
3000 shekels.............................Make 1 talent
1500 ounces.............................Make 1 talent

It is interesting to keep in mind that Moses was instructed to make all things according to the divine design. Only three buildings were ever erected from plans furnished by direct revelation from God. (1) The Ark of Noah (Gen 6:14-16), (2) The Tabernacle of Moses (Ex 25:8), and (3) The Temple of Solomon (1 Chron 28: 11, 12, 19).

We read in Ex 25 a stern command to Moses, Ex 25:8-9 *"Let them construct a sanctuary for Me, that I may dwell among them. 9 "According to all that I am going to show you, as the pattern of the tabernacle and the pattern of all its furniture, just so you shall construct it..."*

And then the Hebrews 8:5 reminder to us when referring to the Tabernacle *These serve as a copy and shadow of the heavenly things, as Moses was warned when he was about to complete the tabernacle. For He said, Be careful that you make everything according to the pattern that was shown to you on the mountain.* (Holman Christian Standard Bible)

I love the NET Bible's revelation on this Scripture; *The place where they serve is a sketch and shadow of the heavenly sanctuary.*

I would say these instructions, which we will see in more detail as continue, are enough to cause a serious study of its entire construction.

Most people have little idea of its beauty and cost. God promised to take up residence in the midst of His people, provided they gave Him a beautiful and costly palace-temple for a dwelling. It must be made of gold, silver, and other suitable materials (Ex 25:1-7). To most people, they view the later temples of Solomon and Herod, as far surpassing this poor portable tent. However, may I point out that the writer of the New Testament book of Hebrews, passed by those two grand structures as if of no consequence when compared to the Tabernacle from whence they came. That writer speaks of its holy places, of its golden vessels, of its veil, of its ark and cherubim, of its servants and priests and high priest—it is of these that he so vividly describes showing their spiritual significance —all of Christ. All were symbolic and pointed to the reality in heaven, the person of Christ. So, access to God, is the lesson the Tabernacle and its vessels teach.

Consider the space allotted in the sacred Scriptures to describe this Tabernacle. Much more is said about the Tabernacle than about Solomon's temple, in both the Old and New Testaments. Nearly three hundred verses in Exodus are devoted to the tabernacle and its furniture. The description of the temple and its furniture in 1 Kings and 2 Chron is comprised in less than half that number.

Think of just the single words and phrases in the New Testament that come from the Tabernacle verses. William Brown[1] lists "Veil," "Mercy seat," "Propitiation," "Laver of Regeneration," "Lamb of God who taketh away the sin of the world," "Washed," "Cleansed," "Purged," "Reconciled," "Sacrifice," "Offering," "Atonement," "Without shedding of blood is no remission," "Gave Himself for us," and "Bore our sins in His own body on the tree." Wow, all those would be lost if not for the Tabernacle.

The Exodus description begins with the inner most compartment, **The Holy of Holies**. Briefly, the details directed by God:

The Ark of the Covenant *They shall construct an ark...* (25:10-22). The single piece of furniture in the Holy of Holies.

> A type of the throne of God, 3 ¾ x 2 ¼ x 2 ¼ (LxWxH). All dimensions are converted to feet.
> All overlaid with pure gold.

---

[1] Brown, William, *The Tabernacle and its Priests and Its Services, Described and Considered in Relation to Christ and the Church*, Oliphant, Anderson & Ferrier, Edinburgh and London, 1899.

To contain the two tablets with the Ten Commandments given to Moses, a jar of manna (God's constant provision), and Aaron's rod (confirmation of Aaron as high priest).
Covered by a Mercy Seat (a lid on top), 3 ¾ x 2 ¼.
Sprinkled with blood once a year.
Two cherubims of gold not *attached* to Mercy Seat, rather as *one piece with it*.

Depth of Bible Words and Places
Ark of the Covenant

A wooden chest that was covered with gold. On the top were two golden figures of angels, which faced each other. Inside were The Ten Commandments on two tables, a pot of manna, and Aaron's rod. It was located in the inner place of the Tabernacle.

` Depth of Bible Words and Places
Cherubim

Cherubim are angelic beings who do God's bidding. They are protectors of God's majesty: they protected the Garden of Eden (Genesis 3:24), they flank or support God's throne (Psalms 80:1; 99:1; Isaiah 37:16; Ezekiel 1:4-28; 10:1-22). They were present in the Tabernacle and the Temple. In the Tabernacle, the Israelites wove cherubim into the curtains covering the inner walls of the Tabernacle tent as well as in the veil that separated the Holy Place from the Most Holy Place. In addition, God ordered two cherubim to be placed on the "mercy seat" which covered the Ark of the Covenant. The cherubim appear again in Revelation 4:6-9, where they surround God's throne protecting his majesty.

The Holy Place included *three pieces* of furniture.

1 Table of the Bread of Presence *You shall make a table*... (vv 23-30).

3 x 1 ½ x 2 ¼. Made of indestructible shittim wood.
Overlayed with pure gold.
Also, dishes, bowls, and spoons, all of pure gold.
Bread was always to be on the table. *I am the bread of life* (John 6:58).

Depth of Bible Words and Places
Shittim

Found in Ex 25:5, 10. Also called *acacia*. A large genus of trees and shrubs especially suited for hot, dry climates. The bark content included tannin, which was used in processing leather. Produce attractive, highly figured hard wood.

2 Golden Candlestick *Then you shall make a lampstand...* (vv 31-40).

All made of pure gold.
Made from a single piece of gold; shaft, branches, bowls, and flowers.
Seven lamps.

3 Altar of Incense (described later in 30:1-10 *you shall make an altar as a place for burning incense*
1 ½ x 1 ½ x 3.
Shittim wood overlaid with pure gold.
Located immediately outside the Holy of Holies.
Incense burned every morning.

Curtains (for covering the Tabernacle) 26:1-
Tent covering of fine linen, (36:8) decorative and viewable from the inside.
Pure linen, dyed blue, purple, and scarlet.
Figures of cherubim were interwoven by weavers.
Placed as the first layer over the Tabernacle and down the inside walls (not touching the ground).
Each identical in size, 42 x 6.
Five sewn together to form a single set.
Two identical sets of five curtains.
Loops of blue (the heavenly throne of God) to join the two sets together.[1]

Eleven of goat's hair, the usual material for tents. *Then you shall make curtains of goats' hair.* Perhaps the white of the Angora goat.

---

[1] Ex 26:3-6 "Five curtains shall be joined to one another, and the other five curtains shall be joined to one another. 4 "You shall make loops of blue on the edge of the outermost curtain in the first set, and likewise you shall make them on the edge of the curtain t hat is outermost in the second set. 5 "You shall make fifty loops in the one curtain, and you shall make fifty loops on the edge of the curtain that is in the second set; the loops shall be opposite each other. 6 "You shall make fifty clasps of gold, and j oin the curtains to one another with the clasps so that the tabernacle will be a unit."

The second layer (of four layers), immediately above or on top of the linen. It is also possible that the white Angora was interwoven with the lined to create a most beautiful layer.
Not viewable.
Each to be 45 x 6. Longer than the linen layer and reaching to the ground, viewable below the decorative linen.
The eleventh curtain was perhaps sewn to one of the sets of five and extended beyond the fine linen layer.

Ram's and Badger's skins, the 3rd and 4th layers of covering;

The top two layers.
Ram skins not viewable, probably dyed as red leather.
Badger skins were the outer most covering, and the only viewable layer from the outside.
The Hebrew word is difficult to translate. It is the skin of some type of aquatic animal, perhaps porpoise.
Least attractive of any layer. *He has no stately form or majesty That we should look upon Him, Nor appearance that we should be attracted to Him* (Isa 53:2).

The Tabernacle Structure (vv 15-37). Two compartments, (1) The Holy Place (2) The Holy of Holies.

The Foundation for the Tabernacle consisted of 100 silver *sockets* forming a continuous base of silver. (26:19).[1] Those silver sockets, two for each board, were arranged in a rectangle of 40 on north and 40 on the south. There were 16 along the west end and 4 on the east end for the entrance veil to the Holy of Holies. They were placed on the ground and fit together in a construction method similar to a dovetail fit; at least we know it was a method which God designed.

Next was the *Tabernacle outer Wall* of sixty Gold Covered Boards. Each long side of the rectangular wall was 20 boards, each of which was 1 ½ cubits, making each side 30 cubits, or 45 feet. The narrow west and east had ten boards. The Tabernacle measured 10 cubits wide, or 15 feet, and 15 feet in height. Five

---

[1] Ex 38:27 *The 100 talents of silver were for casting the sockets or bases of the sanctuary and of the veil; 100 sockets for the 100 talents, a talent for a socket.*

rows of gold bars went along the sides of the three walls[1], passing through the gold rings fixed to each board.

Nine Pillars overlaid with gold provided the support for the Outer Veil (five pillars, entrance to the Holy Place) and the Inner Veil (four pillars, entrance to the Holy of Holies).

There were two entrances (veils) to the Tabernacle, (1) an Inner veil separating the Holy Place from the Holy of Holies (2) an Outer Veil at the entrance of the Tabernacle.

> *The Outer Veil* was made of blue, purple, and scarlet. Ex 26:33 *the veil shall serve for you as a partition between the holy place and the holy of holies.*

Blue, the heavenly throne, speaking of Christ's deity.
Purple, the royal color that combines heaven with the cross.
Scarlet, the blood of Christ.
Suspended from the five pillars.[2]
> *The Inner Veil* was also made of blue, purple, and scarlet.
Cherubim figures woven in to the fabric.[3]
Suspended from the four inner pillars of gold.
Separated the Holy Place from the Holy of Holies.[4]

Courtyard Structure

Courtyard[5] (Outer Court, 27:1-15) a double square, 150 x 75.
South side, 150 feet, 20 brass-covered shittim wood pillars on brass sockets, 7 ½ in height, 7 ½ feet between each.
North side, identical to south side.
West, 75 feet, 10 pillars on sockets.
East, identical to the West.
Fine twined linen hangings suspended from the pillars.

---

[1]Ex 26:26-27 *Then you shall make bars of acacia wood, five for the boards of one side of the tabernacle, 27 and five bars for the boards of the other side of the tabernacle,*
[2] Ex 26:37 *You shall make five pillars of acacia for the screen and overlay them with gold, their hooks also being of gold*
[3] Ex 26:31 *You shall make a veil of blue and purple and scarlet material and fine twisted linen; it shall be made with cherubim, the work of a skillful workman*
[4] Heb 9:3 *Behind the second veil there was a tabernacle which is called the Holy of Holies,*
[5] Ex 27:9 *You shall make the court of the tabernacle.*

The pillar caps were overlaid with silver. What a beautiful site, a bright silver cap contrasting with feet of bronze.

Silver rods extended through silver hooks, from pillar to pillar to steady the pillars, forming a beautiful silver railing.

Two pieces of furniture; all overlaid with brass (copper).

1. **Bronze Altar** of shittim wood—an acceptable sacrifice was brought by a worshipper, bound, lifted to the altar. Blood was caught by the priest in a basin.
2. **Bronze Laver**, a basin of water; priests had to clean their hands and feet before entering the Holy Place.

The Gate into the Outer Court

Blue, purple and scarlet, fine linen, hanging curtain
30 feet wide.
Hung down on four pillars, four sockets.
The *Order and Arrangement of the Furniture* in the Courtyard and Tabernacle were important.
First, at the one entrance was the Bronze Altar upon which the sacrifice of a spotless lamb was burning continually.
Next was the Laver at which the priest washed his hands and feet; then, entering into the Holy Place.
At the right was the Table of the Bread of His Presence and on the left was the Golden Candlestick.
Just before the entrance to the Holy of Holies was the Altar of Incense.
In the Holy of Holies stood the Ark of the Covenant, the blood-sprinkled Mercy Seat, and the Overshadowing Cherubim.
Finally, notice, the articles of furniture are placed in the shape of a cross—the main shaft was made by the Brazen Altar, the Laver, the Altar of Incense, and the Ark of the Covenant; the Table of Shewbread and the Candlestick made the two arms.

3.6.3.   The New Testament book of Hebrews devotes three chapters (8-9-10) to the tabernacle and its typology of Christ.[1]

---

[1]The great importance attached to the Tabernacle is shown by the extra-ordinary care in describing it.

3.6.4.   This period at Sinai is very important in our Old Testament journey.[1] Note that prior to the one year at the mountain:

    3.6.4.1.   God's glory had never resided among the Israelites

    3.6.4.2.   There was no central place of worship

    3.6.4.3.   No formal priesthood

    3.6.4.4.   No structure for sacrifices or feasts to teach them.

    3.6.4.5.   So this one year, this twelve-month period of Leviticus, establishes the foundation of the nation.

    3.6.4.6.   In Genesis we saw *a people falling*

    3.6.4.7.   In Exodus we saw *a people rescued*

    3.6.4.8.   Next in Leviticus, we have *a people worshipping.*

4   The Scriptures continue with one of the books that most of you have "sort of passed over": Leviticus. Am I right?

A Basic Outline of Leviticus
FOUR THEMES

1.   Offerings Cps 1-7
2.   Priesthood Cps 8-10
3.   Cleansing Cps 11-16
4.   Holiness Cps 17-27

Depth of Bible Words and Places
Leviticus Key Word: *Blood*

Found in 1:5, 3:7, 4:7, and 8:15. We must understand the vital place of the shedding of *blood.* The connection or scarlet thread runs through the Old Testament.

From God shedding the first blood in Genesis, through each book, to the *"rising of the Son of Righteousness with healing it its wings"* in Malachi 4. Blood is always associated with life in the Old Testament, always pointing to Christ. Hebrews 9:22

Today, we do not follow the system of offerings in Leviticus. The New Testament makes it clear that from Pentecost forward, the church, the body of Christ is under the authority of the new covenant, not the old Hebrew's Covenant.

Seven cps of detail are given to Moses in cps 25-31. Then five cps are devoted to the execution of the temple work and inventory in 35-39; and then more description on setting it up!

[1] Ex 19:1; Num 10:11

> *Jesus in Leviticus…The High Priest.* He is the only intercessor to God you need. Jesus presented Himself as the final sacrifice for every person.

4.1.1.   The name Leviticus, which was not inspired, wasn't assigned as a title, until the Hebrew was translated into Latin, called the *Latin Vulgate*. Leviticus in Latin means "Matters of the Levites" taken from the tribe of Levi.

4.1.2.   The Hebrews called it by the first few words *"And He called."*

4.1.3.   The historical time period of Leviticus is clear because we are told in the last verse of the book, they were at Mt Sinai. Moreover, since we acknowledge the Exodus occurred around 1491 BCE and realize the tabernacle was finished one year later, the date is established.

4.1.4.   Leviticus records some of the regulations and guidelines given to Moses for the people.

4.1.5.   More than twenty times Leviticus confirms that its contents are God's direct words to Moses. Twenty of the twenty-seven begin *"and the Lord spoke to Moses."*

4.1.6.   In Leviticus, the Lord says to His people *"You are to be holy to me because I the Lord am holy."*

    4.1.6.1.   What does "holy" mean? If we are to be holy as God is holy, what is it? Many books have been written describing this subject, so more than a few words are needed. Many think of being almost perfect. Others just think of "a holier than you" concept.

    4.1.6.2.   Since it appears some six hundred times in the Bible, it is vital to understand it.

    4.1.6.3.   Our motives, thoughts, and even attitudes must be in conformity with God. Unite with Him, and the result will be a resemblance to holiness. Put Him in your daily thought life. Think on His Word as often as you can. Let God remake you into His image. Be like Jesus.

    4.1.6.4.   Psalm 29:2 speaks of "the splendor of holiness." It must be attractable and attainable. The answer is in the word itself. The word in Hebrew means "wholeness."

4.1.7.   In the first sixteen chapters of Leviticus, three themes provided instructions on gaining *access to God* and our personal inadequacy to do so. This was shown by various sacrifices.

    4.1.7.1.   Offerings

4.1.7.2.   Priesthood

4.1.7.3.   Cleansing.

4.1.8.   The final eleven chapters taught them how to *maintain fellowship*; what God expects from our response in living for Him apart from the world and connecting and maintaining that fellowship with Him.

4.1.8.1.   This is still His desire for each of us...come *TO* Him and remain *IN* him. I'm always reminded of Paul's message in the New Testament. He uses *"in Christ"* at least 160 times in his Epistles! You and I are born-again, *INTO* Him; then have to *STAY* there. The great lesson of Leviticus is that a holy God must have a holy people, and holiness must embrace the whole of life.

4.1.9.   Five types of offerings are given, to draw people *TO* Him; and notice with me, each type is nothing more than what we are to do directly, without any animal, meal, or symbol. The object is the same.

4.1.9.1.   #1, *Burnt Offerings*[1] (See Lev 1) were a dedication by worship. We dedicate ourselves...by our direct worship, in several forms. Whatever that form is, as long as it's heart-directed, do it. Keep doing it...worship Him in spirit and truth! All the sacrifices in Leviticus point to *"Christ who takes away the sin of the world"* (John 1:29).

Depth of Bible Words and Places
Burnt Offering

The burnt offering was a gift to God, which was burned on an altar. This offering was to be a perfect animal of the first year, the best of the heard, usually a lamb or ram. These were always given for cleansing for sin. Hands were laid on the sacrifice, identifying oneself with the transfer of sin.

4.1.9.2.   #2 *Grain or Meal Offerings* (See Lev 2) were thanks to God. No blood was involved; a variety of sacrifices could be used.

4.1.9.2.1.   Fine flour baked into cakes

4.1.9.2.2.   Ears of corn

4.1.9.2.3.   Oil was involved as well as fire, each pointing to Christ

---

[1]Lev 1:3 If his offering is a burnt offering from the herd, he shall offer it, a male without defect

180

4.1.9.2.4.   We have a great privilege in going directly to Him in Jesus' name and thanking Him. The curtain of separation was torn from the top to bottom by the cross of Christ.[1] Thank Him for the air you breathe, the job you have, kids of yours, the daily steps you take.

4.1.9.3.   A third type, the *Peace Offerings* (See Lev 3) expressed a fellowship; similar to the burnt offering, except the offerer received back some of the animal to feast on; fellowship. Both God and the family shared the offering. Live in peace, not conflict.

4.1.9.4.   Then a fourth type of offering, *Sin Offering* (See Lev 4) acknowledged guilt. We note that more blood was involved with this—sprinkled and applied more liberally. [2]He cannot look upon sin; however, every failure can be forgiven. Never run FROM Him...Run TO Him. Shame screams..."run," Grace offers..."come." Each of these four offerings, the Scriptures say was *"a soothing aroma to the Lord."*[3] He still loves these types of offerings.

4.1.9.5.   The fifth offering was the *Trespass or Guilt Offering* (See Lev 5 and 6a), for intentional sin. This offering was always an unblemished ram; offered for a trespass against the Lord or against man.

Depth of Bible Words and Places
Scapegoat

In Leviticus 16, the term refers to the second of two goats. One was sacrificed, the second was released after praying and laying on of hands to signify the sins of the people being transferred and released into the desert. This was only done annually on the Day of Atonement. The word comes from an Arabic word meaning *remove*. This Day of Atonement is the spiritual "center" of this book of Leviticus.

4.2. We note the order of these sacrifices.

4.2.1.   God begins with the burnt offering, the giving of His Son to the work of redemption. However, in our way of thinking, the offerings are in reverse order. We see ourselves first as having

---

[1] Matt 27:51 *And behold, the veil of the temple was torn in two from top to bottom*

[2] Lev 4:17-18 *the priest shall dip his finger in the blood and sprinkle it seven times before the Lord, in front of the veil. 18 'He shall put some of the blood on the horns of the altar which is before the Lord in the tent of meeting; and all the blood he shall pour ou t at the base of the altar of burnt offering which is at the doorway of the tent of meeting.*

[3] Lev 1:9, 2:9, 3:16, 4:31 *a soothing aroma to the Lord. The AMP reads for a sweet and satisfying fragrance*

committed all kinds of individual sins, *Trespass* Offering. As conviction sets in, we realize that yes indeed we are sinners, *Sin* Offering. Then the Spirit reveals Jesus, the One who made peace by His blood, *Peace* Offering. In addition, as we grow in that grace we learn that we are "accepted in the Beloved" *Meal* Offering. The result of all this is a complete dedication to Christ. Burnt Offering Heb 10:14

God's Order	Man's Order
Burnt	Guilt
Meal	Sin
Peace	Peace
Meal	Meal
Guilt	Burnt

4.2.2.　　Beginning in cp 11, God sets down many guidelines for His people. These laws concerning *the diet, cleanliness* (told not to touch a dead carcass, for example), told to be *holy* and different from the nations around them, *leprosy* and how it characterized sin.

4.2.3.　　Right in the midst of all these guidelines, God emphasizes *atonement* thru the blood; life is in the blood and the sacrifice was to be treated with respect. For us today, realize that the precise following of the Old Testament laws were done away, with the fulfillment of the Law in Jesus (Col 2:11-17).

4.2.4.　　The last section of Leviticus sets down *Seven Feasts* where they were to enjoy being with God. Each one was a picture of Christ. The five offerings we detailed, spoke of the blood that saves, the seven feasts that we now review, speak of a food that sustains.

4.2.4.1.　　Note the order of the feasts. Their year begins with *Passover*, the death of Christ: followed by *First Fruits* the resurrection; next came 50 days later, the coming of the Holy Spirit, *Pentecost.* Then *Feast of Trumpets* is the gathering of God's people when Christ returns, followed quickly by a cleansing of Atonement. Of course the climax, the blessings of a future Kingdom, the feast of Tabernacles.

Depth of Bible Words and Places
Feasts

Feasts are a reference to celebrations and dinners in the Old Testament. Also, include Jewish religious holidays.

The First Coming
of Christ

Month	Day(s)	Feast	Looks Back On...	Looks Ahead To...	Scripture
1st	14	Passover	Redemption of Firstborn	Christ's Redeeming Death	First Corinthians 5:7
					First Peter 1:18-19
1st	15–21	Un-leavened Bread	Separation from Other Nations	Holy Walk of Believers	First Corinthians 5:7–8
					Galatians 5:9, 16–17
1st	16	Firstfruits	Harvest in the Land	Resurrection of Christ	First Corinthians 15:20–23
				Revelation 1:5	
3rd	6	Pentecost	Completion of Harvest	Sending of the Holy Spirit	Acts 2:1–47
					First Corinthians 12:13

The Second Coming
of Christ

Month	Day(s)	Feast	Looks Back On...	Looks Ahead To...	Scripture
7th	1	Trumpets	Israel's New Year	Israel's Regathering	Isaiah 27:12–13
					Matthew 24:21–31
7th	10	Day of Atonement	Israel's National Sin	Israel's National Conversion	Zechariah 12:10
					Romans 11:26–27

| 7th | 15–22 | Tabernacles | Israel in the Wilderness | Israel in the Kingdom | Zechariah 14:4–16 Revelation 7:9-17 |

4.2.4.2. The seven annual holy feasts were seasonal and each pointed to Christ:

4.2.4.3. The Spring Festivals.

4.2.4.3.1. Passover marked a new year, a new beginning for the Israelites (Ex 12:1-2). The entire community was required to participate.

4.2.4.3.2. Unleavened Bread commemorated Israel's hurried escape from Egypt. The *matzah* was made in a hurry, with no yeast.

4.2.4.3.3. First-fruits; reserved for when they were settled in the land of Canaan. There they would have fields and harvest

4.2.4.3.4. Pentecost; outpouring of the Holy Spirit of Christ, fifty days following His resurrection.

4.2.4.4. The Autumn Festivals.

4.2.4.4.1. Trumpets; Looks to Israel's regathering by Christ

4.2.4.4.2. Atonement; Reminder to each of us of the sacrifice of Christ. The Day of Atonement in Israel's future is described in detail in Zech 12:10 and 13:1

4.2.4.4.3. Tabernacles; A feast of rejoicing, speaking of the future millennial kingdom that God promised to the Jews, and follows a great harvest. We are reminded of a rest and reunion with Christ.

Depth of Bible Words and Places

Passover and *Unleavened Bread:* Death Christ
First fruits: Resurrection of Christ
Pentecost: Outpouring of the Holy Spirit of Christ
Trumpets: Israel's regathering by Christ
Atonement: Sacrifice of Christ
Tabernacles: Rest and Reunion with Christ

4.2.4.5. Christians can celebrate a personal relationship every day. On our knees, we experience a fullness of joy because of being *IN Him*. Our life in Christ is so much better than the offerings and the feasts. Let us never lose sight of our great privilege.

ELEVEN

Wilderness

1   One month after the tabernacle was erected, a census was taken, which places our journey in *Numbers.*

Basic Outline of Numbers

#1 THEIR TRAVELS	#2 FIVE PERSONS
1. At Sinai, Cps 1-10	1. Moses
2. Sinai to Kadesh, Cps 11-13	2. Aaron
3. Wandering Around Kadesh, Cps 14-21	3. Miriam
4. On the Banks of Jordan, Cps 22-36	4. Joshua-Caleb

Depth of Bible Words and Places
Numbers Key Word (1): *Wilderness*

The first of two **KEY Words** in Numbers is *wilderness*. It is a key because it's found forty-eight times in the book and always refers to a land of little vegetation and very little rain.

Depth of Bible Words and Places
Numbers Key Word (2): *Anointed*

Anointed is a verb that means, "To wet or dab a person with olive oil." Read it in 3:3, 6:15, 7:1, and 10. Priests and prophets were anointed at the beginning of their service. It set one apart for God's special purposes. Even the tabernacle itself was anointed during the Exodus. The anointing oil was a very exquisite and expensive blend of oil and spices.

Jesus in Numbers...A Pillar of fire by night, A Pillar of cloud by day. He is always with you, and will lead you each step of your journey in life.

1.1. Numbers, which covers thirty-nine years, was most likely written in the final year of Moses' life, 1451 BCE. (See detail of JEDP authorship theory).

1.2.   The events recorded in 20:10 through the end of the book occur in the 40th year after the Exodus, and conclude with Israel camped on the Eastern side of the Jordan, looking across at Jericho, and poised to conquer Canaan (36:13). The book is primarily concerned with the journey from Sinai to Moab.

1.3. We note, as in several books of the Bible, the book title was not assigned until the Septuagint in 250 BCE, long after the book itself was written. The name "Numbers" was used in reference to the two separate numberings of the people.

1.4. Again, we see the Hebrews simply referred to this place in Scripture, by using the first words, *"in the wilderness."* As you will discover while reading this book, we might call it "a book of murmurings."

    1.4.1.   This book relates the story of a people who have come out of Egypt, however, have not reached Canaan. They came out of bondage but have not yet settled in peace.

    1.4.2.   The first nine and a half chapters of Numbers take place at Sinai, with no moving around. During that year, God taught them about His Law and how to worship in truth. The tabernacle is dedicated in cp six with this wonderful blessing given over the people.[1] Other instructions are given such as

        1.4.2.1.   Arrangement of Israelites around the tabernacle

        1.4.2.2.   Levites, their numbering and their duties

        1.4.2.3.   Nazirites and their vows

        1.4.2.4.   Dedication of the Tabernacle

        1.4.2.5.   The Passover celebration identified

    1.4.3.   Chapters eleven, twelve, and thirteen, record how they packed and moved from Sinai to Kadesh and explored Canaan—many miles north. We read that 80% of the spies were negative (and we seem to live today in the midst of a highly negative society), with only Joshua and Caleb positive and excited about the land. God wanted them in His Promised Land at that time.

Depth of Bible Words and Places
Kadesh (Numbers 13)

Kadesh-barnea was an important location in Israelite history, between the Sinai desert and the southern boundary of

---

[1] A prayer which will live forever; many churches use it to close every service. Numbers 6:24-26. *24 The Lord bless you, and keep you; 25 The Lord make His face shine on you, And be gracious to you; 26 The Lord lift up His countenance on you, And give you peace.*

Located in 1979 CE on a silver "credit card" size piece of silver, were inscribed these w ords. Perhaps the oldest written scriptures we have, dated back to the seventh century BCE.

Canaan. Moses sent twelve spies into Canaan from here. Perhaps Kadesh-barnea was regarded as a potential base for the invasion of Canaan. The place was an important crossroads, from which routes run in every direction. Today it is an obscure waterhole. Since 1905 CE, fortresses have been excavated at the location in northern Sinai. Today, it is an obscure waterhole. Since 1905 CE, fortresses have been excavated at the location in northern Sinai.

1.4.4. Chapters fourteen through twenty-five, are the years of moving around from place to place, in or around Kadesh.

1.4.5. Then chapters twenty-six through thirty-six are on the banks of the Jordan.

1.5. Let's look a little deeper at Numbers. The rules and laws had been set down for this peculiar nation...the glory-God was in their midst, and God was ready for them to enter into a land He had for them.

1.5.1. They are numbered in chapter one, one month after the Tabernacle was erected. The first numbering was of twenty-year old men and younger (those soldier-age men totaled 603,550 (1:46). The total population of the new nation was around three million, approximately the same number who crossed the Red Sea on dry land.[1]

1.5.1.1. Twelve princes representing the twelve tribes are appointed and bring forth a special offering of oxen and wagons, which were to be used for the transportation of the Tabernacle and its equipment. This was not to include the special items in the Tabernacle, Ark of the Covenant, Golden Lampstand, Altar of Worship, and the Table of Shewbread. Those items were to be borne on shoulders.

1.5.1.2. The Levites were consecrated, the Passover celebrated, and Moses made two silver trumpets as signals to alarm or call an assembly.

1.5.2. And quite suddenly, the cloud of God's glory over the tabernacle was lifted and trumpets were sounded...and with the Ark in the center, Judah (praise) in the lead, and Dan (the smallest tribe, meaning "judgment") in the rear...they started towards the Promised Land.[2][1]

---

[1] I love the idea of numbering. Not one individual is unimportant. 600,000 men of over twenty years of age, 3,000,000 people, each one important. Organized and arranged with duties assigned to various people. God is the great organizer, ignoring no one. The Lord knows by name all that are His!

[2] Num 10:14 *The standard of the camp of the sons of Judah, according to their armies, set out first...*

1.5.2.1.   Each tribe had its own Standard and Prince in the lead. Moses stepped forward, Numbers 10.[2]

1.5.2.2.   Three million people start to move. And within three days...murmuring![3] Again, I remind you, this is "the book of murmuring."

Depth of Bible Words and Places
Murmuring (Complain)

Complaining is nothing less than unbelief. Unbelief always leads to spiritual death. As recorded in Exodus, the Lord did not chastise them for their many expressions of murmuring. However, this time He does not let it pass without a condoning of sin. By now they should have known better!

1.5.2.3.   Moses says (Numbers 11:14) *I alone am not able to carry all this people, because it is too burdensome for me.* And our merciful God appoints seventy elders who were given a spirit of wisdom, which had rested on Moses. They assisted with the load. It is believed that the Sanhedrim, the ruling body of Israel, originated with the Seventy Elders.

1.5.2.4.   They arrive at Kadesh where God instructs them to send the chief of each of the twelve tribes and spy out Canaan. You're here! I've brought you to the land!

1.5.2.5.   They return with their reports after forty days with the "fruit of the land" in their hands—a large cluster of grapes, pomegranates, figs, milk, and honey.

1.5.2.6.   Caleb and Jacob, the "positive two," did their best to encourage...but the "negative ten" win out...and the entire population propose a vote to elect a new captain and purpose to stone Caleb and Jacob. This is the written record of many a believer's life. Many giants are faced: greed, fear, selfishness...all "strong and tall."

1.5.2.7.   God is upset and He is ready to disinherit the nation and make a greater and mightier people from the descendants of Moses. Never before had they refused to

---

[1] *The Ark:* His Word in their midst *A Silver Trumpet:* The sound of His leadership *A Pillar and Cloud:* The comfort of the Holy Spirit.

[2] Numbers 10:35 *" Rise up, O Lord! And let Your enemies be scattered, And let those who hate You flee before You."*

[3] Num 11:1 *Now the people became like those who complain of adversity in the hearing of the Lord;*

go forward; never before had they turned back towards Egypt and bondage.

1.5.2.8. Because of Moses' insistence and intercession for the people, God allows the people to again break camp...but thirty-eight years of wandering would follow...and every man above the age of twenty (except Joshua and Caleb), over 600,000 men would die in a desert. We can be sure many others died during those years also.[1]

1.5.2.9. They leave Kadesh, becoming nomadic wanders for these next years. They moved from location to location, many times stopping with their animals for grazing on the hills, and other times stopping several days or more for rest.

1.5.2.10. Cps 9-12 describe the experiences in a wilderness, much of it murmuring. At the root of all the wandering, was unbelief; they did not trust God's Word. Many Christians are delivered from Egypt by the blood, but do not enter into their inheritance "in Christ."

1.5.2.11. In approximately 1451 BCE, the Hebrew nation returned to Kadesh where they had started just a few miles from the Promised Land, forty years earlier. Israel had wandered a year for each day that had been spent in the exploration of Canaan.

1.5.2.12. During the last encampment at Kadesh, Miriam died and was buried, and Moses in impatience struck a rock twice rather than obeying exactly the instructions from God. This disobedience kept him from going into the land of promise.

1.5.2.13. Numbers 25 is significant. Israel for the first time experiences the attraction of Baal worship. Moreover, this experience plagued them for centuries — all the way to the rebuilding of Jerusalem, late in the Old Testament period. Repeatedly, the seed of idolatry planted, as recorded in Chapter 25, would be a downfall and curse as they allow it to become the fruit of their life.

1.5.2.14. Before they cross the Jordan into the land, a second numbering/census was taken. Moses was

---

[1] A side-bar. Remember the "negative ten?" The ten spies with a negative report were victims of a plague. Also, the people quickly repented but it was too late. They attempted an invasion without God's assistance, and were turned back by the Amalekite and Canaanite warriors.

instructed to take a census of the children of Israel (26:1-51) because they were about to enter the land to war against its inhabitants and to receive their share of the inheritance. This second census is almost the same as the first...less than a single percentage fewer. Only two names appear in both numberings.[1]

The Second Census (Numbers, Chap. 26)

26:1–51 Again Moses was instructed to take a census ... of the children of Israel, since they were about to enter the land to war against its inhabitants and to receive their share of the inheritance. There was a decrease of 1,820 people from the first census, as seen in the following numbers:

Tribe	Census (Chap. 1)	Census (Chap. 26)
Reuben (vv 5–11)	46,500	43,730
Simeon (vv 12–14)	59,300	**22,200**
Gad (vv 15–18)	45,650	40,500
Judah (vv 19–22)	74,600	76,500
Issachar (vv 23–25)	54,400	64,300
Zebulun (vv 26, 27)	57,400	60,500
Joseph (vv 28–37)		
—Manasseh (v 34)	32,200	**52,700**
—Ephraim (v 37)	40,500	32,500
Benjamin (vv 38–41)	35,400	45,600
Dan (vv 42, 43)	62,700	64,400
Asher (vv 44–47)	41,500	53,400
Naphtali (vv 48–51)	43,400	45,400

---

[1] Who were they?

TOTAL	**603, 550**	**601, 730**

Note the slight decrease in numbers over the long period of time between the 603,550 of chapter 1 and the 601,730 in chapter 26--the tribes of Simeon and Manasseh experienced the greatest change. Israel's growth ceased for forty years.

1.5.2.15.   Noting the decrease in numbers over the long period of time between the 603,550 of chapter 1 and the 601,730 children of Israel, Moody comments: "Israel's growth ceased for forty years. So it may be with us today, as churches, and individuals, if we are unbelieving."

1.6. We complete our study of the Pentateuch or Torah, with the fifth book, Deuteronomy. (See the Pentateuch in Chapter THREE). This book records three great addresses by Moses while they were camped east of the Jordan River at Shittim. (This author includes as a fourth address, chapters 31-34). He wanted the people of this second generation to remember their history.

1.6.1.   Deuteronomy is not an accurate title for this book; again we can note it was not inspired. To the Israelites it was called *"These are the words,"* from the first words of the book. That is really a more accurate title than "Deuteronomy."

1.6.2.   The word "Deuteronomy" was actually a translation of 17:18, which in Hebrew was "copy of this law," but the translators used the name Deuteronomy that meant "second law." However, this was not a second law; it was exactly what the first words said. It was actually the words of Moses explaining/repeating the first law. It was the second "stating" of the Law.

1.7. God educated a new generation of the Hebrew nation. Deuteronomy records an interesting summary of the wilderness experience.

Depth of Bible Words and Places
Deuteronomy Key Word: *Covenant*

A KEY WORD in Deuteronomy is really the primary theme of the entire Book. It could be an entire multi-week study.

Covenant. The Hebrew means "a cutting." You have heard the words "to cut a covenant." You remember when Livingston met a tribal chief? To continue on his journey, Livingston literally "cut" an agreement with the tribe's chief. And never did he have a serious problem in his travels. He had an agreement; he had "a covenant." All the chief's integrity and might was now Livingston's.

The formal covenant occurs in Deuteronomy, cp 27 with Moses and all Israel agreeing, verse 9: *Be silent and listen, O*

Israel! This day you have become a people for the LORD your God.

A Basic Outline of Deuteronomy

1. Remember God's Blessings, Cps 1-5
2. Respond to God's Goodness, Cps 6-11
3. Review God's Word, Cps 12-26
4. Renew God's Covenant, Cps 27-31
5. Recite to Israel, Cps 32-34

Jesus in Deuteronomy...The Prophet is coming. He is the Messiah.

Depth of Bible Words and Places
Shittim (A city, Numbers 25)

This was the Israelite's final wilderness encampment before they crossed the Jordan River. Shittim was located just east of Jericho (actual full name was *Abel Shittim*). This is where Moses ascended Mount Nebo, as well as where Joshua dispatched the spies to Jericho. It was here also that Israel fell in to Baal worship. This city has been located showing ruins of houses, a fortress with towers and surrounded by 4' thick walls. Moses gave three addresses to the nation. Note that Jesus, in the wilderness, used these three speeches to rebuke Satan as He began His ministry.[1]

1.7.1.   *Speech # (1)* in Deuteronomy cps 1-4, Moses addressed *their past,* emphasizing God's love, and mercy. *He looks back,* a history lesson of the past forty years reminding them that whenever the nation believed God, they were blessed; when they disobeyed, some form of chastisement occurred. 700 years earlier God promised Abraham and his "seed," the wondrous land upon whose borders they were now standing. Moses was clear concerning the fact they were about to enter a land which God had for them. He refers to *land* over 200 times in Deuteronomy. He encourages the people to *possess the land* (1:8), do *not fear* the enemy in the land (1:21), and realize this land was their inheritance (4:20).

         1.7.1.1.   He reviewed the faithfulness of God in guiding them from Horeb to the plains of Moab. Israel was reminded of how spies had been sent into Canaan and had returned with the report of a land flowing with milk and honey, a Promised Land. However, the people

---

[1] Matt 4

rebelled against God, and did not enter the land due to their fear of the giants there. Therefore, for forty years, God allowed them to wander in the wilderness until all who had rebelled in disobedience, died. Moses records that only Caleb and Joshua were left alive of those adults who had come out of Egypt. Again, they stood on the threshold of destiny. Now they prepared to possess the land before them.

Depth of Bible Words and Places
Horeb

The second verse of cp 1 mentions they traveled from Horeb. Horeb (in the Pentateuch) is a name for Mt Sinai where the Israelites spent one year being taught. It had taken Israel about one year to reach Kadesh from Mount Horeb or Sinai and another year to reach the place where Moses was delivering the messages of Deuteronomy. The thirty-eight years between had been spent wandering. That is why in most of my information concerning dates; I refer to thirty-eight years of wandering.

1.7.1.2.   *Speech # (2),* a long address in cps 5-26, repeating the law. Moses restates the Ten Commandments, the religious training of the children in the home, and obedience and trust in the law. They now heard all this from a man who heard directly from God. *Speech #2 looks within.*

1.7.1.3.   As you read Deut 10:12-13[1] think on the five actions each of us is to take in our day. Perhaps you have never considered Deuteronomy in this way, but we could use a theme of love to describe it; love is repeated at least twenty times in the book. It is the first book in the Bible that emphasizes love.

1.7.1.4.   In 12:1 we read *These are the statutes and the judgments which you shall carefully observe in the land which the Lord, the God of your fathers, has given you to possess as long as you live on the earth.*

1.7.1.5.   In 17:19, in giving instructions for future kings of Israel, God said that a copy of His Law *"shall be with him, and he shall read it all the days of his life, that he many learn to fear the Lord his God, by carefully*

---

[1] Deut 10:12 *"Now, Israel, what does the Lord your God require from you, but to fear the Lord your God, to walk in all His ways and love Him, and to serve the Lord your God with all your heart and with all your soul, 13 and to keep the Lord's commandments and His statutes which I am commanding you today for your good?*

observing all the words of this law and these statures." The king was to read God's law all the days of his life in order to learn to honor the Lord. Too bad every king did not obey this message. We will see where many of them did not refer to His Words.

        1.7.1.6.   In Deuteronomy 18, God tells of Jesus who alone knows the future—not some sorceress.[1]

1.7.2.   *Speech # (3) Moses looks ahead* to the near future in chapters 27-30. It's one of the most important sections in all of Scripture. God warns them of disobedience and a scattering of the people among the nations. However, He also states that He will bring a remnant back to the land. This was fulfilled twice.

        1.7.2.1.   The first scattering was in 586 BCE, which we will review later, when Nebuchadnezzar destroyed the first temple and captured a large group of Hebrews.

        1.7.2.2.   A remnant *returned* fifty years later, in 536 BCE and stated to rebuild the temple under Zerubbabel.

        1.7.2.3.   There was a second scattering in 70 CE when Rome destroyed the second temple.

        1.7.2.4.   A remnant began to *return* in May, 1948 CE.

        1.7.2.5.   Chapters 27 and 28 describe the blessings God promised Israel if they obeyed Him, and the terrible curses that would come on them for disobedience; a scattering, restlessness, and sorrow.

1.7.2.5.1.   They marched toward two mountain peaks, and six tribes were assigned to go up each of the peaks; one group of six tribes called out the curses, while the other group shouted back the blessing. Israel has experienced the truth of these words through the centuries.

1.7.2.5.2.   These warnings are followed by a renewal of the covenant between God and His people, with promises of blessing and prosperity if they *"obey the LORD your God and keep his commands and decrees."* (Deuteronomy 30:10). This covenant appears seven times in cp 29, a reaffirmation between God and his people.

1.7.2.5.3.   So Moses called the people to choose God's way, the way of life (see Deuteronomy 30: 11-20).

---

[1] Deut 18:18 *I will raise up a prophet from among their countrymen like you, and I will put My words in his mouth;* Deut 18:20-21 *But the prophet who speaks a word presumptuously in My name which I have not commanded him to speak, or which he speaks in the name of other gods, that prophet shall die.*

1.7.3.   This author considers a *Speech # (4)*. Moses in Deuteronomy, *Looked Back* in chapters 1-4, *Looked Within* in chapters 5-26, *Looked Ahead* in chapters 27-30, and *Looked Out* to the future in chapters 31-34.[1]

         1.7.3.1.   Speech four described the future leadership of Joshua, prediction of Israel's rebellion, Moses' extensive Song, and Moses' blessing of the Israelites

2   Note some additional details of the book of Deuteronomy.

   2.1. Only Moses, Joshua, and Caleb were from that first group that came out of Egypt (of course there were women and children also).

   2.2. This book of Deuteronomy does not advance historically. Similar to Leviticus it takes place over a one-month period and entirely at one location. From the early verses in Deuteronomy, we see the date for both Numbers and Deuteronomy set at January-February of 1405 BCE. (Refer to the Jewish Calendar.) They next arrived just east of the Jordan River, across from Jericho and Ai.[2]

The Jewish Calendar

Tishri	7th	September-October	30 days
Heshvan	8th	October-November	29 or 30 days
Chislev	9th	November-December	29 or 30 days
Tebeth	10th	December-January	29 days
Shebat	11th	January-February	30 days
Adar	12th	February-March	29 or 30 days
Nisan (Abib)	1st	March-April	30 days
Iyar	2nd	April-May	29 days
Sivan	3rd	May-June	30 days
Tammuz	4th	June-July	29 days
Ab	5th	July-August	30 days
Elul	6th	August-September	29 days

Their year was shorter than ours, with 354 days. Every 3 years, an extra 29-day month was added between Adar and Nisan.

         2.2.1.1.   Deuteronomy is a book concerning the attributes of God. No surprise then that the New Testament quotes from this book over forty times. Only Psalms and Isaiah are quoted more.

         2.2.1.2.   Deuteronomy reveals some great information about God.

2.2.1.2.1.   The Lord is the only God

---

[1] Deut 31:1 So Moses went and spoke these words to all Israel.

[2] Deuteronomy 1:3 records *In the fortieth year, on the first day of the eleventh month, Moses spoke to the children of Israel…*

2.2.1.2.2.   He's a jealous God

2.2.1.2.3.   A Faithful God

2.2.1.2.4.   A Loving God

2.2.1.2.5.   A Merciful God

2.2.1.2.6.   He's angered by sin

2.2.1.2.7.   All of this revealed in Deuteronomy.

2.2.1.2.8.   Over 250 times Moses the writer repeated the words *"the Lord your God."* The Hebrew is *Yahweh your Elohim,* combining two names of God. Your personal God (*Yahweh*) is your powerful God (*Elohim*). He made the strong point to Israel — no room for failure.

2.3. I offer two additional points about this book of Deuteronomy, the first of which is an intentional repeat of earlier comments.

2.3.1.1.   *First,* Moses spends twenty-six cps addressing the people, a second generation, about what happened to their parents. He wanted them never to forget:

2.3.1.1.1.   God's blessings on them,

2.3.1.1.2.   Providing for them,

2.3.1.1.3.   Leading them by His glory,

2.3.1.1.4.   And helping them to respond to their God and living by His word. God has not changed!

2.3.1.2.   The *second* point he discussed. Moses seemed to assume the Israelites would not be able to keep the covenant, so he anticipated in cp 30, in a few of his final words, that there would one day be a new covenant; take time to read this important passage.

Verse 6 touches on this theme concerning a future covenant. "Moreover the Lord your God will circumcise your heart and the heart of your descendants, to love the Lord your God with all your heart and with all your soul, so that you may live. Also, see Expanded Help Paper, Four Covenants, in this volume.
Also verses 11-14 "For this commandment which I command you today is not too difficult for you, nor is it out of reach. 12 "It is not in heaven, that you should say, 'Who will go up to heaven for us to get it for us and make us hear it, that we may observe it?' 13 "Nor is it beyond the sea, that you should say, 'Who will cross the sea for us to get it for us and make us hear it, that we may observe it?' 14 "But the word is very near you, in your mouth and in your heart, that you may observe it.
Then it is made even more clear by Jeremiah in 32:39 and Ezekiel in 36:26; and I will give them one heart and one way, that they may fear Me always, for their own good and for the good of their children after them(Jeremiah 32:39); will give

you a new heart and put a new spirit within you; and I will remove the heart of stone from your flesh and give you a heart of flesh. 27 "I will put My Spirit within you and cause you to walk in My statutes, and you will be careful to observe My ordinances (Ezekiel 36:26-27).

Depth of Bible Words and Places
Altar on Mount Ebal

Deuteronomy 28, as well as Joshua 8, describes an altar constructed on Mount Ebal, after entering Canaan. A similar altar (if not the same one), was discovered in 1980 CE. It is 29' long by 23' wide and filled with layers of ash, animal bones, and constructed of unworked stones. It has been dated around 1200 BCE, only slightly later than "Joshua's Altar."

2.3.1.2.1.   A new covenant would be ratified by the blood of Christ on a cross. Moses says in verse 11, this *is not too difficult for you, nor is it out of reach.* Some versions say "it's not too far off." He's saying "It's not inaccessible." Actually, verses 11-13 apply to Christ cutting the new covenant by His blood.

2.3.1.2.2.   Then I encourage you to read verses 15-20 of this wonderful chapter. This is for every Christian believer. As we read this, keep in mind Galatians 3:13, which make it clear, it is for every one of us: *Christ redeemed us from the curse of the Law, having become a curse for us*.

Deuteronomy 30:15 *"See, I have set before you today life and prosperity, and death and adversity; 16 in that I command you today to love the Lord your God, to walk in His ways and to keep His commandments and His statutes and His judgments, that you may live and multiply, and that the Lord your God may bless you in the land where you are entering to poss ess it. 17 "But if your heart turns away and you will not obey, but are drawn away and worship other gods and serve them, 18 I declare to you today that you shall surely perish. You will not prolong your days in the land where you are crossing the Jordan to enter and possess it. 19 "I call heaven and earth to witness against you today, that I have set before you life and death, the blessing and the curse. So choose life in order that you may live, you and your descendants, 20 by loving the Lord your God, by obeying His voice, and by holding fast to Him; for this is your life and the length of your days, that you may live in the land which the Lord swore to your fathers, to Abraham, Isaac, and Jacob, to give them."*

2.3.1.2.3.   The final verses of Deuteronomy record the change in leadership. Joshua would lead them into Canaan. The poetic Song of Moses is recorded in cp 32. The grand old man of 120 years of age stands and sings a song for Israel.

2.3.1.2.4.   At the age of 120, the three forty-year periods of Moses' life ends. He charged the nation to accept Joshua as their captain and finished the writing of the law...and gave his life while viewing the land. We see a great continuity of leadership and preparation to strongly go in unity.

Depth of Bible Words and Places
Nebo

This is a mountain where Moses viewed the Promised Land. It overlooks the Dead Sea. It is the highest peak of Mount Pisgah, eight miles east of the Jordan. Somewhere in this vicinity angels came down and took Elijah away (2 Kings 2:11).

2.3.1.2.5.   His final place of burial has never been identified. The last three verses of the Pentateuch are a fitting epitaph[1]

2.3.1.2.6.   These four great books...Exodus, Leviticus, Numbers and Deuteronomy, have moved us a long way in our journey in God's plan of redemption. Moses' leading the people out of captivity, receiving and presenting of God's requirements, and building the Tabernacle to worship God, all were the plan of Yahweh.

---

[1] Deuteronomy 34:10 *Since that time no prophet has risen in Israel like Moses, whom the Lord knew face to face, 11 for all the signs and wonders which the Lord sent him to perform in the land of Egypt against Pharaoh, all his servants, and all his land, 12 and for all the mighty power and for all the great terror which Moses performed in the sight of all Israel.*

S E C T I O N 5
The Promised Land

Joshua, Judges, Ruth, 1 Samuel 1-8. The period from 1451 to 1050 BCE

Theme Statement: *"...a good and spacious land...a land flowing with milk and honey."* (Exodus 3:8)

THE KEYS IN SECTION FIVE

Section 5: The Promised Land

Keys to Joshua—

A Key Word: *Rest*

The Key Verses (1:8; 11:23)

1:8 This book of the law shall not depart from your mouth, but you shall meditate on it day and night, so that you may be careful to do according to all that is written in it; for then you will make your way prosperous, and then you will have success.

11:23 *So Joshua took the whole land, according to all that the Lord had spoken to Moses, and Joshua gave it for an inheritance to Israel according to their divisions by their tribes. Thus the land had rest from war.*

The Key Chapter (24)

The Key People in Joshua

Joshua—taught by Moses, led Israel across the Jordan and into the Promised Land (1–24)

Rahab—a prostitute living in Jericho; assisted the two spies; listed in the "seed" line, ancestor of David and Jesus (2; 6:17, 22, 23, 25)

Achan—after the victory in Jericho he kept some items for himself, thus disobeying God; this was the reason Israel failed in the battle against Ai; stoned to death (7; 22:20)

Eleazar—son of Aaron; became high priest; worked closely with Joshua (14:1; 17:4; 19:51; 21:1–3; 22:13–33; 24:33)

Phinehas—son of Eleazar, also a priest; helped to prevent civil war (22:13, 31–34; 24:33)

Keys to Judges—

A Key Word: *Deliverance*

The Key Verses (2:20–21; 21:25)

2:20 So the anger of the Lord burned against Israel, and He said, "Because this nation has transgressed My covenant which I commanded their fathers and has not listened to My voice, 21 I also will no longer drive out before them any of the nations which Joshua left when he died.

21:25 In those days there was no king in Israel; everyone did what was right in his own eyes.

The Key Chapter (2)

The Key People in Judges

Othniel—first judge of Israel; defeated a powerful Mesopotamian king; brought forty years of peace to Israel (1:13–14; 3:7–11)

Ehud—second judge of Israel; brought Israel eighty years of peace by helping to conquer the Moabites (3:15–31)

Deborah—prophet and Israel's only female judge; succeeded Shamgar as fourth judge of Israel (4:4–16; 5)

Gideon—Israel's fifth judge; defeated the Midianite army (6–8)

Abimelech—Son of Gideon; made himself king of Israel; murdered his sixty-nine brothers (8:31–9:57)

Jephthah—judge of Israel, also a warrior; defeated the Ammonites (11:1–12:7)

Samson—given to God from his birth; unusual strength; a judge of Israel who was to defeat the Philistines (13:24–16:31)

Delilah—Samson's lover who betrayed him to the Philistines for money (16:4–21)

Keys to Ruth—

A Key Word: *Kinsman-Redeemer*

The Key Verses (1:16; 3:11)

1:16 But Ruth said, "Do not urge me to leave you or turn back from following you; for where you go, I will go, and where you lodge, I will lodge. Your people shall be my people, and your God, my God.

3:11 Now, my daughter, do not fear. I will do for you whatever you ask, for all my people in the city know that you are a woman of excellence.

The Key Chapter (4)

The Key People in Ruth

Ruth—Naomi's daughter-in-law; marries Boaz; direct ancestor of Jesus (cps 1–4)

Naomi—the widow of Elimelech; mother-in-law of Orpah and Ruth; mentored/advised Ruth (cps 1–4)

Boaz—prosperous farmer who married Ruth, the Moabite; direct ancestor of Jesus (cps 2-4)

Approximate dates of key events in Section 5	
1451 BCE	Joshua succeeds Moses; conquest begins
1445	Canaan apportioned
1443	Joshua dies
1392-1050	Events in Judges
1175	Samuel is born
1392-1050	Events in Ruth during this period
1095	Saul becomes king

TWELVE

The Promised Land

1   We continue our Journey, in Section 5 *THE PROMISED LAND.*

EXPANDED HELP PAPER
The Topography of Israel[1]

Travelling from the Mediterranean coast eastward, we note the land of Israel has four strips or geographical sections.

First is the *coastal plains* of Phllistia and Sharon, terminated at the north by the promontory of Mount Carmel. Further east, moving inland, rise the *central rugged plateau* (about the size of Long Island), dotted with unwelcoming thorns and scrub, seamed and broken by steep and narr ow gorges, and occupied in historical times, from south to north, by the tribes of Judah, Ephraim and Manasseh (these last two forming the core of Samaria). Moving north again we cross into the land's most important inland plain of Jezreel, flanked by Mounts Carmel and Gilboa and merging, on Its northern side, into the slopes of Galilee.

Moving to the east, the country fell sharply into the *Jordan Valley,* which widened, at two points, into the Dead (or Salt) Sea and the Sea of Galilee

And finally, to the east, came *the hilly or mountainous fringe* tracts, not regarded, for millennia, as genuinely Israelite: Edom beyond Judah's Negeb wilderness, and Moab and Ammon across the Jordan.

The entire complex of small, varying, and often mutually hostile Territories (Israel), extended for about a hundred and fifty miles from north to

---

[1] Summarized from Michael Grant, *The History of Ancient Israel,* Orion Publishing Group edition, 2002, p. 7

south, and less than seventy-five across.

1.1. In this section, we will cover Joshua, Judges, Ruth, and edge in to 1 Samuel, covering the next 400+ years of Israel's history...the first years in their own land. In addition, keep in mind, the theme found in Exodus 3:8: *"...a good and spacious land...a land flowing with milk and honey."*

1.2. The next few Sections will cover what are classified as the Books of History. You may refer to a list of those books in this volume in cp TWO. Interesting to view how these books fit into the Old Testament time line.

2   For nearly 400 years, the Israelites had no homeland.

2.1. Now they have been delivered from Egyptian slavery, living in a wilderness, and dwelling in portable tents for forty years. (However, see Expanded Help Paper, The Topography of the Sinai in this volume).

2.2. Think about this—no fixed location, breaking down tents, moving on, and setting up again. No land or building to say, "This is my home." No garden to plant. No business to start. Wondering while wandering.

2.3. Husbands, dads, and surely some mothers, were dying every day in a strange land...not very pretty!

2.4. The time came for the chosen people to take hold of the Promise Land.

2.4.1.   This "promise land" or "land of promise" is the usual reference given to the territory of the inheritance, which God promised to His people. Exodus 6:4 and Deuteronomy 32:49 call it *Canaan*. This name applied to the land until after the time of the Judges.

2.4.2.   Joshua 11:22 calls it *the land of the Sons of Israel,*

2.4.3.   Judges 20:6 calls it *The land of Israel's inheritance,*

2.4.4.   Other peoples later called it Palestine following the captivity of 586 BCE.

2.4.5.   The boundaries of the land are defined in several scriptures, originally to Abraham in Genesis 15:18; then to Moses in Exodus 23. Palestine was situated on the major trade routes between Egypt and the countries to the east. Before the Hebrews arrived, the land was inhabited mainly by Canaanites; also Joshua 3:10 mentions some other "ites" who were there.

Depth of Bible Words and Places

Prior to the entrance into the Promised Land, the population of this land consisted of seven main groups:

Hittites, located northwest (modern day Turkey). They had a few small settlements in the land.

Amorites, a general ethnic people located in portions of Babylon.

Girgashites, located east of the Sea of Galilee.

Canaanites, a term for the people of the Holy Land, specifically the inhabitants near the Jordan Valley.

Perizzites, near the hill country, which was eventually a part of the tribes of Judah, Ephraim, and Manasseh.

Hivites, located in the Lebanon region.

Jebusites, and independent clan near Jerusalem until David captured Jerusalem.

Additional information of many of these is offered in this volume.

3   We travel next to the conquest of Canaan and the struggles prior to establishing a monarchy under Judges. It is true, the land was given to God's people, but it still had to be possessed by them. We read from Obadiah 17 *And the house of Jacob will possess their possessions.* What a lesson for each of us. God said in Joshua 1:3 *Every place on which the sole of your foot treads, I have given it to you.* God gave; the people had to possess! (Today, we too must "see the land before us, take action by getting ready, then marching into the situation, and take it"). It is one thing to have title to an inheritance, but quite another thing to make it one's own.

3.1. Take hold of all the spiritual life that you desire.

3.2. It is abundant and full of riches

3.3. It will not be easy, but it will end in victory

4   We begin the book of Joshua.

4.1. Tradition says that Joshua is the author, 24:26 records *And Joshua wrote these words in the book of the law of God.*

4.2. The Book of Joshua covers a period from 1405-1385 BCE, approximately 20 years. His name means "God is salvation" or "Jehovah the Helper" and is almost identical to the Hebrew word for Jesus. Both come from *Yeshua. Yeshua,* translated *Jesus* in the New Testament, contains all the elements of the names of God in the Old Testament!

4.3. I love the book of Joshua. It links with the New Testament book of Ephesians (the author has written a study book entitled *Travel Through Ephesians*). Every Christian should master the contents of both Joshua and Ephesians. Both books have wonderful, personal promises, and will help in your travel through life. Keep in mind, the book of Joshua parallels the walk of every believer:

4.3.1.   A journey into a promised land

4.3.2.   The battles with the world system

4.3.3.   Overcoming the forces of the enemy

4.3.4.   Spiritual warfare

4.4. We note by overview, after crossing the Jordan

4.4.1.   Joshua set up an altar of twelve stones at Gilgal

4.4.2.   The city of Jericho was captured, highlighted by the walls falling down at the sound of trumpets

4.4.3.   The city of Ai taken by a trick

4.4.4.   The defeat of an alliance of southern peoples led by the king of Jerusalem.

4.4.5.   The defeat of the alliance of northern kings.

A Basic Outline of Joshua

1. Preparation for Conquest, Cps 1-5
2. Conquest of Canaan, Cps 6-13
3. Settlement in Canaan, Cps 14-22
4. Two Speeches of Joshua, Cps 23-24

Depth of Bible Words and Places
Joshua Key Word: *Rest*

The key word in Joshua is found in 1:13, 3:13, 10:20, and several other references. Joshua is a book of *rest*. It literally means, *"To be at peace."* Rest implies freedom from anxiety and conflict. God's promise of a land to settle in was a promise of *"rest,"* but would depend on God's command for His people to drive out the Canaanites. The New Testament speaks of Christians who are told that heaven will bring *"rest"* from death and all other earthly struggles (Hebrews 4:1).

Jesus in Joshua...The Captain of your salvation. He is the only way to eternal life with God.

4.5. Joshua continues the story from the first five books of Scripture. In Deuteronomy, many times the book of Joshua was grouped with the first five books, and together called "The Hexateuch" or "Six Scrolls."

Together they are one story. Generally, the book of Joshua is grouped with the historical books.[1]

4.5.1.   Joshua, the son of Nun from the tribe of Ephraim, was the companion of Moses for many years, so it was natural that he became the new leader, now sixty years of age. His original name was Oshea (Numbers 13:8, 16) meaning "helper," later changed to Joshua "Jehovah the Helper."

4.5.2.   He was appointed by Moses as the military commander after the Exodus, spied out the land forty years before (along with the other eleven spies), and then heard the wonderful words of Moses in Deuteronomy 31:23.[2]

EXPANDED HELP PAPER
A Quick Overview of The Conquest of Canaan[3]

After crossing the Jordan, Joshua camped awhile at Gilgal, and then was directed to take Jericho and Ai. Afterward he returned to Gilgal (Joshua 1-8).

Joshua made peace with Gibeon, then moved through the Valley of Aijalon and defeated the five Amorite kings (Joshua 9-10).

From Makkedah, Joshua launched a southern campaign against Lachish, Hebron, Debir, and Gaza Gob. Victorious, he returned to Gilgal (Joshua 10).

In a northern thrust, Joshua moved from Gilgal all the way to Hazor (Joshua 11).

4.5.3.   Israel was camping on the east side of the Jordan and plans were being made to attack a very strong, fortified city— Jericho.

Depth of Bible Words and Places
Jericho

---

[1] The Hebrew Old Testament included three groupings of Scriptures. 1. The Law (first five books, Pentateuch); 2. The Prophets (eight books, Prophets); 3. The Writings (eleven books, poetical, historical). Later, a four-fold structure developed. 1. Law; 2. History (twelve books, Joshua-Esther); 3. Wisdom (five books, Job-Song of Solmon); 4. Prophets (seventeen Prophets).

[2] Deuteronomy 31:23 *"...Be strong and courageous, for you shall bring the sons of Israel into the land which I swore to them, and I will be with you."* What a great Word from God!

[3] From Nelson's Illustrated Bible Dictionary, Copyright © 1986, Thomas Nelson Publishers

Jericho, located twelve miles north of the Dead Sea was called "the city of palm trees" (Deut 34:3) and strategically positioned. The city controlled the vital water supply for the entire area. It was one of the largest urban centers in the land of Canaan. The economy of Jericho had advanced beyond food gathering to production of food during that period. Pottery was made by the year 4500 and records indicated massive walls enclosed a population of perhaps two thousand.

Archeology has revealed cobbled streets, shops, storerooms, and living quarters of a bustling economy. The stone wall surrounding Jericho was approximately fifteen feet tall. Archeologists have discovered a small portion of the city wall that did not fall when all else was destroyed.[1] The section that remained standing was nearly eight feet high, with a house built against it, still intact.[2]

4.5.3.1.   The invasion into a strange land begins with a strange plan and a scarlet cord.

4.5.3.2.   Plans are being made to attack the strongly fortified city of Jericho. Joshua sends two spies from the camp to obtain information about the city. They entered the city and secured lodging with an innkeeper named Rahab. A literal translation of Joshua 2:15 reads, *"Her house was against the vertical surface of the city wall, and in the city wall she lived."*

4.5.3.3.   Rahab hides the two spies among "stalks of flax" drying on her roof because the king of Jericho heard they were in the city. From a window of her house built on the wall surrounding Jericho, a scarlet cord allows the two to slip away from the enemy. The cord would also be the sign to Joshua's army to protect her household.

4.5.3.4.   This woman's name, Rahab, is listed in the genealogy of Jesus (Matthew 1).[3] She is also listed in the Hall of Faith, Hebrews 11. It was *"by faith...Rahab did not perish."*

4.5.3.5.   Rahab had to lie to protect the spies. Let's remember that whenever the laws of a city, state, or nation are in contradiction to the Law of God, the choice must always be His Way. She lied and I hope I would have

---

[1] Joseph P. Free, *Archaeology and Bible History*, rev. and exp. Howard F. Vos (Grand Rapids: Zondervan, 1992), 109

[2] Bryant Wood, *The Walls of Jericho, Creation*, March 1999, www.answersingenesis.org

[3] Matthew 1:5 *Salmon was the father of Boaz by Rahab*.

also lied. Always remember to be on God's side, not the side of the world.

4.5.3.6.   God did not destroy the people of Jericho without warning. He loved them and did not want them to perish. Read Joshua 2:10 and the verses, which follow.[1] Rehab said *we have heard.* She seems to be the only one who acted in faith.

4.5.3.7.   It is the priests who begin the invasion. They arouse the people and they move about a half-mile to the edge of the Jordan River.

4.5.3.8.   And for three days the people sanctified themselves before the Lord; they had their hearts and minds right...and on the 3rd day, as priests' feet touched the water, the river rolled back...and they crossed on dry land and set up a camp just outside the fortified Jericho.

4.5.3.9.   The crossing of the Jordan is quite similar to the crossing of the Red Sea. This crossing is *IN* to their land; the first crossing was *OUT* of a strange land.

4.5.3.10.   We note that the crossing of Jordan was as the priests stood in the waters, carrying the Ark of the Covenant. After all the people crossed over, the Ark was carried out of the dry riverbed. Immediately the river returned to normal.

4.5.3.11.   They established their camp at Gilgal and it served as the headquarters for the invasion into the land.

4.5.3.12.   The invasion is underway.

4.6. We will look at the invasion in three campaigns: Central, Southern, and Northern. Remember that faith brought them *OUT* of Egypt. It will take the same faith to *ENTER* and then *CONQUER* the Promised Land.[2]

4.6.1.   We note a discovery in 1896 of a black granite marker, the only account of Israel in Egyptian records.[3] Below two images of the god Amon were written in hieroglyphics, the details of an

---

[1] Joshua 2:10 *For we have heard how the Lord dried up the water of the Red Sea before you when you came out of Egypt......*

[2] Before they marched IN, they paused and honored God and received INNER strength to conquer. The first thing they did was to celebrate the Passover for the first time since coming out of the desert (see Passover). This celebration looked back at the deliverance and encouraged the people for what was ahead. At this time the manna they had lived on for those forty years, ceased. Now they were in a land of food. The "corn flakes" were behind, "food" was before them.

[3] The Merneptah Stele, *NIV Archaeological Study Bible: An Illustrated Walkd through Biblical History and Culture,* ed. Walter C. Kaiser, Jr., and others (Grand Rapids: Zondervan, 2005), 360

invasion of Canaan, in which Israel was in battle. The time frame was *c.* 1231 BCE and verifies that Israel was already an established power by this year, *allowing* for a much earlier date for the exodus. See Two Possible Pharaohs of the Exodus in this volume.

Depth of Bible Words and Places
Gilgal

Gilgal was the site of the Israelites' first camp after crossing the Jordan River. There, Joshua set up stones as a memorial (Joshua 4:20-24). Gilgal remained the religious location in Israel until David brought the ark to Jerusalem. It was also the site of Saul's later confirmation as king, and the place where he disobeyed Samuel's instructions, resulting in his being rejected by God as king. Today there is remaining only a small cluster of mounds just northeast of Jericho.

4.6.2.   Jericho is taken in the *first campaign*, in the central territories of the land. This was the first obstacle before them, one that required a march of faith and trust in God's leadership.

    4.6.2.1.   The wonderful and quite unusual method of warfare in Jericho (it was a twenty-minute walk from the Israelites' camp at Gilgal). I believe this unique method, instructed by God, was miraculous to show His people that they could do anything as long as they trusted Him.

    4.6.2.2.   They had no powerful weapons of warfare, no real organized army. The faith chapter of Hebrews eleven tells us how every battle is won.[1]

    4.6.2.3.   We read about the obedience to the plan of God: Seven priests bearing seven trumpets led the company; marching around the wall six days followed on the seventh day by marching around the wall seven times followed by trumpets sounding and the shout of the people. I imagine the people inside the walls mocked and laughed at the unusual site of priests leading a parade around their tall, strong walls, carrying a table! And not a sound for six days. But the seventh day came, and when the silence was broken by trumpets and people shouting, the walls of Jericho fell outward not inward, as they normally would have. Quite an unusual battle plan, the only time we have a record of this method of warfare.

---

[1] Heb 11:30 *By faith the walls of Jericho fell down*

4.6.2.4.   We then note that the house of Rahab on the wall was not destroyed. She became an honored mother in Israel, the mother of Boaz, who in turn became the husband of Ruth, the grandmother of King David.

4.6.2.5.   The city of Jericho was uncovered years ago and they found that the walls had fallen outward. See Jericho in this volume.

4.6.2.6.   *This* plan came from God's messenger following Joshua's prayer.[1]

Expanded Help Paper
Theophany

Theophany was the direct, visual manifestation or apparent incarnation of the presence of God in the Old Testament. The key word is visual, since God makes His presence and power known throughout the Bible in a variety of ways. However, even in a theophany a person does not actually see God Himself.

Theophanies proper are limited to the Old Testament, mostly common in Genesis and Exodus. The most frequent visible manifestation of God's presence in the Old Testament is the "Angel of the Lord." Other appearances that would be considered theophanies are the burning bush (Exodus 3:1-6), the pillar of cloud and the pillar of fire (Exodus 13:21-22), the cloud and fire of Sinai (Exodus 24:16-18), and the cloud of the glory of the Lord (Exodus 40:34-38). Theophanies are never given for their own sake or to satisfy a curiosity about God; rather to convey some revelation or truth about Him.

4.6.3.   The city of Ai was next (Joshua 9). It was the "key city" in taking central Canaan and would divide the land in half. This central plateau was the heart of the country, and whoever controlled this land, controlled the entire Promised Land. Coming from the east across the Jordan River, the city of Jericho guarded the approach. Next was this key city of Ai. Again, spies were sent out. They came back and said, "Oh, just send a few soldiers, easy pickings."

4.6.3.1.   But they suffered defeat in the first attempt to take Ai, not because of sending too small an army, (God is not limited by size) but because sin was in the camp. Had it not been for the hidden sin, Israel would have

---

[1] An Old Testament appearance of Jesus Christ is called a "theophany." With the appearance as a man, He would talk and give instructions to His chosen leader.

defeated Ai easily. God wanted a holy people, honest before Him. The sin issue was dealt with, and as soon as it was cleared, the Israelites experienced another victory.

4.6.3.2.　　　The men of Ai came rushing towards the Hebrews, expecting an easy victory, and at first, it seemed as though they were correct. However, they left their city unprotected[1] and Joshua's 3000 men, who were in hiding, launched a surprise attack on the city. Some 12,000 inhabitants of Ai were killed. The city was burned, but the spoils and the cattle were given to the Israelites.

Depth of Bible Words and Places
Ai

Ai, "heap of ruins," was Located east of Bethel. It was small in size—Joshua needed only 3,000 to capture it. Archeology has revealed a gate of the fortress located on the north side. Abundant ash, burned pottery, and stones remain as evidences of destruction by fire. (Joshua 8:28).

4.6.3.3.　　　Also note that it is not recorded that Joshua prayed before making plans to attack AI (as he did before Jericho).

4.6.3.4.　　　Following these victories, Joshua called the people together and they renewed their covenant with God. The people responded "amen" to each blessing as the Levites pronounced the blessings and curses commanded by Moses.

4.6.4.　　　They turned south for the *second campaign* (Joshua 9 and 10).

4.6.4.1.　　　The Canaanites, west of the Jordan were by this time afraid. They heard about Jericho and Ai. So they unified and formed a confederacy against this very strange army![2]

4.6.4.2.　　　A Few miles from Ai and close to Jerusalem... was Gibeon, a trading center...a key city in the land.[3] The

---

[1] Josh 8:17 *So not a man was left in Ai or Bethel who had not gone out after Israel*

[2] Archaeologists have found evidence of Canaanite culture of Joshua's time where the people practiced child sacrifice, religious prostitution, and snake worship in the ceremonies. Moses already knew this and had long ago warned his people to destroy them or their influence would ensnare them.

[3] Jerusalem is named for the first time in the Bible, in Joshua 10:1 *Now it came about when Adoni-zedek king of Jerusalem heard that Joshua had captured Ai.......*

people of this city knew the Hebrews were coming to defeat them. So they had to act quickly.

Depth of Bible Words and Places
Gibeon

This was the only Canaanite city to make peace with Joshua. It was located a few miles northwest of Jerusalem and became an important place of worship. Solomon had come to offer sacrifices at this city when God spoke to him in a dream.

Today it is being excavated at the present time. It was a strategic city, ruling several other cities (Joshua 10:2). The Gibeonites came to Joshua at Gilgal and deceived him into an alliance (which he honored). Later, he made them servants because of it.

4.6.4.3.   Gibeon was full of fear...so some of the Gibeonites disguised themselves in old garments, shoes, even had old, moldy bread— and lied to Joshua.[1] They told him they would serve the God of this new group of people, so a treaty was made to protect them. Note that again Joshua did not ask God for direction.[2] Perhaps he was over-confident and acted in his own wisdom.

4.6.4.4.   Joshua marches toward Gibeon to take the city, but the people of Gibeon reveal themselves as the ones having the treaty. Joshua does not like it, however he honors the treaty he had made with them and pulls away.

4.6.4.5.   The confederacy, which had been formed, turns against Gibeon because of their association with the Hebrews. Again the Gibeonites say *"Hey Joshua, how about the treaty?"* Joshua's word was his character, absolute, unbreakable. (See Expanded Help Paper, Integrity, and Character, in this volume).

4.6.4.6.   And again, Joshua honors the agreement/his word; marches back toward Gibeon and eventually defeats the five-king confederacy. Late in the day, OR

---

[1] Josh 9:4-5 ...*took worn-out sacks on their donkeys, and wineskins worn-out and torn and mended, 5 and worn-out and patched sandals on their feet, and worn-out clothes on themselves; and all the bread of their provision was dry and had become crumbled.*

[2] Josh 9:14 *So the men of Israel took some of their provisions, and did not ask for the counsel of the Lord.*

early in the morning he needs more time to defeat them, so he prays.[1]

EXPANDED HELP PAPER
Sun, Stand Still

Many explanations have been offered. I agree with what Spurgeon said: *"How He did it is no question for us, it is not ours to try and soften miracles, but to glorify God in them."* (From Spurgeon's Devotional Bible.)

Perhaps the next verse, 14, helps us.[2]

What is amazing is that God did not initiate this miracle as He usually did/does. A man did! God did as Joshua asked!

The earth actually stopped revolving (or the earth and sun revolved together). This allowed Joshua to complete the battle with total victory.

Also note what a Yale professor, (Totten, *Our Race*), in addition to reports from Egyptian and Chinese research and several other prominent scholars, have calculated that one full day is missing in the astronomical calendar.

An interesting and quite likely explanation of this story may be presented. To understand this, we must first become familiar with the physical features of the land. We realize that Joshua was responding to the agreement he made with the Gibeonites.[3] He and his military force-marched during the entire night, thus arriving at Gibeon in the dark just before dawn. This cover of darkness allowed an element of surprise upon the five kings. We then understand that Gibeon sits east of the Aijaolon Valley.[4] In relationship to their location, the sun was east, the moon was west, and the only time of day for this arrangement, was sunrise. Because Joshua came towards Gibeon form Gilgal, it means at the time of attack, the sun was in the eyes of those he attacked. As he pursued them to the west, the enemy looked back towards Joshua with the sun in their eyes. Fighting would have been almost impossible as they retreated west. Joshua requested that the sun remain in the east at dawn keeping the sun remaining in their eyes. So it was more likely that Joshua commanded the

---

[1] Josh 10:12-13 *"O sun, stand still at Gibeon, And O moon in the valley of Aijalon."* 13 *So the sun stood still, and the moon stopped.*
Archeologists have excavated this area, and dated a violent battle, which took place 1400 BCE.
[2] Josh 10:14 *There was no day like that before it or after it, when the Lord listened to the voice of a man*
[3] Josh 9:14-15 *So the men of Israel took some of their provisions, and did not ask for the counsel of the Lord. 15 Joshua made peace with them and made a covenant with them, to let them live; and the leaders of the congregation swore an oath to them.*
[4] Josh 10:12 *"O sun, stand still at Gibeon, And O moon in the valley of Aijalon."*

sun from rising, rather than the common thought of commanding the sun from going down.

4.6.5.   Next, a *third campaign*; this one to the north.

4.6.5.1.   Another confederacy, the last Canaanite group that Joshua had to face, is formed as fear spreads throughout the territory. Joshua was moving rapidly north. This time Joshua is not fooled. As he continues his northerly advance, the new confederacy gathers north of the Sea of Galilee. They thought their united army would be strong enough to hold off God's "little nation." [1]

4.6.5.2.   However, God says to Joshua in 11:6 *Do not be afraid because of them, for tomorrow at this time I will deliver all of them slain before Israel;*

4.6.5.3.   Wow, I don't know about you but this was an enemy to be feared. (*three hundred thousand armed footmen, and ten thousand horsemen, and twenty thousand chariots).* I hope that all I would need is His Word.[2]

4.6.5.4.   And of course...this huge enemy who had Israel full of terror is defeated and scattered. God spoke, Israel trusted, the enemy ran!

4.6.5.5.   You can do this when facing your enemy. Find a Word, have faith to stand on it, and watch God work His Word for you.

4.6.5.6.   Moreover, as we noted before, archeologists have excavated the cities of four of these kings, and dated their destruction...you guessed it... *c.* 1400 BCE.

---

[1] Note something written in 93 CE. Flavius Josephus (see details of his life in this Volume) was a great Jewish historian and general in the wars of the Jews against the Romans when they destroyed the Temple. We have today his works. In one of them, "Antiquities of the Jews", (I quote from that work: §18 [5.18]). It's quite educational to read his works along with the scriptures of the same period. Here's an example:

"*So the kings that lived about Mount Libanus, who were Canaanites, and those Canaanites that dwelt in the plain country, with auxiliaries out of the land of the Philistines, pitched their camp at Beroth, a city of the Upper Galilee, not far from Cadesh, which is itself also a place in Galilee. Now the number of the whole army was* three hundred thousand armed footmen, and ten thousand horsemen, and twenty thousand chariots; *so that the multitude of the enemies afrighted both Joshua himself and the Israelites; and they, instead of being full of hopes of good success, were superstitiously timorous, with the great terror with which they were stricken."*

[2] *Do not be afraid because of them, for tomorrow at this time I will deliver all of them slain before Israel;*

4.6.6.   During the conquest of the entire land, in three campaigns, thirty-one kings were defeated. However, the Canaanites had retained strongholds that later caused many difficulties. The Israelites did not complete the conquest according to God's instructions.

Depth of Bible Words and Places
Hazor

The largest city/territory in Cannan during the second millennium BCE. Hazor is the largest archaeological site in Israel. It remained important even after the Israelite conquest. Remaining fortifications and residential buildings date from the tenth century BCE until its destruction in 732 BCE (2 Kings 15:29). It is located 8.5 miles northeast of the Sea of Galilee. It was heavily fortified with walls as wide as 24'. In 1962 CE, a clay tablet was found with its name on it (discovered by a tourist!).

"Hazor formerly was the head of all those kingdoms" — thus wrote the chronicler of the Book of Joshua (11:10), and the source before him was undoubtedly reliable and accurate. Of all the sites mentioned in the Book of Joshua as having been conquered by the Israelites, none is as important as the destruction of Hazor. As a result of this victory, *"Joshua took all this land ... the mountains of Israel and its lowlands from Mt. Halak and the ascent to Seir, even as far as Baal Gad in the Valley of Lebanon below Mt. Hermon"* (Josh 11:16-17).

During thirty excavation seasons conducted at the site of ancient Hazor, it became clear that this was the largest and most important city-state in the Land of Israel in the second millennium BCE. Hazor spanned 200 acres, 10 times the size of Jerusalem in the days of King David and King Solomon.

The magnificent find uncovered within the Ceremonial Palace of the Canaanite period point to extensive commercial, cultural and artistic ties with the centers of power in the region, from Babylon in the east, through the Hittite kingdom and Egypt, all the way to Cyprus and Greece in the west. Hazor's days of grandeur ended with its fall into the hands of the Israelite tribes that settled the land. As clearly shown by the famous Merneptah Stele, dated to the last decade of the 13th century BCE, the Israelites were present in Canaan. They are credited with having brought down the Canaanite Hazor.

The visitor to Israelite Hazor has the unique opportunity to witness the reliability of the Biblical historiography first-hand and to cast his eyes upon the structures attributed to the days of the monarchs of the Kingdom of Israel, from Solomon, through Ahab and Jeroboam II, until the days of Pekah son of Remaliah.

Evidence of the Joshua-destruction by fire has been discovered with a date of Joshua's time. Excavations have revealed its total destruction. Judges 4 records that Deborah and Barak continued, "Until they destroyed" Jabin (who ruled at Hazor).

4.6.7.   Beginning in Joshua 13, we understand that the wars of Canaan were largely at an end. We read that the land was to be cleared and developed. It was not enough for the people to enter and conquer the land. They had to possess it by faith. It was God's to give. It was theirs to possess. Therefore, Joshua commands them in the first verse *"very much of the land remains to be possessed."* Perhaps if the land was divided and assigned to twelve tribes, each one would "clear its own territory of enemies." The land was divided even while other peoples were present (see the various "ites," listed in this volume).

    4.6.7.1.   The division of land for the remaining nine and one-half tribes had to be settled. The tribes of Gad, Reuben and one-half of Manasseh already chose their land east of the Jordan, before the invasion. Now Joshua releases them to return to their land and families.

    4.6.7.2.   The tribe of Levi was not given any land. But there were still twelve tribes who receive land. The tribe of Joseph had been divided into two tribes, (his sons Ephraim and Manasseh, in Genesis 48: 17-20).

    4.6.7.3.   The Levites were made helpers to all the other tribes and were dispursed among the forty-eight cities and six cities of refuge. The other tribes paid a tithe to support the Levites, who were the priests of the nation (Numbers 35:2-5; Joshua 21:1-42). The Levites were made helpers to all the other tribes and distributed in convenient locations, including east of the Jordan. We note that the cities were only *designated* as Levitical sites and did not require that all of them served that purpose.

    4.6.7.4.   The land was divided to the twelve tribes.[1]

---

[1] Note that the tribe of Dan later abandons their God-given inheritance in the south, and migrate north (Judges 18:1) to a land that was located in the 20th century CE, an archeological discovery called "tel Dan" at the foot of Mount Herman. Pottery and stone evidence has been found identifying this settlement. It is said they traded their southern land for a cool, shady northern location. It could also be noted that Dan migrated north because of the Philistines who were attempting to move east into Canaan. It was also

EXPANDED HELP PAPER
Division of Land

The people were divided into twelve territories, becoming twelve tribes.

Each tribe represented the people descending from one of Jacob's twelve sons. Each of the sons had been at their father's deathbed and received his prophecy concerning their future.

Interesting to note, Joseph's two sons represented two of the tribes, Ephraim and Manasseh, while Levi received no land but was given 48 cities with land around them.

The apportionment of land in the Book of Joshua. We would note that Judah was honored of God in a very special way and had the first portion, being allotted land in the high country, south and west of Jerusalem. The other tribes' lands divided by casting of lots.

- To Judah, 15:1-63
- To Ephraim, 16:1-10
- To Manasseh, 17:1-18
- To Benjamin, 18:11-28
- To Simeon, 19:1-9
- To Zebulun, 19:10-16
- To Issachar, 19:17-23
- To Asher, 19:24-31
- To Naphtali, 19:32-39
- To Dan, 19:40-48

Reuben and Gad had received their land east of the Jordan before Joshua led them across. Also, Manasseh had received one-half of their total allotted land on the east side, before the crossing into Canaan.

Caleb, now eighty-five years of age, was given land inside Judah for his part in the conquest, 14:6-13. He took possession of the land, drove the Anakims out of the city, and changed its name to Hebron.

Depth of Bible Words and Places
Jews

Any member of the tribe of Judah was referred to as a Jew. Later, any descendant of Abraham, and followed the Jewish religion was called a Jew. See the Expanded Help Paper, Israel and Judah in this volume; Also see Hebrews detailed in this volume.

discovered Dan had turned immediately to idols...and the tragedy? The grandson of Moses served as priest! (Judges 18:30)

4.6.7.5.　　　Cities of refuge were important, but only briefly mentioned in chapter 20. There were to be six cities established in the land. I emphasize their importance because of the special mention of them in the Scriptures. Ex 21:13, Num 35:6, 9-28, Deut 4:41-43, and Deut 19:1-10 allow an understanding of the cities.

4.6.7.6.　　　There were three east of Jordan and three west. The roads leading to each were to be clearly marked so that one who had slain another without premeditation, might quickly flee to a refuge. The cities were not available to one who was guilty of deliberate murder.

4.6.7.7.　　　The names of the six cities had meaning. Kadesh (*the sanctuary*), Shechem (*a shoulder)*, Hebron, (*communion),* Bezer (*fortress),* Ramoth (*the heights*), and Golan (*is rejoicing).*

Depth of Bible Words and Places
City of Refuge

Six cities were established for persons who accidentally killed someone in order that they could receive protection until a fair trial could be held.

Depth of Bible Words and Places
Ramoth Gilead

Ramoth Gilead was one of three cities of refuge in Trans-jordan (with Bezer Golan). In the Israel-Syrian wars, Ahab fought at Ramoth Gilead and was mortally wounded (1 Kings 22:1-40). Today, the ruins of Gilead may be viewed. Gilead died here.

4.6.7.8.　　　Similar to what Moses did, and also similar in age, Joshua, 110 yrs old, gives his final two messages to the leaders. He reviews what has happened and charges them to obey the Lord *"choose you this day whom you will serve..."* (24:25)

4.6.7.9.　　　Joshua sets down the statutes and writes them into the book of the Law.

4.6.7.10.　　　So he dies...and nowhere is there any record of his committing sin against God during his 110 years. May we have a similar report! It was *his* name, Joshua, translated into the Greek as "Jesus."

THIRTEEN

Judges

1   We go forth into Judges.

The name "Judges" is a fitting name, referring to the unique leaders God sent to preserve them from enemies. The name means "deliverers" or even "saviors." The book is not a chronological book, rather it is thematic.

Samuel probably wrote both Judges and Ruth. 1 Sam 10:25 reads *Then Samuel told the people the ordinances of the kingdom, and wrote them in the book and placed it before the Lord.*

Judges spans a period from Joshua to immediately before Saul, approximately 1392 to 1050 BCE.

Judges is a sequel to Joshua, continuing the story of conquest and settlement. They also formed one book along with Ruth, in the Hebrew Bible.

A Basic Outline of Judges
1. Review and Preview, Cps 1-2
2. Times of Judges, Cps 3-16
3. Time of Decay, Cps 17-21

Depth of Bible Words and Places
Judges Key Word: *Deliverance*
Found in 15:18, and few other places. It's more of a theme of the book. *Deliverance*. A different word from the key word in Exodus, which was *delivered*. This word in Judges means "victory" or even "safety." The Bible always associates this

deliverance...with God. He is the one who brings victory or safety. Psalm 51:14 and 71:14 praise Him for it. Psalm 33:17 records deliverance is not found in horses but only in the Lord. Psalm 108:12 says it is not in the capabilities of people.

Jesus in Judges...He is The Judge and Lawgiver. Failure happens! He is the savior of a fallen people.

---

2   After Joshua's death, Israel had work to do. And the Lord had told him already back in Joshua cp 13 these words:[1]

2.1. There were many Canaanites surrounding the new borders, separating the Central Tribes from the Northern and Southern groups.

2.2. We must realize the difficulties during this period.

    2.2.1.   The Israelites were still living in open camps

    2.2.2.   They entered a land full of difficult people

    2.2.3.   They were struggling to carve a new existence/homeland. As a result, Satan takes advantage of their separation.

    2.2.4.   When Israel entered Canaan, it had to be content to live in the mountains...for it *"could not drive out the inhabitants of the valley, because they had chariots of iron"* (Judges 1:19). Realistically, the tribes were functioning individually and were fragmented, moving separately into particular areas on their own initiative. Note the Psalmist.[2]

    2.2.5.   Immediately in Judges 1 we see the sequence begin...idolatry is working its way into Israel. In addition, we will see this idolatry plague the Jews until they return from captivity in 536 BCE—over 800 years of idolatry.

    2.2.6.   A four-part sequence repeatedly occurred during this time in Israel. A cycle or circle of similar events:

        2.2.6.1.   Israel's turning from God

        2.2.6.2.   God's allowing military defeat and enslavement

        2.2.6.3.   The people would then pray for deliverance

        2.2.6.4.   God would raise up a "judge" to defeat the enemy and deliver them

---

[1] Joshua 13:1...*the Lord said to him, "You are old and advanced in years, and very much of the land remains to be possessed*

[2] Ps 105:11 *"To you I will give the land of Canaan As the portion of your inheritance,"* 12 *When they were only a few men in number, Very few, and strangers in it.*

2.2.6.5. God tells them if you leave the Canaanites in you midst, they will be as thorns and "a snare" to you. However, His word was not obeyed.

2.2.7. Israel was a group of separated territories with no central government and no leader to replace Joshua. They forgot the past blessings, and did what was evil in the sight of the Lord. [1] Judges is a book about the unsurrendered life. The book begins with compromise and ends with confusion, similar to today concerning an unsurrendered life. [2]

2.2.8. Keep your eyes on Him. Distractions cause weakness, which leads to destruction.

2.3. This book of Judges was a period of very loosely unorganized territories, with confederacies and foreign territories separating them. We find a people who God loved so much, that even though they fell to spiritual lows, He provided leaders to rescue them. They were not Judges as we think of Judges; rather most of them were military "deliverers." We see a period of six cycles.

2.3.1. Six apostasies[3], six bondages to other nations, six prayers for deliverance, and six deliverances.

2.3.2. Rather than driving out the "ites" from their land, they intermarried with them, sharing their land and beliefs. The result was a falling away from a strong belief in God and accepting other gods.

2.3.3. In each case God raised up a judge to free some or all of the tribes. There wasn't a single judge over all the tribes. In fact, in some cases there was more than one judge in the same period over separate tribes, making exact dates difficult to determine. They could be considered "local" judges. They seemed to be marked out, called, set apart, by Yahweh.[4] See The Period of Twelve Judges below.

2.3.4. A total of fourteen deliverers are named, six of them were military leaders; two were an example to illustrate spiritual

---

[1] Judg 3:7 *The sons of Israel did what was evil in the sight of the Lord, and forgot the Lord their God and served the Baals and the Asheroth.*

[2] This confusion is summarized in Judges 17:6 *In those days there was no king in Israel; every man did what was right in his own eyes.* There was confusion in their religious life (17:18), in their moral life (cp 19), and in their political life (cp 21)

[3] Apostasy is a giving up of the life you have. It's voluntary embracing of a different state of life; we tag a Christian who gives up his faith as apostasy.

[4] Judg 3:10 *The Spirit of the Lord came upon him, and he judged Israel* (Othniel); Judg 11:29 *Now the Spirit of the Lord came upon Jephthah;* Judg 14:6 *The Spirit of the Lord came upon him mightily* (Samson).

contrast: Eli a bad example and Samuel a good example. Five of the judges are listed among the heroes of faith in Hebrews 11: Barak, Gideon, Jephthah, Samson, and Samuel.

Depth of Bible Words and Places
Gaza

Gaza was a major Philistine city (located in the territory given to Judah) from the time of the judges until its destruction by Alexander the Great following the close of The Old Testament. Located in the strip of land, which today is called Gaza Strip.

The Period of Twelve Judges*, approximately 1392-1050 BCE

Reference in Judges	Oppressor	Years of Oppression**	Deliverer/Judge	Years of Peace Following **
3:7-11	King of Mesopotamia, Chushan-Rishathaim	8 1400-1392 BCE	**Othniel,** Tribe of Judah, son of Kenaz, brother of Caleb	40 1392-1352 BCE
3:12-30	King of Moab, Eglon	18 1360-1342 BCE	**Ehud,** Tribe of Benjamin, son of Gera	80 1342-1262 BCE
3:31	Philistines	1	**Shamgar,** foreigner	unknown
Cps 4,5	King of Canaan, Jabin	20 1280-1260 BCE	**Deborah/Barak,** Tribe of Ephraim	40 1260-1220 BCE
6:1-8:32	Midianites	7 1240-1233 BCE	**Gideon,** Tribe of Manasseh, son of Joash	40 1191-1151 BCE
10:1-5		3 1200-1197 BCE	**Tola,** Tribe of Issachar, son of Puah/**Jair,** Tribe of Manasseh	45 1197-1152 BCE
10:6-12:15	Ammonites	18 1153-1135 BCE	**Jephthah,** Tribe of Manasseh/**Ibzan,** Tribe of Judah or Zebulun/**Elon,** Tribe of Zebulun/**Abdon,** Tribe of Ephraim	6 7 10 8 1035-1104 BCE
13:1-16:31	Philistines	40 1141-1101 BCE	**Samson,** a Nazarite, Tribe of Dan	

* Eli and Samuel were also Judges (not in Book of Judges); there were a total of 1 4 Judges.

**There were several years of overlap in different territories. Compiled by Thomas Hiegel

2.3.5.   We will not detail every judge. Allow me to summarize the highlights of this period.[1]

2.4. The cycles of Judges

2.4.1.   The *first cycle* began from the northeast and forced the tribes into oppression for eight years. When they finally cry out to God, He sends them Caleb's nephew, named Othniel, to deliver them, and forty years of peace follow. He was one of the better judges; entirely because of what is recorded about him in Judges 3:10, *"The Spirit of the Lord came upon him..."* God can and does use a seemingly weak man to do His work. (There is hope for you and me!)

    2.4.1.1.   After his death, there was no leader, so idolatry slips back in and causes oppression, and the cycle continues.

2.4.2.   Next, a Moabite invasion from the southeast under King Eglon of Moab begins the *second cycle,* and they capture Jericho. Oppression continues for eighteen years until God raises up Ehud

    2.4.2.1.   Ehud (meaning "red hair") was a left-handed judge. Very little strength is found in this man. We only know he gained access to and then killed the king of Moab, Eglon, resulting in thousands of lives being saved.[2]

    2.4.2.2.   Shamgar was also a very ordinary man, used by God in cp 3. He used what he had, an "ox goad" and killed six hundred Philistines who invaded from the southwest. Israel did not have access to any iron weapons (see Philistines detailed in this volume); this judge used what he had. Eighty years of peace followed.

Depth of Bible Words and Places
Ox goad

Found in Judges 3:31. A rod about eight feet long sharpened to a point and sometimes covered with iron. It was used in driving animals. Ecc 12:11 *The words of wise men are like goads, and masters of these collections are like well-driven*

---

[1] A tablet found in 1896 CE in a Pharaoh's temple is the only Egyptian record which mentions Israel. This Pharaoh invaded Israel about the time of the Judges. It recognizes a group of people in Canaan called Israelites.

[2] Eglon was so fat that the dagger used to kill him by Ehud was hidden in Eglon's layers of fat. Ehud escaped because the soldiers did not see the dagger and thought Eglon was sleeping. Moab, located east of the Dead Sea, invaded, and established a headquarters in Jericho. Ehud collected tribute from the Israelites. The abandoned palace of Eglon was located there in 1933 CE. (Judges 3).

nails. An animal injuring itself by coming against the sharp point of the goad is the metaphor used by Christ to Saul in Acts 9:5.

> 2.4.2.3.   May each of us use what we have! Moses used his rod, David used five stones, and a little boy used five loaves and a few fish.
>
> 2.4.2.4.   Certainly we have seen that the first three judges had little ability; they used what was available to them. Quite a lesson for each of us.

2.4.3.   A *third cycle* of oppression follows a period of religious corruption in Israel. Jabin, king of Canaan with a great army and nine hundred chariots held the Israelites in slavery for twenty years. He ruled from Hazor.

> 2.4.3.1.   Deborah & Barak in cps 4 and 5 met King Jabin on a battlefield at Megiddo. Barak raised an alliance of six of the tribes (perhaps unprecedented in the era of Judges). For the first time they succeeded in smashing and routing a force of chariots in open battle, proving they could meet the military might of the Canaanites. Confusion brought by a sudden storm resulted in eventual victory. Deborah, a mother not looking for a "job," was raised up by God to call upon a weak general to "go, move forward." This weak general, Barak, is shown hiding behind Deborah in cp 4.[1]
>
> 2.4.3.2.   Deborah seemed to love Israel, and for their sake went with Barak against the enemy. Deborah, also a prophetess, saw a total victory that would eventually come. She was perhaps Israel's most outstanding judge.
>
> 2.4.3.3.   Her song in cp 5, following the short-lived defeat of the Canaanites, is one of the first recorded songs of the human race. It alludes to a lack of men to take leadership, so she assumed that place, for the sake of Israel.

2.4.4.   Chapter 6 records, that following forty years of freedom, Israel again returned to evil practices. The *fourth cycle* begins. This time invasion comes from the east from the Midianites and

---

[1] *Now she sent and summoned Barak the son of Abinoam from Kedesh-naphtali, and said to him, "Behold, the Lord, the God of Israel, has commanded, 'Go and march to Mount Tabor, and take with you ten thousand men from the sons of Naphtali and from the sons of Zebulun. 7 'I will draw out to you Sisera, the commander of Jabin's army, with his chariots and his many troops to the river Kishon, and I will give him into your hand.'" 8 Then Barak said to her, "If you will go with me, then I will go; but if you will not go with me, I will n ot go."*

Amalekites along with various tribes as numerous "as grasshoppers."

2.4.4.1.   The Israelites fled into caves and again "cried out unto the Lord." Archeologists have located these caves.

2.4.4.2.   The Midianites of this period was a band of wandering tribes. They would raid territories of Israel, taking food and anything they needed, then moving on to other locations. A new "discovery" made it possible for the Midianites to terrorize Israel...the taming of the camel.

2.4.4.3.   Gideon, son of Joash, of the tribe of Manasseh is raised up during this period, and certainly does not appear to be a deliverer or hero. He is first seen threshing wheat in secret *DOWN* by a wine press. He is afraid of the Midianites (they had killed his brothers previously), and is hiding away from the usual location of threshing which was *high on* a hill.

2.4.4.4.   The pre-incarnate Christ appears to him in 6:12 and commands him to destroy Baal's altar that his father had built. He obeyed and then erected an altar to Yahweh.[1]

2.4.4.5.   I love how God calls things that are not, as though they are. A seemingly weak man is called by God, using the spoken Word, calls him *"o valiant warrior."*

2.4.4.6.   Gideon and his 32,000-man army that he gathered...are reduced by God to 300 qualified men (1%). With their only weapons of lamps, pitchers, and trumpets, they defeat the thousands of warriors of the Midianites. God causes the Midianites to fight each other as He brings about confusion in their midst. Isaiah and Paul both mention Gideon in their writings.

Depth of Bible Words and Places
Lamps, Pitchers, Trumpets

The sight of trumpets and torches, at first concealed in clay pitchers, when suddenly revealed, would be dramatic! Each

---

[1] Judges 6:12 *The angel of the Lord appeared to him and said to him, "The Lord is with you, O valiant warrior." 13 Then Gideon said to him, "O my lord, if the Lord is with us, why then has all this happened to us? And where are all His miracles which our fathers told us about, saying, 'Did not the Lord bring us up from Egypt?' But now the Lord has abandoned us and given us into the hand of Midian."*

light could indicate a legion behind it, indicating a large enemy may soon attack. Each of the 300 men had a trumpet in one hand, and an empty pitcher with a lamp burning inside it, in the other. Imagine...breaking the pitchers (which would have protected the torch from any breeze), holding the lamp in their left hands, and then crying *"The sword of the Lord and of Gideon."* 301 trumpets (including Gideon) blaring forth and a sudden cracking of pitchers revealing lamps were indeed startling. The Midianites fled!

2.4.4.7. After the conquest, the central tribes offered to make Gideon their king, but he refused, consenting only to serve as their judge. Eventually he retired to private life, passing on *at a good old age* (Judges 8:29).

2.4.4.8. His son, Abimelech, attempted to become king of Israel by taking control of Shechem. His rule was violent, never called a judge. His skull was cracked, and was killed by his armor bearer.

2.4.4.9. Other Judges follow; Tola and Jair ruled for specific periods.

2.4.5. The tribes of Judah, Benjamin, and Ephraim, located in the center of the land were invaded and oppressed by the Ammonites for eighteen years, the *fifth cycle*. They cry out and God said *"No I will not deliver you any more, go cry to the gods you have chosen."* (10:13-14). Does even God run out of patience?

Depth of Bible Words and Places
Shechem

A great fortress has been excavated there. It lasted until Abimelech destroyed it. The impressive gate was 54 feet wide and 44 feet deep. Evidence of massive destruction has been found, dating to Abimelech (Judges 9:45).

2.4.5.1. However, God decides later to send another deliverer, Jephthah, who judges for six years.

2.4.5.2. Japhthah was an illegitimate child, son of a harlot. Later in Proverbs, we will read of a young lad who is advised to keep clear of *"a strange woman,"* in reference to this same type. Israel thought of harlots as being strangers from a foreign land. Jephthah is an example of this belief. Gilead had married a foreign woman who gave birth to Japhthah. Because she was thought of as *"a strange woman,"* Japhthah was cast away by his own brothers.

So this judge doesn't have much of a foundation to be used by God, similar to the other judges who each seemed to have a weakness. Japhthah is an illustration for us today: a person with an unhappy childhood need not grow up to be unsuccessful. God uses the seemingly unusable. He knows what He is doing.

2.4.5.3.   So when Israel is attacked by Ammonites, they immediately thought of Jephthah to come to their aid. He had developed into the leader of a small military community and agrees to help them as long as he could rule them as a judge, when finished.

2.4.5.4.   Later, he becomes a little frightened, for he goes from being in exile to a judge. He seems to refer to the Lord (11:9), as though they were closely acquainted. Apparently Jephthah had not rejected the God of the people and family who had rejected him. Victory is experienced through Jephthah as the Spirit of the Lord became his helper. Again God used an unlikely man to deliver His people.

2.4.5.5.   There were three more judges, of who very little is mentioned. I don't know why they are listed. God knows. Ibzan, Elon, and Abdon.

2.4.6.   Then a well-known deliverer in cps 13-16, the *sixth and final cycle*.

2.4.6.1.   The Southern tribes, who had returned to idolatry, have now served the Philistines for forty yrs. The Philistines invade, first oppressing two tribes, Dan and Judah, followed by some of the other territories. So again a deliverer was raised up.

2.4.6.2.   Sampson, from the tribe of Dan, raised as a strict Nazarite (Numbers 6:1-21), with great physical strength but great moral weakness, was to deliver the Central tribes.

Depth of Bible Words and Places
Palestine

Palestine was a nation who occupied a territory along the southern coast of the Mediterranean Sea, (Gaza today). We may also refer to the Philistines/Philistia. It gradually was the name used when referring to the entire territory between Egypt and Syria.

Depth of Bible Words and Places

Philistines

These were among the several groups of *sea people* occupying Philistia, the region along the southern coast of the Mediterranean Sea. The Philistines were the enemies of the Israelites, invading Canaan in the 12th century BCE, and well-attested, from Samson's slaying of a thousand Philistines (Judges 15) and David's battle with the Philistine giant Goliath (1 Samuel 17).

The Philistines were traders and seafarers who lived in the area between what is now Gaza and Tel Aviv from 1200 to about 600 BCE. They spoke a language of Indo-European origin.

They were also said to have been experts in making wine and oil, certainly not lacking in culture. Described by Rameses III as tall, slim warriors wearing tasseled kelts and ribbed helmets, originating from Cyprus or Crete. The attempted to invade Egypt in 1177 BCE but were turned away. They retreated to Canaan and settled in previously conquered land, a fertile strip forty miles long and fifteen miles deep along the Mediterranean coastal plain. The Philistines were in competition with God's nation during most of the Old Testament period. Saul also fought "the Philistines" on Mt. Gilboa, another site in the north (1 Sam 41) where "the Philistines" hung the bodies of Saul and his three sons.

They were ahead of the Hebrews in technology because they mastered metallurgy, making use of metal to perfect spearheads and battle-axes. Sea Peoples' javelin heads found at several northern sites have an elongated blade, which very close parallels Aegean and Cypriot forms. They controlled much of Palestine and worshipped Canaanite gods. David conquered them, but they still had battles with both the Northern and Southern Kingdoms during the following centuries. Recent discoveries reveal they were a people who did not practice circumcision, ate pork and dog, and were experts in making wine and oil. They assimilated to the civilization of the Canaanites and intermarried with them. Even their language was eventually replaced by a local Canaanite dialect.

2.4.6.3.   During Samson's time, the Philistines began to overrun the Israelites. They held closely the secret of smelting iron (1 Samuel 13:19-22) which allowed a supremacy over the Hebrews because of strong weaponry. However, by the end of David's reign Israel obtained this advanced knowledge also. It was David who broke the power of the Philistines approximately in 1000 BCE.

2.4.6.4. Samson's life is preached and taught probably by every preacher and teacher ever born. What a life!

2.4.6.4.1. The 300 foxes in a grain field,

2.4.6.4.2. A thousand Philistines massacred with a jaw bone,

2.4.6.4.3. The attempt to capture him; he tore loose the posts and gate at Gaza and carried them off into the hills.

2.4.6.4.4. Picking up gates was easy...it was the charms of Delilah that were too much for him to handle!

2.4.6.4.5. Of course that last great victory.[1]

2.5. The days, which followed, were filled with confusion and civil war. The reason is recorded in both 18:1 and 19:1.[2] They should have accepted the King of Kings.

2.5.1. A war then broke out between the tribe of Benjamin and the other eleven tribes, which almost destroyed Benjamin; only 600 men escaped and hid. It was many years before Benjamin had any standing again in Israel.

2.5.2. This is the period when the tribe of Dan journeyed northward establishing a new settlement for their tribe, founding the city of Dan (Judges 18). Their original territory, west of Benjamin, brought them up against the Philistines and other tough enemies in the south.[3] They failed to conquer their assigned land and moved to the far north. Dan established a form of worship contrary to Hebrew law and became a main center of idolatry in northern Palestine.

2.5.3. The final words in the book of Judges again tell the story.[4]

3 The next book, the book of Ruth, is really a sequel to Judges. It covers eleven or twelve years and bridges Judges to Kings. The book is named after the woman who is the focal point in the story, and takes place near Bethlehem.

3.1. The valuable ancestry in the final verses of Ruth verifies the lineage of Ruth with David, and is also listed in the New Testament, Matt 1:5 and Luke 3:32.

---

[1] Judges 16:30...the dead whom he killed at his death were more than those whom he killed in his life

[2] In those days there was no king of Israel;

[3] Judg 1:34 Then the Amorites forced the sons of Dan into the hill country, for they did not allow them to come down to the valley;

[4] Judg 21:25 In those days there was no king in Israel; everyone did what was right in his own eyes.

A Basic Outline of Ruth
1. Naomi and Ruth, the ten years of Cp 1
2. The two years of Boaz and Ruth, Cps 2-3-4

Jesus in Ruth...He is the redeemer shown in the life of Boaz

Depth of Bible Words and Places
Ruth Key Word: *Redeemer*

Found in 2:1, 20; 3:9, 12, 13. The Hebrew word ga'al *Kinsman-Redeemer* is illustrated in the story of Ruth. It means to "play the part of a kinsman." It refers to a close relative who becomes protector. He was to guard the family rights; a redeemer. In Old Testament Law, a near relative had the right to act on behalf of a person in trouble or in danger. When persons or possessions were in the grip of a hostile power, the kinsman might act to redeem (to win release and freedom).

The marriage of Boaz to Ruth involved buying back Naomi's family land, and meant that their son would carry on Naomi's family line. Jesus, by taking on humanity, became our near Kinsman, with the right to redeem you and me.

Jesus is called our Redeemer in 1 Peter 1:18-19.

3.1.1.   It takes place during a time of oppression followed by a famine in the land; the setting God uses to give us this beautiful story.[1]

3.1.2.   First recognize the characters in the early section of the story: Naomi, her husband (Elimelech), their two sons (Mahlon and Chilion), and two daughters-in-law (Orpha and Ruth), all living in Moab. After ten years and following the death of all three men, three widows are left with no children and remain in Moab.

Depth of Bible Words and Places
Moab

A land located east of the Jordan, settled by the descendants of Lot's son, Ammon. They became a numerous people expanding their land to include the area from the plain of Heshbon to the wady Kurahi. It was in this land that the Israelites had their last encampment. Eglon, king of Moab, invaded Israel and oppressed the people until the Judge Ehud delivered them. Ruth was a Moabite.

---

[1] Ruth 1:1 *there was a famine in the land*

3.1.3.   Naomi decides to return to her home in Bethlehem with her two dauthters-in-law. However, Orpha returns to Moab while Ruth remains with Naomi[1]

3.1.4.   We make special note of one reason the book is preserved for us: Ruth, a Gentile, gives birth to the grandfather of David, whose royal line, thirteen centuries later, gives us the "Babe of Bethlehem" our Savior! The final verses of the book contain this striking revelation:[2]

3.2. It is easy to misunderstand some of the story here, unless we grasp the customs of those ancient days.

3.2.1.   For instance, when Ruth went at night to the threshing floor where Boaz and his men were threshing wheat, and lay down at his feet, no immorality is suggested (3:6-9). This was a symbolic act expressing Ruth's willingness to place herself under the protection of Boaz (the son of Rahab from Jericho, which made him part Canaanite).

3.2.2.   Similarly, the discussion at the gate, and the taking off the sandal, reflect Old Testament customs. The city gates were where the older men gathered and where business could be transacted in front of many witnesses. Taking off the sandal and passing it had the same force in Israel in those days as signing a contract has in ours.

3.2.3.   Consider some lessons for each of us, from Ruth :

     3.2.3.1.   We see redemption of all believers in 2:12. I remind you, Ruth was from the land of Lot, a Moabites, a Gentile.

     3.2.3.2.   Women are co-heirs with men, of salvation.

     3.2.3.3.   God takes care of ordinary people

     3.2.3.4.   Also as already mentioned, we see David's "right to the throne," traced back to the tribe of Judah.

3.3. By the providence of God, Ruth in Bethlehem, seeks and finds work gleaning in the field of a wealthy man, Boaz. It was springtime in Bethlehem during barley harvest when Naomi and Ruth returned.

---

[1]Ruth 1:16 *But Ruth said, "Do not urge me to leave you or turn back from following you; for where you go, I will go, and where you lodge, I will lodge.*

[2] Ruth 4:16-22 *Then Naomi took the child and laid him in her lap, and became his nurse. 17 The neighbor women gave him a name, saying, "A son has been born to Naomi!" So they named him Obed. He is the father of Jesse, the father of David. 18 Now these are the generations of Perez: to Perez was born Hezron, 19 and to Hezron was born Ram, and to Ram, Amminadab, 20 and to Amminadab was born Nahshon, and to Nahshon, Salmon, 21 and to Salmon was born Boaz, and to Boaz, Obed, 22 and to Obed was born Jesse, and to Jesse, David.*

The only living relative refused to conform to the Hebrew law (Deuteronomy 25:5-10) which allowed a childless widow to marry her husband's nearest relative. A similar law was followed by Assyrians and Hittites.

3.3.1.　　　Boaz favored Ruth and soon came to love her, marry her and together they had a son named Obed.

SECTION 6
The Kingdom Begins

1 and 2 Samuel, 1 Chronicles 10-29, Psalms 32, 52
The period from 1100 to 975 BCE

Theme Statement: "Your house and your kingdom shall endure before Me forever" 2 Sam 7:16

THE KEYS IN SECTION SIX

Section 6: The Kingdom Begins

Keys to First Samuel—

A Key Word: Hears

The Key Verses (13:14; 15:22)

13:14 "But now your kingdom shall not endure. The Lord has sought out for Himself a man after His own heart, and the Lord has appointed him as ruler over His people, because you have not kept what the Lord commanded you."

15:22 Samuel said, "Has the Lord as much delight in burnt offerings and sacrifices as in obeying the voice of the Lord? Behold, to obey is better than sacrifice, and to heed than the fat of rams.

Key Chapter (15)

The Key People in 1 Samuel

Eli—judged Israel for forty years; also a high priest; not a good father; trained Samuel (1:3–28; 2:11–4:18)

Hannah—Samuel's mother who dedicated him to the Lord when he was a baby (1:2–2:11, 21)

Samuel—ministered as priest, prophet, and judge of Israel; used by God to anoint Israel's first two kings (1:20; 2:11, 18–26; 3:1–21; 7:3–13:15; 15:1–16:13; 19:18–24; 25:1; 28:3–16)

Saul—chosen by God to be the first king of Israel; failed God; attempted to kill David; turned to a sorcerer and soon was killed (9:2–11:15; 13:1–19:24; 20:24–33; 21:10, 11; 22:6–24:22; 25:44–27:4; 28:3–31:12)

Jonathan—Saul's son and close friend of David; protected David against his father, Saul (13:1–14:49; 18:1–23:18; 31:2)

David—greatest king of Israel; also a shepherd, musician, and poet; direct ancestor to Jesus Christ (16:11–30:27)

Keys to Second Samuel—

A Key Word: Ark

The Key Verses (7:12–13; 22:21)

7:12 "When your days are complete and you lie down with your fathers, I will raise up your descendant after you, who will come forth from you, and I will establish his kingdom. 13 "He shall build a house for My name, and I will establish the throne of his kingdom forever.
22:21 "The Lord has rewarded me according to my righteousness; According to the cleanness of my hands He has recompensed me.

The Key Chapter (11)

The Key People in 2 Samuel

David—(See above Key People from 1 Samuel)

Joab—David's military commander (2:13–3:39; 8:16; 10:7–12:27; 14:1–33; 18:2–24:9)

Bathsheba—committed adultery with David; mother of Solomon; direct ancestor of Jesus (11:1–26; 12:24)

Nathan—prophet and advisor to David; used by God to reveal David's sin, urged him to repent (7:2–17; 12:1–25)

Absalom—David's son who attempted to overthrow the throne of Israel (3:3; 13:1–19:10)

Approximate dates of key events in Section 6	
1105-1055 BCE	The Events of 1 Samuel; Samuel's anointing of the united kingdom's first king, Saul

1055-1015 BCE	The Events of 2 Samuel; David

FOURTEEN

The Kingdom Begins

1   The books of Samuel begin Section 6: *The KINGDOM BEGINS.*

1.1. This next period of time can be a little confusing. I'll do my best to clarify the period. We'll look at the two books of Samuel, 1 Chronicles, and a couple of Psalms which fall into the period of history following Judges; *c.* 1100 through 975 BCE, approximately 125 yrs.

1.2. Originally, the two books of Samuel were a single work in the earliest Hebrew manuscripts. They became two when the Hebrew was translated into Greek and also Latin. The original name for the *single book* was "Samuel," after the man God used to establish the kingship in Israel.

1.3. Now stay with me…The Latin Vulgate Translation named these books "First and Second Kings" and the present books of 1 and 2 Kings, were named "Third and Fourth Kings." So the books of Samuel and Kings present one continuous story. The books of Chronicles repeat much of these four books (Samuel and Kings)—only with a different emphasis. See details for Structure of the Old Testament in Chapter TWO in this volume. It is pretty well accepted that the author of 1 and 2 Samuel is unknown.

1.4. The theme of this section comes from 2 Samuel 7:16 *Your house and your kingdom shall endure before Me forever;*

A Basic Outline of 1 Samuel
PERSONS
1.   Samuel: the last Judge, and first Prophet, Cps 1-7
2.   Saul the first king, Cps 8-15
3.   David and Saul, Cps 16-31

A Basic Outline of 2 Samuel
DAVID
1.   David rules Judah, Cps 1-2 David rules all Israel, Cps 3-5

2. David's Glory years, Cps 6-8
3. David's Troubles, Cps 9-20
4. David's Final years, Cps 21-24

Depth of Bible Words and Places
1 Samuel Key Word: *Hears*

Read 1 Samuel 1:13; 2:23; 7:9; 8:18. An important word used over 1,100 times in the Old Testament. It meant "total attention"; much more than listening; it also included obedience. God delights to use the one who hears and then acts. A "doer."

Depth of Bible Words and Places
2 Samuel Key Word: *Ark*

In 2 Samuel we read the Key Word, *ark* in 6:2,4,20,12,17; 15:24. This was a wooden chest overlaid with gold and the "home" to the two tablets of Moses. It was always placed in the Holy of Holies, and represented His Covenant with them. The word itself just meant "a chest."

Jesus in Samuel...He is our *future king anointed by God*.

In addition, 1 Chronicles fits in this period.

A Basic Outline of 1 Chronicles
1. Genealogies Cps 1-9
2. Saul Cp 10
3. David Cps 11-29

Many of the Scriptures in 1 Chronicles are similar to 1 and 2 Samuel, so we will not read many of the duplicates. (Refer to Bible that includes cross references.) Samuel emphasized the historical side while Chronicles is the spiritual side, both during the same period.

1.5. Samuel was Israel's final judge (the 14th)...AND...its first Prophet. So the first eight cps of 1 Samuel close the period of judges and set the stage for the Kings. It brings the two together.

1.6. Samuel was born in answer to the prayer of his mother, Hannah (1 Sam 1:11). Momma quickly dedicates him to the Lord. He later became God's man of prayer:

1.6.1. As a child (1 Samuel 3:1-19)
1.6.2. Victory came through prayer (7:5-10)
1.6.3. Prayed when the nation wanted a king (8:6)

1.6.4.   Intercessory prayer was his life (12:19-23)

1.7. He was trained in the temple at Shiloh by the priest Eli, who was the thirteenth Judge. Eli's story is not always a good one. God shows us a spiritual contrast in these two final judges, Eli and Samuel.

Depth of Bible Words and Places
Shiloh

Shiloh was located north of Jerusalem. Samuel was raised there, and mentored under Eli the high priest.

This also was where Joshua erected the tabernacle, making Shiloh Israel's religious center for the next 300 years. Shiloh was destroyed by the Philistines in the early 11th century BCE.

Excavations have revealed a large building complex prior to 1050 BCE.

1.8. God personally called Samuel during his childhood, speaking to him during the night hours, telling him of the destruction of Eli's household.

1.8.1.   Samuel did not realize that God was speaking to him. God called to young Samuel again and again, until he realized Who was speaking to him.

1.9. Eli's sons were idolaters, and later were killed in a battle with the Philistines. The Ark of the Covenant was carried off to Dagon's temple. The Philistines experience nothing but trouble from this time forward.

1.10.   A great failure on the part of a father who refused to discipline his children. When Eli hears of the death of his boys he falls at the city gate and breaks his neck.[1] He died at the age of ninety-eight after judging Israel forty years. Eli's wife died from the shock of giving birth. See the next Expanded Help Paper.

EXPANDED HELP PAPER
A Lesson For Fathers

1 Samuel 2:12 *Now the sons of Eli were worthless men; they did not know the LORD.*

---

[1] 1 Sam 4:18 Eli fell off the seat backward by the side of the gate. His neck was broken and he died, for he was an old man and heavy.

First realize Eli was a preacher, a priest. As we read this story in 1 Samuel, we discover Eli's sons defied God's instructions, 1 Samuel 2:17. Thus the sin of the young men was very great before the LORD, for the men despised the offering of the LORD.

The question arises to me: "Why did the sons of a preacher, the sons of a good man, of all people, turn out to be *worthless men*?" What was wrong in their training, to cause this?

It went back to dad. I see the answer in 3:13 *"For I have told him that I am about to judge his house forever for the iniquity which he knew, because his sons brought a curse on themselves <u>and he did not rebuke them</u>."*

Eli saw the errors in his sons, and looked the other way. He thought God would understand and also take no action. This will work out on its own. However, God does not "understand," and the job of correction was up to Eli.

May I offer four suggestions from this story? Perhaps this will help families:

One, families that disintegrate, has parents who are preoccupied with an occupation to the exclusion of family needs.

Eli was a busy priest and judge, but that was not the problem. Eli failed to give his boys the proper attention and discipline.

It makes me stop and think. My daughter saw me teach, pray around a table, and take her to church. But I realize that was not enough. Is that all she knew of her father? I would hope she learned to know me as her dad, one who was always there for her, and yet disciplined her when it was needed. One thing I believe she learned, was when I said something, it was done. I did not back off what I said.

"The sons of Eli knew not the Lord" because their father was not with them enough. They did not really know dad.

Proverbs 19:18 *Discipline your children while there is hope. If you don't, you will ruin their lives.* (NLT).

Two, families that disintegrate have parents who refuse to face the severity of their children's actions.

Eli knew how difficult his sons had become, yet he did nothing!

Too many parents deny there is a problem.

Always remember your children, who are now very young, are impressionable

Three, families that disintegrate failed to respond quickly and thoroughly to the warnings of others.

Take the early reports seriously and get involved.

Listen to what you are taught by good teachers; your pastor or youth pastor; friends.

Do not always jump to your child's defense!

Do not be like Eli. He did not listen to a man of God who came to him (1 Sam 2:27) and he later paid dearly for his negligence.

Families that disintegrate rationalize wrong behavior and thereby become part of the problem.

Eli participated in his sons' behavior.

Eli rationalized and excused the sins of his sons while eating meat that had been stolen from the altar.

Fourth, I find a final thought, much later in 1 Sam 8:1-4. Samuel, who was also raised in Eli's home, must not have learned much concerning children. For we find that he too failed this area. Read it in 1 Samuel 8:1-4.

As this is pondered, evaluate your family. Then put action with your thoughts. Only on the rarest occasions does the Lord bless someone for merely listening to Him. Faith is an action. Problems like those of Eli do not solve themselves. They multiply and intensify with the passing of time. If the willful acts of rebellion are permitted and never resolved, they become unwelcome gifts when your children make their own choices.

1.11. The Ark of the Covenant was carried to the Dagons' temple in Ashdod where it remained seven months. Each morning the Philistines' idol was found lying face downward before the ark; also, the Philistine people suffered plagues. The Philistines decided (in wisdom!) to return the Ark to Israel. When the Ark was placed in a new cart, only drawn by two cows, it was transported directly to the land of Israel.[1] Sadly, it remained in the home of Abinadab in Kirjath-jearim for approximately one hundred years.

Depth of Bible Words and Places
Ashdad

Located some twenty miles from Gaza (Josh 13:3; 1 Sam 5:1), it was one of five Philistine cities. One of the cities never taken by the Israelites (Josh 15:46-47). When the ark was captured by the Philistines, it was placed here in the temple of Dagon (1 Sam 5:1-8). Egypt besieged Ashdad for 29 years.

Depth of Bible Words and Places
Kirjath-jearim

A town of the Gibeonites (Josh 9:17) on the boundary line between Judah and Benjamin (Josh 15:9; 18:14-15). It fell to

---

[1] 1 Sam 6:12 And the cows went straight toward Beth-shemesh along the highway, lowing as they went, and turned not aside to the right or the left

Judah (Josh 15:48, 60; Jud 18:12). It was here the ark remained twenty years after the Philistines sent it back to the Israelites (1 Sam 6:19-7:2). It was also called Kirjath-baal (Josh 15:60; 18:14) and Baalah (Josh 15:9, 11).

2   Samuel became recognized as judge and leader of the people following the battle that carried away the ark. He made his home in Ramah where he was born. He also died there. He annually travelled to various locations, leading the people in worship. Few men have exercised a greater influence on the spiritual life of their time.

2.1. Around him at Ramah was gathered the first of the "schools" of young prophets. His death was a time of national mourning (1 Samuel 25:1).[1]

2.2. So the people in 1 and 2 Samuel clamor for a king. Moreover, I guess I cannot really blame them—I emphasize again, the cycles of Judges continues over and over.

2.3. The cycle of judges continues:

    2.3.1.   Territorial disputes

    2.3.2.   Nations invading them, even living in their midst

    2.3.3.   Idolatry consuming them

2.4. So their cry becomes *appoint a king for us.*[2] I can think of three reasons for their desiring a king.

    2.4.1.   The people wanted a leader to direct them in times of war. The Philistines continuously threatened them. They had iron weapons, had carried away the Ark, and had levied taxes on Israel. Enough!

    2.4.2.   Samuel was growing much older, so his age and decline of leadership were reasons to appoint a king. His sons disqualified themselves by their life style. Enough!

    2.4.3.   The Israelites desired a royal court with pomp and ceremony. The newfound unity of sorts, made them desire to be like the nations surrounding them. A theocratic (under God) form of government was exchanged for a monarchial (ruling king) form. Enough!

2.5. God never intended Israel to have a king other than Himself. He would have sent them leaders who would receive their orders from Himself. They settled for God's second best. It is with joy and anticipation, we realize God's form of government will be set up in the eternal future!

---

[1] 1 Sam 25:1 *Then Samuel died; and all Israel gathered together and mourned for him*

[2] 1 Sam 8:5 *appoint a king for us to judge us like all the nations.*

2.5.1. The establishment of a real kingdom was not understood...a kingdom consisted of a king reigning over a domain...a Kingdom...the King of Kings desired to reign over His own domain, the real KING DOM, set up on earth, (see Expanded Help Paper, God's Kingdom, in this volume). His Kingdom was to be an extension from Heaven to a colony called earth.

2.5.2. The people demanded to shift from a *theocratic* rule of God, *THE* King, to a *monarchial* rule of *A* king. Israel desires a king. They get one, but not as they requested *"like all the nations."* They get a king but not *like all the other nations* had. In selecting Saul, chapters 8 and 9 show us:

    2.5.2.1. They had the wrong motive *"like all the nations"*

    2.5.2.2. They had the wrong criteria *"a choice and handsome young man.....taller than any of the people"*

    2.5.2.3. Then they chose from the wrong Tribe, Benjamin. Long before this, God had said, *"The scepter shall not depart from Judah"* (Genesis 49:10).

2.5.3. So as we will see later, Saul was the peoples' choice, David will be God's choice; Saul was a man after the people's heart, David, would be a man after God's heart. Moreover, we see, God's Word has never changed; man looks on the outward appearance, God looks on the heart.

2.5.4. Some sort of national unity under an earthly king was being forced on them by the nations around them.

2.5.5. These countries nearby were highly organized, as Israel experienced on several occasions.

2.5.6. And since most of those nations had kings, Israel believed that was the answer. So the Israelites' new kingdom is established by its first two kings, Saul and David. Let's look at these two kings.

2.6. Saul is a tragic story. Blessed with all he needed:

2.6.1. Natural graces and talents

2.6.2. Selected by God

2.6.3. The people honored him and were happy to get a king. Everything "looks" good.

2.6.4. When Saul was made king, the Israelites had been in the Promised Land almost 300 years. And yet they did not possess the entire land. They were in danger of losing a national identity.

2.6.5. His beginning was good. He received volunteers from all the tribes and began to unify the twelve tribes. War with the Philistine's was on the horizon and both nations prepared.

However, Saul's downfall also began early in this period; He stepped in as priest (1 Samuel 13:9-12), in place of the aging Samuel. Also, on other occasions, he disobeyed God's instructions.

2.6.6.   Saul degenerated into a psychopathic condition of rejection, defeat, and suicide.

2.6.7.   Saul's coronation as Israel's first king was the climax of the desire of a nation that had lasted 200 years. Two centuries before this, the Jews tried to make Gideon their king. But he wisely refused; however, the *desire* for a king never left Israel. The desire for a king continued during those 200 years, but division under Judges resulted.

2.6.8.   We have the words recorded in 1 Samuel 8:19.[1]

2.6.9.   Samuel worked hard to get a king. God first chooses the smallest of the tribes, then the smallest of clans, then a family...and finally a man to be their first king...Saul.

2.6.10.   Religion had been dormant in Saul's life as a young man, now it becomes the ruling factor for his future.

2.6.10.1.   This whole experience was kept a secret from his family, but at the age of 40, already with a grown son Jonathan, Saul is anointed king and we note that his "spiritual life" is as weak as his physical life is strong.

2.6.10.2.   At first, he is able to prophecy, but soon his inner life is starved. He lost his conversing with THE king. He certainly had potential for God to use, for He chose him. However, Saul did not choose and seek after God. David later "pants" after God. That is not seen in Saul.

Depth of Bible Words and Places
Anointed

To anoint, to rub with oil, especially in order to consecrate someone or something. Appearing almost seventy times, *mashach* refers to the custom of rubbing or smearing with sacred oil to consecrate holy persons or holy things.

Priests and kings in particular were installed in their offices by anointing. The most important derivative of *mashach* is *mashiyach* (Messiah), "anointed one." Messiah was translated into Greek as *Christos*, thus His designation, "Jesus Christ."

Samuel is the first book to use the word *anointed,* the origin for the word *messiah.*

---

[1] *...the people refused to listen to the voice of Samuel, and they said, "No, but there shall be a king over us...*

2.7. Cp 13 informs us that Saul and his son had the only swords. Those could not have been produced by Israel until much later.

    2.7.1.   They were not organized nor did they have any real plans.

    2.7.2.   They were constantly in danger from surrounding nations. They had little resemblance to a nation under God.

    2.7.3.   Always remember, "Great leaders rise to great occasions." God knew what was inside this man Saul and would use that gift.

    2.7.4.   That spark of leadership inside Saul was fanned into a flame when an enemy threatened to put out the eyes of everyone in the city of Jabesh.[1]

Depth of Bible Words and Places
Jabesh

Jabesh was located in Gilead just east of the Jordan River and south of the Sea of Galilee. It was part of the half-tribe of Manasseh east of the Jordan. The city was named from its geographical characteristic "dry place." That was a common method of naming a person or city:

- Adam "soil"
- Abel "meadow"
- Bethelehem "location of Bread"
- Gath "wine press"
- Ramah "height"
- Zoar "small"

It was Jabesh that Saul rescued when the city was threatened by the Ammonites.

    2.7.5.   Saul is upset! He rallies the Israelite tribes, and for the first time since Gideon, 200 years before, all twelve tribes come together, and they defend Jabesh. A crowing time—Saul now was king.

    2.7.6.   So following this victory, Israel prepares for war against the Philistines who were at the height of their power. God had told His people years before, to go into the land and destroy the enemy. Still, the warlike people (the Philistines) held the most fertile part of Palestine, the land which divided North from South

    2.7.7.   Saul picks an army of 3,000 and makes a two-pronged attack against the 30,000 chariots and 6,000 cavalry of the enemy

---

[1] 1 Samuel 11:2-3 records it; *"I will make that covenant with you on this condition, that I will gouge out the right eye of every one of you, thus I will make it a reproach on all Israel."*

2.7.8.　　His son Jonathan leads part of the attack, and surprises the enemy; confusion is used by God along with an earthquake, to cause the enemy to fight among themselves and scatter.

2.7.9.　　From these two early victories, Saul gains favor. The nation is coming together. The Twelve Tribes had been able to assume their final shape under Saul, comprising all Israel. He then defeats other enemies, Moab, Ammon, Edom and others. As a result, Saul is fully recognized as king of all Israel. These triumphs are the period of Saul's greatest glory. Things are looking good for Israel.

2.7.10.　　But his glory is brief. Chapter 15 tells of his failure to follow God's specific instructions. This is the reason any man fails.

EXPANDED HELP PAPER
Saul's Five-Step Failure

1.　His presumption at the altar of God

1 Samuel 13:8-9 Now *he waited seven days, according to the appointed time set by Samuel, but Samuel did not come to Gilgal; and the people were scattering from him. 9 So Saul said, "Bring to me the burnt offering and the peace offerings."*

2.　His cruelty to his son

1 Samuel 14:44 Saul said, *"May God do this to me and more also, for you shall surely die, Jonathan."*

3.　His disobedience concerning Amalek

1 Samuel 15:20-23 *Then Saul said to Samuel...I did obey the voice of the Lord,* "But the people took some of the spoil," Samuel said..." *For rebellion is as the sin of divination And insubordination is as iniquity and idolatry. Because you have rejected the word of the Lord, He has also rejected you from being king."*

4.　His jealousy and hatred of David

1 Samuel 18:29 *then Saul was even more afraid of David. Thus Saul was David's enemy continually.*

5.　His appeal to a witch

1 Samuel 28:7 *Then Saul said to his servants, "Seek for me a woman who is a medium that I may go to her and inquire of her."*

2.7.11.　　We read the story of a man named Agag, who Saul paraded as a prize rather than killing him in battle as God instructed.

2.7.12.   We read in these verses: [1]

2.7.13.   Agag became a type for sin, "your agag." Sin must be put down, destroyed in one's life.

2.7.14.   Saul's life is at a turning point. Fear and suspicion take over his mind. Rather than running fear out, he allows it in.[2]

2.7.15.   His servants send for David, a musician, who sooths Saul's heart...for the moment.

2.7.16.   David defeats a giant with a stone, and leads the soldiers to other victories against the Philistines, which only aroused Saul's jealousy.

2.7.17.   Why did David pick five stones? Did he not trust God and carry only one? Remember the giant, Goliath had four brothers? They could have immediately retaliated against David. He was ready. Perhaps we conclude, Goliath plus four brothers equals five stones!

2.7.18.   Twice Saul tries to kill David and fails. So he reduces David to a captain over 1,000 men. He couldn't dismiss him because of his great popularity; so he demotes him.

Depth of Bible Words and Places
Ziklag

Listed as one of the 29 towns in Negev and was assigned to the tribe of Simeon (Joshua 15:31; 19:5). It was apparently controlled by the Philistines during King Saul's rule, and was given by King Achish of Gath to David when he was running from Saul. David used it for a home base for raids against various groups who threatened the southern borders of Judah (1 Samuel 27). After being away one time, he returned to find it ransacked by the Amalekites.

2.7.19.   More frustrations set in as fear and jealousy grows; Saul orders his men to murder David. While in pursuit, twice David refuses to touch the king. Integrity...character. May you be a person of character! May I offer you some help concerning *Integrity and Character*?

---

[1] Samuel 15:23 *Rebellion is as sinful as witchcraft, and stubbornness as bad as worshiping idols. So because you have rejected the command of the Lord, he has rejected you as king.* 28 *And Samuel said to him, "The Lord has torn the kingdom of Israel from you to day and has given it to someone else—one who is better than you.* (NLT)
[2] Proverbs 29:25 *The fear of man brings a snare.*
Job 3:25 *For what I fear comes upon me.*

EXPANDED HELP PAPER
Integrity and Character

Integrity relates to our behavior before other people, whether or not they are watching. Proverbs 20:7 *The righteous man walks in his integrity*. Psalm 26:1 *...for I have walked in my integrity*. Proverbs 10:9 *He who walks with integrity walks securely*.

By approaching every aspect of our lives with a concern for what God thinks, and a commitment to live with purity, we can develop confidence in our character. He is holy (Deuteronomy 7:6; 14:2), humble (Psalms 34:2), righteous (Isaiah 60:21), and upright (1 Kings 3:6). Someone said, *"We need to be known for our integrity as Tiffany's is known for jewelry."* God's people must be people of truth and unimpeachable integrity. How can that happen? Through fewer words and more deeds. That is the way to build consistent evidence of a new and credible lifestyle with lasting impact.

Psalms 15 lists ten marks of integrity. How does your life compare?

- Walks uprightly
- Works righteousness
- Speaks the truth
- Does not backbite
- Does no evil to a neighbor
- Does not take up a reproach against a friend
- Honors those who fear the Lord, not the ungodly
- Keeps his word, even when it is costly
- Does not practice usury
- Does not take bribes

There are many Old Testament examples of people with integrity. Two examples

Job's determination to hold fast his righteousness and integrity was remarkable. Though Job believed that God had taken away a fair trial, he would not put away his integrity. He persevered despite the discouraging words of his wife and friends.

Consider Joseph. He had no support system for his beliefs or values and no one to turn to for godly counsel as he made far-reaching decisions. In spite of the environment he was in, he walked with integrity:

He maintained his moral integrity when facing the advances of Potiphar's wife (Genesis 39:7–10).

He kept doing his best even when the situation was the worst when unjustly thrown into prison, (Genesis 39:22–23).

2.7.20.   Saul continues his downward fall and turns to a fortune-teller, and soon dies in discouragement, falling on his own sword on a battlefield against the Philistines, near the plain of Jezreel.

2.7.21.   What a picture of two lives: Saul's hate and David's love.

2.7.22.   Saul failed as a king; however, a champion was already in the picture...chosen to replace him...as Israel's second king.[1] I love that God selected *a shepherd* to lead His people. A shepherd of sheep becomes the shepherd of Israel.

2.7.23.   With the death of Saul...the path to the throne was being cleared for David.

> 2.7.23.1.   Just over thirty yrs old,
> 2.7.23.2.   Popular with the people,
> 2.7.23.3.   Unquestioned courage,
> 2.7.23.4.   Anointed of God.

Depth of Bible Words and Places
Hebron

The word means *fellowship* or *communion*. Hebron is located twenty miles south-west of Jerusalem. Abraham lived there and established his family burial site. Joshua defeated the ruler of Hebron and gave the city to Caleb. Later it was a city of refuge. David ruled from Hebron before ruling all of Israel.

Depth of Bible Words and Places
Shepherd

Shepherds were responsible for the physical survival and welfare of the flock. In comparison with goats, which tended to fend for themselves, sheep depended on the shepherd to find pasture (Ezekiel 34:2, 9, 13), and they required "quiet" water (Psalm 23:3). Shepherds also had to provide shelter, medication, and provision for lameness and weariness. Without the shepherd, the sheep were helpless.

He entertained himself by making music on a readily made reed pipe (Judges 5:16). The shepherd would count his sheep twice a day, one by one, probably calling each by its own name. He would talk to his sheep until each one recognized his voice (John 10:4).

---

[1] 1 Samuel 16:1 *Now the Lord said to Samuel, " How long will you grieve over Saul, since I have rejected him from being king over Israel? Fill your horn with oil and go; I will send you to Jesse the Bethlehemite, for I have selected a king for Myself among his sons."*

For the most part, the shepherd's long days and nights in the field made for a lonely life.

At night, the shepherd gathered his sheep into a group for protection against beasts, thieves, and the weather.

This selfless, caring attitude of the shepherd is attributed to Jesus throughout the New Testament. "We are the people of his [God's] pasture and the sheep of his hand"

Many of the best-known Old Testament persons, including the patriarchs and the prophets, had personal experience as successful herdsmen. Moses, who learned sheep tending from the seven daughters of Jethro and for a time tended the flock of the priest of Midian (Exodus 2:15-3:1); David, who when Samuel found him was "keeping the sheep" (1 Samuel 16:11); and Amos of Tekoa, an under shepherd whom "the Lord took from following the flock" and commanded to "prophesy to my people Israel" (Amos 7:15; 3:12).

David's experiences at Bethlehem were an ideal training for a future king and spiritual leader. His occupation developed prudence, promptitude, and prowess. His long night vigils allowed a solitude which directed him to God.

2.8. When Saul was defeated and killed, his son and heir Jonathan lost his life in the same battle. Saul's fourth son Esh *baal* survived to inherit the now diminished kingdom. The Philistines again were in occupation of most of the land.

2.9. At this time, David is the king of only one tribe…his own…Judah. And for seven and one-half years, he reigns from the city of Hebron, gaining popularity. The other tribes had some leadership in the form of another one of Saul's sons, Ishbosheth.

2.10. However, many in leadership were assassinated at various times, and soon the tribes struggled.[1]

2.11. During a convention of 280,000 persons, representing all twelve tribes, David is made king of a united Israel, at the age of 38. If God were not to rule as King of His domain, at least He would have a loving King on earth, that would eventually lead to a future Kingdom ruled by God.

2.12. What a great king he was! What accomplishments. They were both brilliant and permanent. His first two decades were spent in aggressive wars.

2.12.1. He founded a national capital at Jerusalem. *So David lived in the stronghold and called it the city of David* (2 Samuel

[1] 2 Samuel 3:1 *Now there was a long war between the house of Saul and the house of David; and David grew steadily stronger, but the house of Saul grew weaker continually.*
All in God's plan

5:9). This was perhaps the greatest thing he did for Israel. It was here that his son built the Temple where today the Dome stands.[1]

Depth of Bible Words and Places
(A short history of) Jerusalem

Jerusalem existed as far back as the eighteenth century BCE, before the arrival of the Israelites. During that Middle Bronze Age II to Iron Age I (archaeological terms), it was a tiny area south of the Temple Mount, known today as the City of David. However, it did include a massive fortification, recently excavated. It consisted of approximately 11 acres with a population of 500-700 persons.

The city grew in population to the time of Kings David and Solomon in the 1000-800 BCE period. Solomon expanded the city to forty acres, mostly by way of the temple and related buildings. The population reached 2000-3000 persons.

During the next period, the Western Hill was added to Jerusalem. More than a hundred acres became land in Jerusalem. Archeologists have well documented this addition of territory. The fall of the northern kingdom of Israel at least partly accounted for the great increase in population.

The city expanded outside the walls, north, with a total population exceeding 7500. Sennacherib laid siege upon Jerusalem in 701 BCE causing a reduction in population to around 6000. When Babylonia destroyed the city in 586 BCE, the population was further reduced. Shortly before the time of the destruction of the Temple by the Babylonians, the walled city of Jerusalem consisted of approximately 160 acres. Following the destruction, a few habitants remained in the original territory of the City of David. When the Persians took Jerusalem from the Babylonians, Jerusalem again was only a small territory, with a population reduced to around 400-700, living on the forty acres.

During the remainder of the BCE period, Jerusalem grew in population to approximately 8000 in a slightly expanded territory. But then came the next archeologically documented period slightly before the 70 CE destruction by the Romans. This is the time when Jesus was there. Estimates of the population vary, but the better number would be 20,000. The Christian city of Jerusalem gradually grew in size and population until it reached a peak as high as 100,000 in the

---

[1] What a great story. Many had failed to capture this city; most of the people thought any invading force could never capture it. Jerusalem was not a city controlled by the Hebrews. So David, using a tunnel which brought fresh water into the city, sneaked in and captured the city! Truly to become "city of David."

fifth-sixth centuries and then steadily decreased to 15,000 by the seventh century.

In 637 CE, the Muslims besieged Jerusalem and the Islamic Jerusalem resulted. By the tenth century, the population was approximately 7000.

2.12.2.   David defeated Israel's enemies, breaking the power of the Philistines (2 Samuel 5:17-25).

2.12.3.   Established a peace that lasted a century.

2.12.4.   He returned the Ark to Jerusalem and reestablished worship of Yahweh (another of his great accomplishments).

2.12.5.   He enacted many social reforms, organizing the government with overseers, recognizing and utilizing their individual gifts. These men became a king's cabinet.

2.13.   This was a king after God's heart.

2.14.   Those accomplishments are detailed in 2 Samuel cps 5-10.

2.15.   He also expanded the kingdom of Israel from 6,000 square miles to 60,000! The only land which had not come under David's control was Phoenicia, the northern coastal area along the Mediterranean.

2.16.   But then comes cps 11-24

2.16.1.   It has been written that Abraham Lincoln died at his peak....if he had lived longer his life might have been tarnished with mistakes.

2.16.2.   Well, David lived past his peak...and made a mistake...his great sin. Psalms 51 was written at this time. Let's read from Psalms 51. Read this heart-felt, earnest talk with God.

Psalms 51:1

Be gracious to me, O God, according to Your lovingkindness;
According to the greatness of Your compassion blot out my transgressions.
Wash me thoroughly from my iniquity
And cleanse me from my sin.
For I know my transgressions,
And my sin is ever before me.
Against You, You only, I have sinned
And done what is evil in Your sight,
Purify me with hyssop, and I shall be clean;
Wash me, and I shall be whiter than snow.
Make me to hear joy and gladness,
Let the bones which You have broken rejoice.
Hide Your face from my sins
And blot out all my iniquities.
Create in me a clean heart, O God,
And renew a steadfast spirit within me.
Do not cast me away from Your presence

And do not take Your Holy Spirit from me.
Restore to me the joy of Your salvation
And sustain me with a willing spirit.
17 The sacrifices of God are a broken spirit;
A broken and a contrite heart, O God, You will not despise.

2.16.3.　　　What an honest confession. Both adultery and murder are recorded in his life. David just says *Against You, You only, I have sinned*. The wages of sin is always death.

2.16.4.　　　The prophet Nathan denounced David for his sin, and David knew it was the voice of God pronouncing judgment.

2.16.5.　　　What a great picture of God's grace is shown in David's choice with Bathsheba and his planning the death of her husband. Law demanded David be *stoned* for adultery and *killed* for murder. However, God extended grace. True confession and repentance...always win.

2.16.6.　　　Grace...covers...then...removes. Not to be used as a blanket over sin, rather a true repentance activates grace.

EXPANDED HELP PAPER
Grace

GRACE is favor or kindness shown without regard to the worth or merit of the one who receives it and in spite of what that same person deserves. Grace is one of the key attributes of God. The Lord God is "merciful and gracious, long-suffering, and abounding in goodness and truth" (Exodus 34:6).

Therefore, grace is usually associated with mercy, love, compassion, and patience as the source of help and with deliverance from distress. The grace of God is always free and unearned. I define His Grace as *"God lavishing on us ALL that He is, All of His benefits, even though we really deserve none of them."*

2.16.7.　　　And judgment did come. It occurred in David's family. Four tragic events in David's life are the result of the seeds planted. David was never the same, even though God was gracious.

2.16.8.　　　One of his sons, Absalom kills one of the other sons and is driven away.

2.16.9.   After three years, Absalom returns and leads a rebellion against his Father. David, being the superior soldier, defeats Absalom who is then killed by Joab, David's earlier military leader.

2.16.10.   David later faces more and more strife in his household, finally dying at an early age of seventy, after forty years of being king.

2.16.11.   David in every way was remarkable. He was as human as he was great. He was in love with God! Oh! That I would love God in heart, attitude, and action. His life reflects the weaknesses and characteristics of a harsh age. In spite of that, David stands as a spiritual monument. His constructive energy and versatile genius had bestowed upon Israel an unparalleled epoch of prolonged peace and prosperity. In addition, one of his outstanding qualities, and one of his greatest contributions to his country, was a passion for music. And, he was a man of grace:

2.16.11.1.   As a soldier,

2.16.11.2.   A poet,

2.16.11.3.   A politician.

2.16.11.4.   He had every quality that makes a man lovable. Where is the man who could claim equal fame as soldier, political leader, poet, and musician?

2.16.11.5.   From the depths of despair under the yoke of the Philistines, Israel climbed to a position of power, esteem, and greatness because of the work of David.

2.16.11.6.   David serves as an example to every man who loves God, makes mistakes, turns TO God rather than FROM Him, and continues to love and honor God—God of grace.[1]

---

[1]The last words of David reveal the greatness of Israel's most honored hero. 2 Sam 23:1-7 *Now these are the last words of David. David the son of Jesse declares, The man who was raised on high declares,*
The anointed of the God of Jacob, And the sweet psalmist of Israel, 2 "The Spirit of the Lord spoke by me, And His word was on my tongue. 3 "The God of Israel said, The Rock of Israel spoke to me, 'He who rules over men righteously, Who rules in the fear of God, 4 Is as the light of the morning when the sun rises, A morning without clouds, When the tender grass springs out of the earth, Through sunshine after rain.' 5 "Truly is not my house so with God? For He has made an everlasting covenant with me, Ordered in all things, and secured; For all my salvation and all my desire, Will He not indeed make it grow? 6 "But the worthless, every one of them will be thrust away like thorns, Because they cannot be taken in hand; 7 But the man who touches them Must be armed with iron and the shaft of a spear,
And they will be completely burned with fire in their place."

Increase your Bible knowledge from 1 Chronicles: What Did David Accomplish?

> Built an army (11:10-26)
>
> Constructed a palace (14:1-2)
>
> Brought the Ark home (cp 15)
>
> Psalmist (16:8-36)
>
> Defeated surrounding enemies (cps 18-20)
>
> Planned the Temple (22:2-19)
>
> System of worship (cps 23-26)
>
> Organized the kingdom (26:20-28)

David's Specific Psalms. We learn many things about David

Psalms 7	I Samuel 24:11-12	David Hides
Psalms 18	II Samuel 22:1-51	David Delivered
Psalms 30	II Samuel 24:25	David Builds
Psalms 34	I Samuel 21	David Delivered
Psalms 51	II Samuel 11:12	David Sins
Psalms 52	I Samuel 22:9	David Distressed
Psalms 54	I Samuel 23:19	David Distressed
Psalms 56	I Samuel 21:10-11	David Delivered
Psalms 57	I Samuel 24:3-10	David Hides
Psalms 59	I Samuel 19:11	David Watches
Psalms 60	II Samuel 8:13	David Celebrates
Psalms 63	I Samuel 23:14	David Runs
Psalms 142	II Samuel 22:1	David Visits

SECTION 7
Solomon and The Temple

1 Kings 1-11, 2 Chronicles 1-9. The period from 1037 to 975 BCE

Theme Statement: *"Solomon in all his glory."* (Luke 12:27)

THE KEYS IN SECTION SEVEN

Section 7: Solomon and The Temple

Keys to First Kings—

A Key Word: Baal

The Key Verses (9:4-5; 11:11)

9:4 As for you, if you will walk before Me as your father David walked, in integrity of heart and uprightness, doing according to all that I have commanded you and will keep My statutes and My ordinances, 5 then I will establish the throne of your kingdom over Israel forever, just as I promised to your father David, saying, 'You shall not lack a man on the throne of Israel.'

11:11 So the Lord said to Solomon, "Because you have done this, and you have not kept My covenant and My statutes, which I have commanded you, I will surely tear the kingdom from you, and will give it to your servant.

Key Chapter (12)

The Key People in 1 Kings

David—king of Israel; chose his son Solomon to be the next king (1–2:10); also see info for Key People in 1 Samuel

Solomon—third king of Israel; son of David and Bathsheba; builder of the first temple; God granted him his choice to become the wisest man ever born (1:10–11:43)

Rehoboam—son of Solomon; succeeded him as the fourth king of Israel; his evil actions led to the division of Israel into two kingdoms; later became king of the southern kingdom of Judah (11:43–12:24; 14:21–31)

Jeroboam—evil king of the northern ten tribes of Israel; erected idols and appointed non-Levitical priests (11:24–14:20)

Keys to Second Kings—

A Key Word: High Places

The Key Verses (17:22–23; 23:27)

17:22 The sons of Israel walked in all the sins of Jeroboam which he did; they did not depart from them 23 until the Lord removed Israel from His sight, as He spoke through all His servants the prophets. So Israel was carried away into exile from their own land to Assyria until this day.

23:27 The Lord said, "I will remove Judah also from My sight, as I have removed Israel. And I will cast off Jerusalem, this city which I have chosen, and the temple of which I said, 'My name shall be there.'"

Key Chapter (25)

The Key People in 2 Kings

Elijah—a prophet of Israel; faced Ahab and Jezebel; raised a dead boy; called fire from heaven; never physically died; was carried directly to heaven in a chariot of fire (1:3–2:11; 10:10, 17)

Elisha—prophet trained under Elijah; close companion, became Elijah's successor; many similarities in ministry; asked for twice the anointing; saw Elijah taken to heaven (2:1–9:3; 13:14–21)

The woman from Shunem—the woman visited by Elijah in her home; brought her son back to life (4:8–37; 8:1–6)

Naaman—a Syrian warrior who suffered from leprosy; healed by Elisha (5:1–27)

Jezebel—evil queen of Israel; Baal worship introduced; attempted to prevent Israel from worshiping God; eventually killed and eaten by dogs (9:7–37)

Jehu—anointed king of Israel; used by God to punish Ahab's family (9:1–10:36; 15:12)

Joash—king of Judah, saved from death as a child; followed evil advice of younger friends, ultimately assassinated by his own officials (11:1–12:21)

Hezekiah—king of Judah who remained faithful to God (16:20–20:21)

Keys to First Chronicles—

A Key Word: Sons

The Key Verses (17:11–14; 29:11)

17:11 *"When your days are fulfilled that you must go to be with your fathers, that I will set up one of your descendants after you, who will be of your sons; and I will establish his kingdom. 12 "He shall build for Me a house, and I will establish his throne forever. 13 "I will be his father and he shall be My son; and I will not take My lovingkindness away from him, as I took it from him who was before you. 14 "But I will settle him in My house and in My kingdom forever, and his throne shall be establishe d forever."""*

29: 11 *Yours, O Lord, is the greatness and the power and the glory and the victory and the majesty, indeed everything that is in the heavens and the earth; Yours is the dominion, O Lord, and You exalt Yourself as head over all.*

Key Chapter (17)

The Key People in 1 Chronicles

David—king of Israel and ancestor of Jesus Christ; described by God as "a man after My own heart" (2:8–29:30; see Acts 13:22) See Key People information from 1 Samuel and 1 Kings

The mighty men—a special group of soldiers who were dedicated to fight for King David (11:10–28:1)

Nathan—a prophet and advisor to David; told Solomon of God's will for him to build the great first temple (17:1–15)

Solomon—David's son who became the third king of Israel (3:5–29:28)

Keys to Second Chronicles—

A Key Word: Passover

The Key Verses (7:14; 16:9)

7:14 and My people who are called by My name humble themselves and pray and seek My face and turn from their wicked ways, then I will hear from heaven, will forgive their sin and will heal their land.

16:9 "For the eyes of the Lord move to and fro throughout the earth that He may strongly support those whose heart is completely His. You have acted foolishly in this. Indeed, from now on you will surely have wars."

Key Chapter (34)

The Key People in 2 Chronicles

Solomon—a king of Israel and builder of the first temple; asked for/received great wisdom to rule God's people (1:1–9:31)

Queen of Sheba—heard of Solomon's great reputation; visited him seeking information about his success (9:1–12; see Matt. 12:42)

Rehoboam—evil son of Solomon who became a king of Israel; soon divided the kingdom and later led the southern kingdom of Judah (9:31–13:7)

Asa—king of Judah; used very corrupt methods to accomplish God's purposes (14:1–16:14)

Jehoshaphat—son of Asa, followed him as king of Judah; attempted to follow God but made poor decisions (17:1–22:9)

Jehoram—wicked son of Jehoshaphat who succeeded him as king of Judah; promoted idol worship and killed his six brothers (21:1–20)

Uzziah—(also called Azariah) succeeded his father, Amaziah, as king of Judah; mostly followed God, but prideful (26:1–23)

Hezekiah—succeeded his father, Ahaz, as king of Judah; restored the temple; followed God and started religious reform (28:27–32:33)

Manasseh—succeeded his father, Hezekiah, as king of Judah; did evil in the sight of the Lord but repented later in his reign (32:33–33:20)

Josiah—succeeded his father, Amon, as king of Judah; followed the Lord; found the Book of the Law while restoring the temple; took the Book to the people. Brought revival/reforms (33:25–35:27)

Approximate dates of key events in Section 7

C. 1025-975 BCE	The events of 1 Kings 1-11 and 2 Chronicles 1-9; The Solomon era.

FIFTEEN

Solomon and the Temple

1   Next in Kings and Chronicles, Section 7 of our study course *SOLOMON AND THE TEMPLE.*

1.1. We'll cover 1 Kings 1-11 and 2 Chronicles 1-9, a period of about fifty years, 1025 to 975 BCE. The outlines and key words in each of these books will be offered in volume two of this work where we detail the divided kingdom.

1.2. In this section, we will review the life period of Solomon, before the division into two nations.

1.3. The century is from Saul's coronation to Solomon's death and the period of glory for Israel. During that century:

1.4. The united kingdom is established,

1.5. Reaching its highest point of power and prosperity,

1.6. Then beginnings of decline! For purposes of overview:

    1.6.1.   David had left a strong nation in every way for his son Solomon.

    1.6.2.   Solomon, like Saul, walked with God...in the beginning. By brilliant diplomacy he formed alliances with the nations close by. He constructed a spectacular temple.

    1.6.3.   Solomon slipped in to the old pit that we've seen over and over...the one we'll continue to see again and again when we later move to Volume Two of this work: idolatry. When Solomon died, he left a country rotten to the bones, and ripe for disaster and invasion.

1.7. Let's look closer at Solomon. When Solomon was born, the kingdom was at peace. The name given to him meant "the peaceful." This was a time when God looked and smiled on His people; united, prosperous, peaceful.

    1.7.1.   Solomon was the first Jewish king born "from a king," the First Dynasty of Israel. However, it was by no means certain that he had been destined to be David's heir. He was cared for under Nathan the prophet who renamed him Jedidiah "beloved of the Lord." However, this is mentioned only one time, never hearing the name again, for it wasn't a name to be used in public.

1.7.2.   His older brother Adonijah wanted to be king following their father David's death; in fact, he summons a group to attend a banquet where they cry out "long live King Adonijah." Adonijah was trying to take advantage of David's increasing feebleness. It is also known that Adonijah was a strikingly handsome man. David had not disciplined his children, which contributed to the future heartaches, (1 Kings 1:6).

1.8. It is recorded in 1 Kings 1, that David is aging. Nathan informs David concerning Adonijah's plans. David with his last ounce of strength has the high priest declare Solomon as king. David then gives to Solomon the plans for the house of God to be built and the materials, which he had accumulated to build it. See the next Expanded Help Paper, Three Temples. We find this confirmation in 1 Chronicles 29:25, *The Lord highly exalted Solomon in the sight of all Israel, and bestowed on him royal majesty which had not been on any king before him in Israel.*

EXPANDED HELP PAPER
Three Temples

The usual and appropriate Hebrew term for temple is *hekal*, an old word signifying "palace" or "a large building." There were three buildings at Jerusalem, which we refer to with the name of Temple. As these were all built upon the same site and after the same general pattern, they were in nature and design the same, namely, that of the one built by Solomon. A number of texts make clear that Yahweh "chose" Zion to be His own dwelling-place (Psalms 132:13; 2 Kings 8:13; Psalms 9:11).

Solomon's Temple
It is clear that the site of today's "Dome of the Rock" on Jerusalem's eastern hill marks the location of Solomon's temple.

The idea that the wilderness Tabernacle, a temporary building, should be supplanted by a permanent one of stone seems to have been suggested to David by the Spirit. The construction work at the temple was carried on over a period of seven years, during Solomon's 4th through 11th years as king.

The main sources for its design are the accounts in Kings (1 Kings 6; 7:13-51) and Chronicles (2 Chronicles 3-4). The temple building itself was rectangular in shape, the longer sides being those to the north and south. The shorter (eastern and western) sides were 20 cubits long.

Archaeology has shown that the plan of Solomon's Temple was characteristically Phoenician, as would be expected, since it was constructed by a Tyrian architect (1 Kings 7:13-15). However, no stone is left that archaeologists can confidently say belonged to Solomon's Temple. Similar plans of sanctuaries of the general period, 1200 -900 BCE, have been excavated in northern Syria. The temple at Tell Tainat, excavated in 1936 CE by the University of Chicago, is smaller but similar to Solomon's structure.

In 1 Kings 5 we have a description of the diplomatic negotiations that preceded the building of the temple. A treaty was established between Solomon and Hiram king of Tyre by which the latter would supply the necessary timber — cedar (for paneling) and cypress (or pine, for the rough building)—cut from the forests of Lebanon by Hiram's skilled subjects and transported to the sea. There, rafts were constructed, and sent down the coast to a location of Solomon's choosing (2 Chronicles 2:16) to Joppa.

White limestone was taken from the hills surrounding Jerusalem and prepared at the site of the quarries. The bronze items with which the temple and its courtyard were furnished were cast in the lower Jordan Valley by the same Phoenician named Hiram (his mother however, was an Israelite).

The Jewish supervisors were assisted by the skilled workers of Phoenicia ("Hiram's builders") and by "the men of Gebal" (Byblos).

The history of Solomon's Temple has many ups and downs through it's almost four hundred years of existence. At the disruption of the kingdom, the Temple ceased to be the sanctuary of all the Israelite people; Jeroboam erected special places of worship at Bethel and Dan for the use of the revolting ten tribes; but the Temple continued to be the authorized center of worship for the southern kingdom of Judah.

As early as the days of the first king of the Southern Kingdom, Rehoboam (931 BCE), the Temple treasures were plundered by Shishak king of Egypt (1 Kings 14:26), and gold and silver from there were subsequently sent to Ben-hadad, king of Syria, to purchase an alliance against Baasha, king of the northern nation, Israel (15:18-21).

Under Jehoshaphat (*c.* 872 BCE), the outer court was renewed (2 Chronicles 20:5), and under Jehoash (considerable repairs were made upon the Temple itself, 2 Kings 12:5-12).

We learn from 2 Kings: Worst of all was the desecration of the Temple by Manasseh (697 BCE). He caused altars for "all the host of heaven" to be erected in both courts, set up an image of Asherah in the sanctuary (21:4-

5, 7), and erected in the Temple court "houses of the male cult prostitutes" (23:7).

However, King Josiah (640 BCE) purged the sacred place of these abominations (vv 4-8). Soon afterward Nebuchadnezzar captured Jerusalem (606 BCE) and gathered all the treasures of the Temple, including the golden utensils, and carried them off (24:13). Eleven years later Jerusalem was destroyed by the Chaldeans, who burned the Temple to the ground after pillaging it of its remaining valuables, which they took to Babylon (25:9, 13-17; 52:13, 17-23).

Zerubbabel's Temple

Not a lot of information is available concerning this rebuilt temple of the restoration period.

The temple's later history can be traced in some detail in the apocryphal books of 1 and 2 Maccabees and by Josephus' writings.

We do know that during his first year (536 BCE); Cyrus issued a decree by which exiled Jews were allowed to return to their homeland and rebuild the temple of their God.

The first group to return, was under Sheshbazzar's (Zerubbabel's) leadership. Ezra 5:14-16 credits him with beginning the work of rebuilding the temple. The Jews, exclusively, who had returned from Exile, did the work.

In the spring of 515 BCE the temple was finished "by command of the God of Israel and by decree" of the Persian kings (Ezra 6:14).

It may safely be assumed that the second temple shared many features with the first.

The dimensions of the temple area as quoted in Josephus were roughly 150 by 45 m. (500 by 150 ft.).

Kingship was replaced by priesthood during the postexilic period. One of the few other events we know of this time is the Maccabean revolt in 167 BCE and Judas Maccabeus rededicating the Temple. This joyous event is still remembered in the Jewish celebration of Hannukah. Judas' successors appointed themselves as high priests, and the Temple became more of a political institution. Pompey captured the Temple in 63 BCE but did not plunder it.

Herod's Temple

For our knowledge of the last and greatest of the Jewish Temples, we are indebted almost wholly to the works of Josephus, with an occasional hint from the Talmud. The Bible unfortunately contains nothing to assist in this respect.

The Temple as it existed after the captivity was not such as would satisfy Herod the Great. He was a vain man and fond of elaborate display and accordingly undertook the task of <u>re</u>building it on a grander scale. This also could be considered the second Temple.

Herod the Great came to power in 37 BCE and determined that he would please his Jewish subjects and show off his style of kingship to the Romans by making the Jerusalem Temple bigger and better than it had ever been.

Although the reconstruction was practically equivalent to an entire rebuilding, still this Temple <u>cannot be spoken of as a third one</u>, for Herod himself said, in so many words, that it was only intended to be regarded as an enlarging and further beautifying of that of Zerubbabel. Both are thought of and called the "second Temple" by Hebrews.

Work on the temple began in Herod's eighteenth year, 20-19 BCE. The Temple proper, in which priests and Levites were employed, was finished in a year and a half, and the courts over the course of eight years. Josephus reported that there were ten thousand lay workers and a thousand priests. Subsidiary buildings were gradually erected, added to through the reigns of his successors, so that the entire undertaking was not completed until the time of Agrippa II and the procurator Albinus around 64 CE. John 2:20 says that at the beginning of Jesus' ministry the temple had been under construction for forty-six years. The time of Albinus is dated at 62-64 CE.

The interior of the Temple was divided into the Holy Place and the Holy of Holies. "The temple had doors also at the entrance, and lintels over them, of the same height with the temple itself. They were adorned with embroidered veils, with their flowers of purple, and pillars interwoven: and over these, but under the crown-work, was spread out a golden vine, with its branches hanging down from a great height" (per Josephus, Antiquities).[1] The rabbinical writers maintain that there were two veils over its entrance. This inner veil was rent on the occasion of our Lord's crucifixion.

A wall enclosed the temple area. According to Josephus in his Antiquities, each side was about 180 m. (600 ft.) long.

An inscription found among the debris near the southwest corner indicates that, on a tower rising above the wall in this vicinity, a priest would stand to blow a trumpet, announcing the beginning of Sabbath.

The Jerusalem Temple is the focus of many New Testament events. The birth of John the Baptist was announced there (Luke 1:11-20). The offering by Joseph and Mary at the circumcision of baby Jesus, was brought there. Simeon and Anna greeted Jesus there (2:22-38). Jesus

---

[1] Flavius Josephus, Antiquities of the Jews, Book VIII, Chapter III.3, A.D. 93

came there as a boy of twelve (2:42-51) and later taught there during His ministry (John 7:14). His cleansing of the Temple was instrumental in precipitating His death. He knew no earthly temple was necessary to the worship of God (4:21-24). He predicted the Temple's destruction by the Romans, and His warnings to His followers to flee when this happened actually saved many Christians' lives (Mark 13:2, 14-23). Early Christians continued to worship there, and Paul was arrested there (Acts 3; 21:27-33).

After the Jewish revolt in 66 CE, Vespasian, followed by his son Titus, crushed all resistance. In 70 CE, only a few years after its completion, Herod's temple was destroyed. So much gold was carried off from the destruction of the temple that Josephus reported the gold market throughout Syria was glutted: "The standard of gold was depreciated to half its former value."

1.9. Solomon's early reign showed great promise:
- 1.9.1.　　　Great humbleness
- 1.9.2.　　　Capable of great planning and wisdom
- 1.9.3.　　　Places the well-fare of his people first
- 1.9.4.　　　Completes many projects which strengthen the kingdom:
  - 1.9.4.1.　　　Strong alliances
  - 1.9.4.2.　　　Great building programs
  - 1.9.4.3.　　　Builds a solid organized kingdom
- 1.9.5.　　　However, just below the surface—was that older brother. Remember Adonijah? Adonijah still wanted to be king.
  - 1.9.5.1.　　　David's old military leader, Joab, now was in alliance with Adonijah, and together they thought it would be quite easy to overthrow this young, inexperienced king.
  - 1.9.5.2.　　　However, the plot, was for Adonijah to marry David's young wife (she was nothing more than his nurse; 1 Kings 1:1-4), and claim the throne. That would put him rightfully in line to take it. No doubt they thought it would be easy to outwit the young and inexperienced king Solomon.
  - 1.9.5.3.　　　But Solomon realizes the plot when Bathsheba presents the plan to him...and Adonijah is killed. Soon after, Joab was killed at a sacred place where he had fled for safety.

1.9.5.4.   Then comes the familiar dream of Solomon in 1 Kings 3 & 4 and 2 Chronicles 1:1-12.

1.9.5.5.   After a wonderful day of offerings to God and a time of thanksgiving at the altar in Gibeon, Solomon dreams that God appears to him and promises to give him any thing he requests.

1.10.   When Solomon awakes, he realized God had spoken to him using a dream. He passes on all the personal objects he could have asked for, instead asking God for wisdom to rule His people. [1]

1.10.1.   Solomon's wisdom went beyond practical shrewdness in everyday affairs. His wisdom is illustrated in scientific knowledge. He is credited with 3,000 proverbs (1 Kings 4:32), which only a relatively few have come to us in the book of Proverbs.

1.10.2.   1 Kings 11:41 refers to "the book of the acts of Solomon," which we no longer have. [2]

1.10.3.   Even though, the Scriptures utilized many "non-Biblical" sources, we can be assured that the original, inerrant content of the Word of God has been preserved. I have said many times in my teachings, "God preserved what He wants us to have."

Name of Source	Chronicles References
Book of the Kings of Israel and Judah	1 Chronicles 9:1, 2; 2 Chronicles 16:11, 20:34, 25:26, 27:7 and several others.
The Chronicles of David	1 Chronicles 27:24
Book of Samuel	1 Chronicles 29:29
Book of Nathan	1 Chronicles 29:29; 2 Chronicles 9:29
Book of Gad	1 Chronicles 29:29
Prophecy of Ahijah the Shilonite	1 Chronicles 9:29
Visions of Iddo	2 Chronicles 9:29
Records of Shemaiah	2 Chronicles 12:15
Records of Iddo	2 Chronicles 12:15
Annals of Iddo	2 Chronicles 13:22
Annals of Jehu	2 Chronicles 20:34
Commentary on the Book of the Kings	2 Chronicles 24:27
Acts of Uzziah by Isaiah	2 Chronicles 26:22
Letters of Sennacherib	2 Chronicles 32:10-17

---

[1] God responds in 1 Kings 3:12 *behold, I have done according to your words. Behold, I have given you a wise and discerning heart, so that there has been no one like you before you, nor shall one like you arise after you.*

[2] This is quite interesting; the sources of information, which helped develop the books of Kings and Chronicles. We don't usually think of God's Word using other writings, which didn't make it into the canon. But there were many, including oral transmissions. Certainly, all the Scripture came through inspiration and revelation from God. Also at times, God used human sources of information, Luke 1:1-4. So I mention it here, because certainly the writers used many sources of information. Even with other writings, God made sure by the Holy Spirit, that there was no error in His Word. For example 1 Chronicles 9:1 mentions a "Book of the kings of Israel and Judah." Many other sources are listed in the Chart of Sources.

Vision of Isaiah	2 Chronicles 32:32
Words of the Seers	2 Chronicles 33:18
Sayings of Hozai	2 Chronicles 33:19
Instructions of David and Solomon	2 Chronicles 35:4
The Laments	2 Chronicles 35:25

Name of Source	Kings References
The Book of the Acts of Solomon	1 Kings 11:41
The Chronicles of the Kings of Israel	1 Kings 14:19; 15:31; 16:5, and several others.
The Chronicles of the Kings of Judah	1 Kings 14:29; 15:7, 23; 22:45; 2 Kings 8:23; 12:19 and several others.
Book of Isaiah 36:1-39:8	Used in 2 Kings 18:9-20:19
Book of Jeremiah 52:31-34	2 Kings 25:27-29

1.10.4.   Solomon set out to enlarge the territory and protect this people. He expanded his kingdom by making strong alliances with other nations. The first of these alliances was with Egypt because her power was declining, (1 Kings 3:1). He bought chariots and horses from Egypt, and stationed them in the strengthened fortresses of Gezer, Hazor, and Megiddo. His alliance with Phoenicia in the north meant a supply of skilled craftsmen and materials to carry out his building programs.

1.10.5.   Let us remember, God had said HE would enlarge their borders, HE would protect them, and HE would prosper them. I do not see Solomon as understanding that.

1.10.6.   In Solomon's life, having *a king,* replaced having *THE KING!* Solomon followed natural instincts, not spiritual direction.

Depth of Bible Words and Places
Phoenicia

Never organized as a nation, rather it consisted of a group of independent cities along the northern seacoast of Israel. The well-known cities of Sidon and Tyre have been located by archeologists.

They were a people of sea traders of lumber and purple dye. The Phoenician alphabet was borrowed by the Greeks. Solomon sought their help to build the temple. Their practice of human sacrifice influenced and penetrated Judah.

1.10.7.   However, two mistakes are made: 1. He "began to lean on the arm of the flesh" by turning to these countries rather than God, and 2, he marries an Egyptian daughter of a Pharaoh.

1.10.8.   As I understand this, Solomon used that wisdom in the wrong way. He saw skilled craftsman and materials that he could use (perhaps we would have done the same thing). However, WE have the Holy Spirit to guide us and must learn how to hear His voice.

1.10.9.　　　Then for seven years he builds the Temple, which from the time it was being constructed, until it was destroyed, was the Center Point of every King's reign. Interesting to note, he spends seven years on God's temple, but then spends thirteen years on his own home! Shows his real interest.

1.10.10.　　　The Temple was always the Center Point during the 345 years of Judah's existence. Every king's reign, good or bad, was related to this Temple. Quickly:

> 1.10.10.1.　　Solomon raised it
>
> 1.10.10.2.　　Rehoboam found refuge there
>
> 1.10.10.3.　　Abijam withstood a rebellion against it
>
> 1.10.10.4.　　Asa renewed it
>
> 1.10.10.5.　　Jehoshaphat found rest in it
>
> 1.10.10.6.　　Jehoram brought God's retribution on himself there
>
> 1.10.10.7.　　Ahaziah rejected God there
>
> 1.10.10.8.　　Joash restored and repaired the Temple
>
> 1.10.10.9.　　Amaziah could not defend its riches
>
> 1.10.10.10.　　Uzziah received recompense from God because of pride
>
> 1.10.10.11.　　Jotham had respect for the Temple and "ordered his ways before his God."
>
> 1.10.10.12.　　Ahaz made images and rifled the Temple
>
> 1.10.10.13.　　Hezekiah reopened the Temple by reopening the doors and repairing them
>
> 1.10.10.14.　　Manasseh and Amon brought in foreign religions
>
> 1.10.10.15.　　Josiah brought revival
>
> 1.10.10.16.　　Jehoahaz, Jehoaikin, and Jehoiachin were witnesses to the final ravaging of Solomon's Temple
>
> 1.10.10.17.　　And the last king of Judah? Zedekiah witnessed the final blow—a ruination of the Temple; it was burned.

1.10.11.　　　Remember, The Temple was planned, by his father, David. However, because David was a man of war and bloodshed, it was left for his son Solomon, the man of peace, to build the house of God.[1]

---

[1] 1 Chronicles 22:8 *But the word of the Lord came to me, saying, 'You have shed much blood and have waged great wars; you shall not build a house to My name, because you have shed so much blood on the earth before Me.*

1.10.12.   The magnificent details of this great structure are in 1 Kings 5-6-7. Of all the many Scriptures dedicated to Solomon's life, 50% of them center on the Temple. Solomon's temple utilized cherubims, beautiful trees, and flowers to remind the people of the Garden of Eden. It is estimated that Solomon's Temple cost more to build, than twice the debt of WW II! (In excess of 40 billion dollars).[1] The massive platform of the Temple on Mount Moriah, still survives.

1.10.13.   Read what happened at the dedication of that first Temple.[2]

1.10.14.   Following his prayer, Solomon goes to the massive altar, and we have the first recorded example in the Bible of this humbleness on knees (1 Kings 8:54).

EXPANDED HELP PAPER
Old Testament Positions in Prayer

1.   Kneeling
    a.   Solomon 1 Kings 8:54
    b.   Elijah 1 Kings 18:42
    c.   Ezra 9:15
    d.   Daniel 6:10
2.   Standing   1 Kings 8:22
3.   Lifting up Hands
    a.   1 Kings 8:22
    b.   Psalms 141:2
4.   Bowing
    a.   Genesis 24:26
    b.   Exodus 4:31; 3:8

---

[1] We have to make an observation concerning this first Temple. The construction pattern was based on the same design of the tabernacle in the wilderness. An outer area, a holy place 60x30, and the Holy of Holies a perfect 30x30x30 cube. The Ark of the Covenant containing the Law tablets was placed in that cube.

[2] 2 Chronicles 5:13-14 ......*when the trumpeters and the singers were to make themselves heard with one voice to praise and to glorify the Lord, and when they lifted up their voice accompanied by trumpets and cymbals and instruments of music, and when they praised the Lord saying, "He indeed is good for His lovingkindness is everlasting," then the house, the house of the Lord, was filled with a cloud, 14 so that the priests could not stand to minister because of the cloud, for the glory of the Lord filled the house of God.*

5. On One's Face
    a. Deuteronomy 9:24
    b. Numbers 20:6
    c. Joshua 5:14

1.11.   And the climax is recorded in 2 Chronicles 7.[1]

1.11.1.   Solomon fortified Jerusalem so that no vulnerable point might be left. He repaired all the walls, extending them to secure the Temple. He protected his entire domain by a chain of forts built at every point of access. Megiddo was one of Solomon's new chariot corps, which formed part of the king's standing army. He built stalls for at least 450 horses and sheds for 150 chariots. This area was uncovered by archaeolologists who were astonished at its size.

1.11.2.   Following this, a change takes place in Solomon's life. He knew where all his fame and success had come from (1 Kings 8:61), but to *KNOW* and to *DO* are two different things. A lesson for us today. When Solomon first became king, he appeared in public riding a mule. However, later he never rode in public except in one of his glittering Egyptian chariots. It was drawn by magnificent horses and followed by bodyguards uniformed in robes of Syrian purple over hung with glittering weapons. Change in Solomon!

1.11.3.   His "royal throne" was carved in solid ivory, inlaid with gold; His feet rested on a golden footstool.

1.11.4.   As I review this, His reign sounds like a fairy-tale:

1.11.5.   1 Kings 4:26 *Solomon had 40,000 stalls of horses for his chariots, and 12,000 horsemen*

1.11.6.   1 Kings 9:17-19 *So Solomon rebuilt all the storage cities, even the cities for his chariots and the cities for his horsemen, and all that it pleased Solomon to build in Jerusalem.*

1.11.7.   1 Kings 9:26 King Solomon also built a fleet of ships

1.11.8.   1 Kings 10:21 All *King Solomon's drinking vessels were of gold and all the vessels of the house of the forest of Lebanon were*

---

[1] 2 Chronicles 7:1-3 *Now when Solomon had finished praying, fire came down from heaven and consumed the burnt offering and the sacrifices, and the glory of the Lord filled the house. 2 The priests could not enter into the house of the Lord because the glory of the Lord filled the Lord's house. 3 All the sons of Israel, seeing the fire come down and the glory of the Lord upon the house, bowed down on the pavement with their faces to the ground, and they worshiped and gave praise to the Lord.*

of pure gold. None was of silver; it was not considered valuable in the days of Solomon

1.11.9.　　　1 Kings 6:21-22 So *Solomon overlaid the inside of the house with pure gold. And he drew chains of gold across the front of the inner sanctuary, and he overlaid it with gold. 22 He overlaid the whole house with gold, until all the house was finished. Also the whole altar which was by the inner sanctuary he overlaid with gold.*

1.11.10.　　　Solomon's sins were his downfall. All his sins were forbidden in the law, so he knew better! They may not seem like huge sins to us, but the motives of each were deep rooted. Solomon knew what was in the law. Solomon's three actions, which were forbidden in the law of Deuteronomy 17:

    1.11.10.1.　　　Many horses, a sign of militarism, were not to be a center of importance. Multiplying them led to an increase in trade with Egypt. God told Israel NOT to trade and make an alliance with the country they had been delivered from.

    1.11.10.2.　　　Gold and silver were only to be used for the people's poverty. Solomon made it part of his own glory. He was to live with abundance, not greed.

    1.11.10.3.　　　To have numerous wives was forbidden—in particular women from foreign lands. Eventually, he built places of heathen worship for many of his 3,000 wives.

    1.11.10.4.　　　This combination of actions forbidden in the law, were Saul's failure.

1.12.　　　The climax of unexcelled brilliance of his reign came as the Queen of Sheba (Matthew called her "the queen of the south"). When she visits, even with her own position and wealth, admitted that the fame of Solomon was beyond what she heard.[1]

Depth of Bible Words and Places
Sheba

Sheba was the land of the Queen who visited Solomon. The Bible informs us that the Queen, having heard of King Solomon's wisdom, traveled to Jerusalem to test him. It is recorded (1 Kings 10:13) that she returned to her own land."

---

[1] 1 Kings 10:6-7 *Then she said to the king, "It was a true report which I heard in my own land about your words and your wisdom. 7 "Nevertheless I did not believe the reports, until I came and my eyes had seen it. And behold, the half was not told me. You exceed in wisdom and prosperity the report which I heard.*

The land probably was located at the southwest tip of the Arabian Peninsula, the Kingdom of Saba that was well known, (modern day Yemen). Another possible location was on the opposite shore of the Red Sea, Aksum, in Ethiopia (continent of Africa). The location allowed a strong sea trade with both Africa and India. In addition, a strong caravan trade which went through Israel. The Queen visited Solomon to negotiate a trade agreement (a clay script was located revealing this treaty).

1.12.1.   Near Solomon's death, God forsakes Solomon and warns him that his son would only be an heir of part of dad's kingdom. Solomon's punishment came in a very personal way:

   1.12.1.1.   Commerce slowed, no more cash flow, no more material goods, and food problems developed. The economy failed.

   1.12.1.2.   His popularity dimmed,

   1.12.1.3.   His own physical body quickly aged;

   1.12.1.4.   He died very young, at fifty-eight years.

1.12.2.   Very little is said about his son Jeroboam following a rebellion, which he led. We will refer to him again, when we return to "more of the story" in Volume 2.

1.12.3.   King Solomon...sadly, here was a king who had unparalleled opportunities to guide Israel to spiritual greatness. That was God's purpose in the wisdom, the blessings, and specifically the Temple. Instead, he squandered it all and left a nation ripe for division and destruction.

1.12.4.   The story of his reign ends with a brief statement.[1]

---

1 Kings: What Did King Solomon Accomplish?
Centralized the government (Cp 4)
Intellectual accomplishments (4:33)
Wrote 3,000 proverbs, 1,500 songs (4:32)
Constructed the first Temple (cp 6)
Built a palace (7:1-12)
Placed strategic cities (9:15-18)
Increased trade (9:26-28; 10-22)
Organized the kingdom (26:20-28)

---

[1] 1 Kings 11:43 *And Solomon slept with his fathers and was buried in the city of his father David, and his son Rehoboam reigned in his place.*

2   In Volume One, we "travelled" from God's creation of all things, through failure of man to obey God, followed by the plan to redeem man through a Redeemer, then the founding of His peculiar nation and homeland, the Judges and first three Kings. Volume Two of this two-part *Travel Through the Old Testament* will begin with Wisdom and Israelite Poetry.

APPENDIX

CHRONOLOGY OF OLD TESTAMENT HISTORY*			
Egypt/God's people	**Approx. Period of Book;** *date Book was written*	Approx. Date (BCE)	Babylonia, Assyria, other parts of the world. (All dates BCE)
Pre-Adam period	**Genesis Begins**	Undated Past	
		5000	Earliest evidences of civilization found near area of Babylon.
Creation (six days)		4004	Ussher's Date of the creation
Birth of Cain		4003	
Cain kills Abel		c. 3900	
Birth of Seth		3874	
Birth of Methuselah		3500 3317	Pictographs used by Samarians
		c. 3200	Growth of city-states in Mesopotamia
First dynasty of Egypt (King Menes); Upper/Lower Egypt unified; early hieroglyphic writing		c. 3150-2890	
Death of Adam		3074	
Enoch, translated by God; did not experience death		3017	
Death of Seth		2962	
Birth of Noah		2948	
		c. 2900	First dynasty of kings at Ur; first advanced civilization; Nineveh founded by Babylonia; first known use of ink; Babylon destroyed by the Flood
Great pyramids at Gizeh. Old Kingdom Period		2600	
Dark period in Egypt		2500	
Birth of Japheth		2448	
Birth of Shem		2446	
Birth of Ham		2444	
Death of Methuselah; the Flood		2348 2344	
Noah leaves the Ark		2343	
		2350	Sargon I (Sargon the

				Great) King of Babylon
Egypt (Pepi) invaded Sargon's empire		2313		
			2300	Babylonian area repopulated; Ziggurats or temple-towers built about this time; (Sumer) Mesopotamia annexed by Akkadians (Sargon)
Birth of Eber		2281		
			c. 2230	Greece founded; earlier indications of population
Tower of Babel		2242		Ur rises to power; Cuneiform invented
			c. 2240	China, perhaps founded by Noah 2240; Took name from "yellow earth"; earliest records were written in 1500 and record back to the 1600-1046 Shang Dynasty
Birth of Terah		2126		
430 years of sojourn began		2091		Silk industry founded; Hammurabi's Code
Terah's first son, Haran, was born		2056		
			2004	City of Ur falls
			c. 2000	Babylonians use geometry, zodiac; Indoor plumbing use in Crete; Stonehenge, England religious center; Hitittes formed; Written history began
Death of Noah		1998		
Birth of Abram/Lot		1997		
Birth of Sarai		1986		
Call of Abram; death of Terah moves to Canaan; famine caused Abram to leave for Egypt		1921		
Abram and Lot returned to Canaan		1920		
Ishmael born to Hagar		1910		
God made a covenant with Abram; name changed to Abrham;		1897		

Sodom and Gomorrah			
Birth of Isaac		1896	
Ishmael jesting with Isaac; Sarah upset; suggested start of the years of slavery in Egypt		1891	
Isaac taken to Mt. Mariah		1871	
Death of Sarah		1860	
		1859	Assyria starts as a tiny colony of Babylonia; lasts until 607 BCE
Isaac marries Rebecca		1856	
Death of Shem		1846	
Rebecca birthed twins; Jacob and Esau		1837	
Death of Abraham in Canaan		1821	
Death of Eber		1817	Canaanites developed sounds of an alphabet
Hyksos invaded Egypt; captured Memphis and lower Egypt		1775	
Death of Ishmael		1773	
Esau sells birthright Jacob; Jacob flees to Haran, marries Leah, Rachel; Jacob's ladder		1759	
Leah bore Reuben, Jacob's first born		1758	
Birth of Judah		1755	
Egypt has developed papyrus and ink for writing; alphabet devised		1750 1699	Old Babylonia Empire unified under Hammurabi, its sixth king. Code found in 1902 CE; first real dynasty of Babylon; Code of Hammurabi, 282 laws written before God's law. (Many similarities)
Jerusalem established		*c.* 1750	Babylon becoming a center for commerce
Birth of Dinah		1748	
Birth of Joseph		1745	
Jacob fled from Laban; Rachel dies when Benjamin born; Esau and Jacob meet;		1739 1729	

Jacob wrestles with (Christ)			
Joseph sold into slavery		1728	
Joseph interpreted dreams of two officers of Pharaoh's court		1717	First Chinese dictionary
Death of Isaac in Canaan		1716	
Joseph interprets Pharaoh's dream; made ruler under Pharaoh		1715	
Jacob allows Benjamin to go to Egypt		1708	
7 years of plenty ends; migration of Jacob's family to Egypt; 70 Hebrews settle in Egypt		1706	
			Babylon Empire United 1700-648 Kassite's rule until 1160
Death of Jacob in Egypt; body was embalmed		1689	
Joseph speaks of Israelites departure from Egypt; death of Joseph in Egypt	**Genesis Ends**	1635	
	Preferred time of Events in Job	*c.* 1625	
New Empire established in Egypt; Ahmose I; Egypt's greatest period; Hyksos expelled		1570	Hittites strike Babylon
Israelites are enslaved in Egypt			
		1582	Early settlements in Greece
Birth of Aaron		1574	
Amenhotep I orders all male babies killed; raises Moses until 18 yrs old		1573	
Birth of Moses	**Exodus Begins**	1571	
Israelites are in			

bondage; *Hyksos kings driven out of Egypt*		1570	
Moses raised, as a young man, under Thutmose I		1553-1536	Assyrian wars with Hittites
Thutmose II sought to kill Moses		1536	
Birth of Joshua		1534	
Moses fled to Midian		1531	
Birth of Caleb		1529	
Thutmose III made Egypt a power by 17 campaigns; lost in the Red Sea?		c. 1508-1491	
		1501-1447	Early Greek Alphabet; Library of Hittites contains eight languages; Leprosy in India and Egypt
		1500	Babylon conquered, first time; Corinth founded
		1496-1446	Art of shipbuilding perfected, Mediterranean countries
Burning bush		1491	Phoenician letters brought into Greece, become Roman letters eventually used in America
Ten plagues; first Passover; Exodus from Egypt, and into the Wilderness, led by Moses	**Numbers begins**	1491	
Mount Sinai, giving of the Law; Ten Commandments	*Moses wrote Genesis, Exodus, Leviticus, Numbers c. 1491-1451 (see alternant JEDP theory*	1491	
Tabernacle; 12 spies sent into the land		1490	
Death of Miriam and Aaron		1452	
	Exodus Ends	1451	Mexico Sun Pyramid build
		1451	Olmec culture begins in Mexico

	Leviticus (one month); *Moses wrote Psalm 90*	1451	
38+ Years of Wandering; 17 camping stops over the 38 years	**Numbers Ends**	1491-1451	
	Deuteronomy (one month) **Joshua Begins**	1451	
Moses had taken the land east of the Jordan; divided the land to 2 ½ tribes; Moses viewed all the land of promise; death of Moses	*Joshua wrote Joshua*	1451	Ethiopia, located on the Horn of Africa, becomes independent, the first independent country on the continent. Known as "Kush" by ancient Egyptians. Known to be inhabited for several previous centuries.
Weak rule in Egypt under Amenhotep II and Thutmose IV		1447-1391	
Joshua crossing the Jordan; Jericho; manna stopped;		1451	Hittites rise to power in Asia Minor
Conquest of Canaan, Joshua		1451-1445	
Land portioned to tribes		1445-44	
Hebrew alphabet developed beyond earlier form			
Death of Joshua; buried in the city he built, Timnathserah	**Joshua Ends**	*c.* 1424	
Egypt expands trade under Amenhotep III		1420	
First of 14 'judges', (1) Othniel (of Judah); Delivery from oppression of the Mesopotamians	**Judges Begins**	1392	Hittites conquer Mesopotamia and Syria; at height of power
Egypt's greatest splendor; Tutankhamen/ Rameses I		1380-1373	
	Judges written, perhaps by Samuel; **Ruth events,**	*c.* 1392-1050	

	sometime during Judges, probably late Judges		
Judge (2) Ehud (of Benjamin) defeats Moabites	*Ruth written, unknown author*	c. 1342	
		1290	Babylon conquered by Assyrians, but held only for a short time
		1267	First Assyrian Empire founded under Ninus
Judge (3) Shamgar		c. 1260	
Judges (4) Deborah (of Ephraim) and Barak (of Naphthali); defeated Canaanites		c. 1260	
		1250	Shalmaneser I (of 5) first powerful king of Assyria; Trojan war in Greece
Birth of Eli		1214	
		1206	Genghis Khan unified tribes in China
		1200	Philistines occupy Mediterranean coast Hercules; Hittite Empire Ends
Judge (5) Gideon (of Manasseh) defeats Amalekites and Midianites		c. 1233	
Judge (6) Tola		c. 1197	
Philistines suffer a defeat at the hands of Ramesses III		1188	
		1184	Trojan war; fall of Troy
Birth of Samson		1155	
		1152	Cho Dynasty in China
Judges: (7) Jair (8) Ibzan (9) Elon (10(Abdon		1146 1139 1129	
		1117	Philistines expand into Israel

Beginning of Greek History, first evidence of quality civilization, |

			revealed in discovered pottery
(11) Jephthah delivers Israel from the Ammonites; *Upper/Lower Egypt split; weakness begins*		*c.* 1087	
Judge (12) Samson (of Dan) delivers from Philistines, dies;		1101	
Ark moved to temple of Dagon		c. 1100	
		1114-1093	Tiglath-Pileser I rules Assyrian Empire
Birth of Samuel (Israel's 14th Judge). (Also, Eli was a Judge)	**1 Samuel Begins; 1 Chronicles Begins**	c. 1105	
Ark moved again		1096	
Saul anointed first King (41 yr reign)		1095-1056	
Civil war in Egypt		1090	
David is born		1085	
Samuel secretly anoints David as Saul's successor		1070	
David and Goliath		1067	
Jonathan visits David		1064	
David cuts off Saul's robe in Engedi; works for Philistines		1062	
Death of Eli		1061	
Death of Samuel		1060	
Israel a dominant power; Philistines took off the head of Saul; Death of Jonathan	*Many Psalms written (6,11,12,19 26, 58, 59,120,131, and several others)*	1055-1048 1055	
	Judges Ends	1050	
David king over 12 tribes; David captures Jerusalem		1048	
David brings Ark of Covenant to Jerusalem; David broke the Philistine hold		1047	
Mephibosheth restored		1040	

David and Bathsheba; Solomon is born		1037	
		1030-1018	Shalmaneser rules Assyria
Preparations to build the Temple			
Absalom revolts against David		1027	
Absalom took possession of David's kingdom		1023	
Saul's sons hung by Gibeonites		1022	
Birth of Rehoboam		1016	
Solomon anointed king; David Dies		1015	
Reign of Solomon		1015-975	
Solomon marries daughter of Pharaoh		1014	
Temple built at Jerusalem		1012-1005	
	2 Samuel Begins	1010	
Temple dedicated		1004	Mayan Dynasties founded in Central America; refrigeration developed, Chinese
Power extended from Red Sea to Euphrates River			
	Ruth written c. 10th century, unknown author; **1 Samuel Ends 2 Chronicles Begins**	1000	
	Song of Solomon (Songs); *written by Solomon*	c. 980	
	Ecclesiastes; *possibly written by Solomon; alternate date written by others c. 450*	c. 970	
	1 Kings Begins; *1 and 2 Samuel written (single book), unknown*	970	

287

	author		
	Many Proverbs written	950-750	
Southern Kingdom (Judah and Benjamin Tribes) 20 kings, 1 Dynasty **Judah King/yrs** Events/Prophets			Northern Kingdom (Ten Tribes) 20 kings, 9 Dynasties **Israel King/yrs** Events
Rehoboam/17 **975-959**; Solomon dies; division of Kingdom; (a fixed date using 586 date for fall of Judah and Ezek 4:4-5)		975	**1st Dynasty; Jeroboam/22;** established shrines at Bethlehem and Dan 975-954
Foreign domination of Egypt, ruled by Lybia		950-750	
Egypt (Shishak) invades Judah and Israel, takes cities	1 & 2 Samuel written 930	971	Tiglath-Pileser II rules Assyria 967-935
Abijam (Abijah)/3 **958-955;** Abijam wars against Jeroboam, wins; highest casualty rate of any Bible battle.		958	
Asa/41 955-914		955	
Judah Wars against Israel		954	**Nadab/2 954-953** Ben-hadad I, King in Syria; war-like people build the Assyrian Empire; set on conquest of the world
Religious reforms		953	**2nd Dynasty; Baasha/24 953-930**
Birth of Jehoshaphat, son of Asa		949	
Ethiopia invades Judah		941	

			Dynasties	Events/*Prophets*
		940	Ben-haded invades Israel, destroyed much of the Asher and Dan Tribes	
	2nd Possible date Job written	930		
		930	**3rd Dynasty; Elah/2 930-929**	
		929	*Zimri*/7 days; shortest "dynasty" to sit on a biblical throne	
		929	**4th Dynasty; Tibni/Omri/12 929-918**	God chose him as ruler; sets up idols, Baalism; builds Samaria; conquers Moab
Asa's feet diseased		918	**Ahab/21 918-897**	Marries Jezebel; Constant war with Judah; defeated Ben-hadad; death of Omri
Jehoshaphat/25 914-889; Co-regent w/Asa Religious reform Peace with Israel/ Ahab; death of Asa		914		
		914		*Elijah's* 1st miracle; Death of Omri
Death of Jehoshaphat		c. 899		*Elijah* chooses *Elisha*
Joram(Jehoram)/ 8 898-884 (co-rule for six); Married Ahab's daughter; Edomites revolted; set up worship of Baal		898		
		897	*Ahaziah/2 898-897*	Calf worship/war with Judah; fell out of window, dies; death of Ahab
	1 Kings Ends;	897-	*Jehoram/12*	Ben-hadad invades

				Israel
	2 Kings Begins	889	*897-884*	Israel
"J" source of Pentateuch		c. 897		*Elisha 1ˢᵗ miracle, ministry;* Homer in Greece; *Elijah taken to heaven*
Died of disease allowed by God		885		
		845		Israel invaded by Ben-hadad II, King of Damascus (880-842)
Made his son Ahaziah his 2ⁿᵈ in command. His other sons were killed		886	*5ᵗʰ Dynasty; Jehu/27 884-857*	Attempts reform; pays tribute to Assyria; Assyria invades; shrewdest of Israel kings suppressed Baalism for a while
Ahaziah/1; Killed by Jehu		884		
Athaliah/6 884-878; (Queen) Daughter of Jezebel/6; slays all leaders except Joash		884		
Joash (Jehoash) /40 879-839; Hidden in temple/influenced by High Priest, Jehioada; made king at age 7; repaired the temple; Samaria founded		879		Assyrian empire extended; control of Babylonia
		858-824		Shalmaneser III rules Assyria
		857	*Johoahaz/17 857-840*	Baal worship; Marriage to Jezebel
				Alliance of peace with Judah
	Obadiah, alternate date and written date	840		Growth of Baalism/idolatry
		839		Joash visited *Elisha* on his death bed; Death of *Elisha*
				Israel/captures Moab

		843-840	Jehoash/16 840-826	
Amaziah/29 839-811; Invades Israel		839		Syria defeated by Assyria
Jerusalem's walls broken down Flees, hides, assassinated		784	Jeroboam II/41 826-785	Son of Joash; Period of prosperity; Dies in fall from window; killed by Jehu
(Best date) Joel 835-796 (Later option in 600 BCE)	Joel writes Joel 835; alternative date is 400	830		
Uzziah born to Amaziah; Joash died		826	c. 825	Carthage founded
Uzziah (Azariah)/52 810-758; Co-regent w/Amaziah		810		
Isaiah and Joel living		808		Jonah living
		800		Homer "LLiad: and "Odyssey" in Greece; Assyrian power weakened
Prosperity in Judah		784	Zachariah/6mo 772	Israel Invaded by Syria;
		783-773		Shalmaneser IV rules Assyria
		776		First Olympic games; Greek history begins
	Jonah written, unknown author 760; Amos Begins	760		
	Hosea Begins Jonah	755		Greece, Hellenic outlook emerged
			753-509	Royal period of Rome
		772	6th Dynasty; Shallum/1 mo 772	Uproots Baal
		772	7th Dynasty; Menahem/10 772-762	Pays tribute to Assyria; King Pul of Assyria invades Israel
Birth of Ahaz, son of Jotham		761	Pekahiah/2 761-760	Turns in desperation to God
Isaiah saw the		759	8th Dynasty;	

glory of God			**Pekah/11** **759-739**	
Jotham/16 758-742; Co-regent with Uzziah (leprosy) at first; the "E" source of Pentateuch	**Micah Begins;** **Possible date that Joel takes place**	750		Jezebel killed, left for dogs; Idolatry on a grand scale; Great Britain settled by the Celtics
	Amos Ends *Amos writes Amos*	*c.* 750		Assyria attacked by Media
		748		Rome was founded; Babylonia (Nabonassar) under Assyrian rule; Tiglath-pileser III rules
				Takes back the cities lost by his father
Isaiah, Micah	**Isaiah Begins**	742		
Ahaz/16 **742-726;** Co-regent with Jotham at first (759); Idolatry; wicked King; Becomes ruler; Edom, joined by Philistines invaded Judah, took captives; Jotham dies		742		Dentistry advances made in Italy, false teeth; Rome institutes a 10 month calendar
Asks Tiglath-pileser III to help against Syria and Israel; Ahaz becomes a servant to Assyria		740-720		Assyria regains power, pushes west; Tiglathpileser III ("Pul" king of Assyria invades Israel
	Micah writes Micah c. 740-710			
Egypt captured by Assyria		*c.* 735		Israel invaded by Tiglath-pileser III, takes much land, captives to Assyria
		730	**9th Dynasty;** **Hosea/9** **730-720**	Last King of Israel; Pays tribute to Assyria; restored order in Israel
Death of Ahaz		726		
		722-	FALL OF ISRAEL;	Shalmaneser V attacks

		721	some of the northern Israelites go south to Judah		Samaria, Sargun II completes the victory; captured many Israelites, carries them away; 254 yrs following division of the Kingdom.
Hezekiah/29 726-697; reforms temple worship following death of his father, Ahaz		726			
Many other reforms introduced; eventually turns from God, destroys Moses' brazen serpent; father of Manasseh		726			
	Hosea Ends; *Hosea writes Hosea c. 722*	722			Samaria (Israel) captured; *Hosea*
		722-705			Assyrian Empire expands; Sargon II rules
Jerusalem, full of foreigners, sees no need of God		711			
Attempted siege of Jerusalem God Intervenes!	*Isaiah writes Isaiah 700-680; two alternative writers may have written cps 40-66*	709			
Hezekiah's tunnels; rebels from Assyria; Sennacherib comes to regain control; Judah survives and outlasts the Assyrian empire		705-681 705			Sennacherib reigned in Assyria; made war on Egypt and Asia Sennacherib war against Judah; killed many Jews; marched to Egypt, took captives
Manasseh/54 697-642; Evil Rule, idolatry, cruelty; thought to have sawn Isaiah in half	**Micah Ends** **Isaiah Ends**	697 680		Assyria captured Babylonia; became united	Murdered by Hoshea Babylon rebuilt under Escrhaddon (681-669)

		690		God intervenes; Sennacherib killed by his own sons; new kingdom of the Medes
Manasseh carried captive into Bablylon		677		Greek city-state emerges
Egypt conquered by Assyria		671		
		657		Assyria took the Medes
		660		Japan recognized as a country
Thebes captured by Assyrians		664		
		650-625		Damascus falls to the Assyrians
		650		Jeremiah born
Death of Manasseh after he returned from captivity		643		
Amnon/2 642-640; Evil reign		642		
Josiah/31 640-609	Zephaniah Begins	640		
	Nahum Begins	635 630		All Asia joins Medes to attack Assyria
Josiah's Great religious reform comes; cleanses Judah from idolatry; Jeremiah's call		629		
	Jeremiah Begins	628		Pays tribute to Assyria
	Nahum writes Nahum 630-620			Puppet king under Assyria
	Jeremiah writes Jeremiah 627-585 Zephaniah writes Zephaniah 625	626		Nabopolassar rules Babylonia 626-605
Josiah finds "Book		624		**Fall of Israel**

of The Law"				
Ezekiel was born	**Nahum Ends; Zephaniah Ends**	622		Captured by Sargon III
Jehoahaz/3mo; taken to Egypt 610 Josiah killed at Megiddo; his son was Jehoahaz		612		
		607		Kingdom of Babylon destroyed
	Habakkuk Begins *Last of the Psalms written*	612		Time of Buddha; Nineveh, Haran captured by Babylonia; Temple of Artemis built in Ephesus
Many in Judah taken by Egypt		605		Babylonia in power, Nebuchadnezzar II 605-562
Jehoaikim/11 (Eliakim) 607-596; rebelled against Nebuchadnezzar (Beginning of 3 captivities) by Babylonia; Jehoaikim was chained and carried to Babylon; Daniel also taken		607		
Reigns as vassal of Nebuchadnezzar Nebuchadnezzar, as a General, takes rule of Jerusalem; 1st Deportation to Babylon; 70 years in Babylon begins; *Egypt falls to Assyria;* Baruch records words of Jeremiah	*Habakkuk writes Habakkuk c. 607;* **Daniel Begins**	606		Birth of Confucius
Nebuchadnezzar's rule		c. 606-561		

Raruch again records the words of Jeremiah		605		
Daniel taken captive to Babylon Nebuchardnezzar, Daniel have dreams		604		
				History of Japan begins
Jehoakim rebels against Babylon; Nebuchadnezzar's army destroyed Judah		600		
Obadiah uttered a prophecy against Edom	**Obadiah** (best date)	600		Nabopolasar, father of Nebuchadnezzar, rules Babylon; unsuccessful invasion of Egypt
Jehoiachin (Jeconiah)/3 mo 598; 2nd Deportation to Babylon Nebuchadnezzar invades Jerusalem, takes captive 10,000 including Ezekiel, Jehoiachin; Mordecai and Ezekiel taken captive	**Habakkuk Ends**	598		Birth of Cyrus
Zedekiah/11 597-586; Last king of Judah, evil reign; refused invitation from Jeremiah	**2 Kings Ends**	597		
Ezekiel's vision; Baruch read all his journal to all the captives in Babylon; Ezekiel carried by the Spirit to Jerusalem	**Ezekiel Begins** in Babylonia; *Ezekiel writes Ezekiel 592-570*	594		Olive tree brought to Italy from Greece

and then back to Babylon			
The Glory departs the temple		592	
		589	Nebuchadnezzar's father breaks from Assyria, aligns with the Mede's, independence of Babylon; Babylon destroys much of Egypt
Zedekiah rebels against Babylonia; final siege on Jerusalem		588	
Jerusalem and the Temple destroyed by Nebuchadnezzar 3rd Deportation to Babylon; many other biblical dates are established by counting backward from this known "point"	**Jeremiah Ends; 1 and 2 Chronicles Ends**	586	
"D" source of Pentateuch	**Lamentations**	586	
Jerusalem develops subterranean water tunnels			
END OF JUDAH		586	
Captives to Babylon; a few Jews left in Judah	*Obadiah writes Obadiah c. 586-553*		
	Jeremiah writes Jeremiah c. 585-580		
Jeremiah, Baruch, and others taken away to Egypt		585	Persian Empire 559-330 BCE;
"P" source of Pentateuch	*1 and 2 Kings written (single book);*	*c. 580*	

	unknown author			
Ezekiel "sees" the Israelites restored		575		
		570		Nebuchadnezzar builds Hanging Gardens; grows proud
		571		Nebuchadnezzar conquered Egypt; kills many Jews there; he dreams and Daniel explains; acknowledged the power of God; took Tyre
		562		Nebuchadnezzar II died; Aesop's fables.
	Ezekiel Ends	571		
		c. 560-539	Babylon descends, Belshazzar last king; writing on the wall in 539	
Ezekiel died				
		559-530	Cyrus II (the Great) reigns in Persia	Builds battering rams; defeated Belshazzar; capture of Babylon
		550		Birth of Buddha; Birth of Confucius (one year later)
	Jeremiah writes 1 Kings and 2 Kings 560-550; Jeremiah writes Lamentations c. 545	559-549 545	Cyrus the Great of Persia conquers Media; Cyrus conquers Lydia; built battering rams	Darius born, 549
	Some Psalms written in Babylon;	539	Cyrus conquers Babylon and adds it to Medo-Persian Empire, resulting Persian Empire is huge, powerful	Darius the Mede ruled the kingdom Cyrus gave him, Babylon; Michael the angel appears to him
		538		Darius subdues all the countries from Syria to the Red Sea
		536	Decree of Cyrus permitting Jews to	

			return to Palestine	
Lions' den	**Ezra Begins**; *Daniel writes Daniel 537-530*	537	End of 70 years of captivity	
First return to Jerusalem under Zerubbabel (Sheshbazzar). As many as 43, 360 returned. Begin to rebuild temple, but held up by Samaritans Daniel dies	**Daniel Ends**	536 525	King Cyrus develops a messenger system using horses Persian Empire (Cambyses) conquers Egypt; king of Arabia made a league with Cambrysees Aramaic language begins to replace Old Hebrew in Palestine	
		529	Death of Cyrus; his son, Cambyses rules Persia 530-522; wars, conquers, Egypt	
Artaxerxes sent letter forbidding the rebuilding of Jerusalem		522	Death of Cambyses; Artaxerxes stopped the rebuilding of Jerusalem	
		521	Buddha's study of philosophy began	
Haggai encourages the Jews to persevere in the work in Jerusalem	**Haggai Begins Zechariah Begins**; *Haggai writes Haggai c. 510*	520 522-485 520	Darius the Great's rule in Persia Greeks use papyrus	
Darius says continue the building of the temple		520	Edict of Cyrus located	
Temple is completed by Zerubbabel	*Zechariah writes Zechariah c.*	516		

	520-518		
Esther marries King Ahasuerus		515	
Haman plots against the Jews		510	
Haman hanged/Mordecai made Prime Minister		509	Expansion/founding of the Roman Republic
Rescues her countrymen from tragic fate (in Persia)		508	Treaty between Carthage and Rome
	Haggai Ends	505	
		c. 500	Rise of democracy at Athens
		492-479	Graeco-Persian Wars; Persia attempts to conquer Greece
		490	Greeks Battle of Marathon
	Esther, Jewish Queen	485-474 480	Death of Darius, 479 in battle; Reign of Xerxes in Persia Persian wars; took Greece; burned many temples in Asia; Xerxes took Athens Battle of Salamis Socrates in Greece 470-399 Pericles in Greece
		480	Death of Buddha; death of Confucius (one year later)
	Zechariah Ends	518	
		474-425	Artaxerxes Longimanus, son of Xerxes, rules Persia
Second return under Ezra and a	Ezra Ends; Esther	467	Persian army driven out of Asia,

large group	written 460-400		Persian wars end
Begin Daniel's 70th week to Christ		454	
		450-430	Age of Pericles at Athens, golden age of Greek Art; temple of Zeus built
	Ezra writes 1 & 2 Chronicles, Ezra, and Nehemiah 450-420		
Third return to Jerusalem under Nehemiah, who is appointed Governor of Judah. Walls rebuilt. Law of Moses is read, reforms made. Feast of Tabernacles; Sanballat and Tobiah; Ezra read the law of God	Nehemiah	454	
		448	Greece at peace with Persia
Nehemiah governor of Judah		445-430	Construction of Parthenon at Athens
Last datable events in O.T. history: Nehemiah returns to Jerusalem after visit to Persia	Ezra wrote Nehemiah written 430-420	442	
		431-404 424-404	Peloponnesian War in Greece Reign of Darius II in Persia
	Malachi; Malachi written, unknown author 430-420	c. 441-425	

		438	Spartacus; Parthenon in Greece completed
		425	Artaxerxes died; his son Xerxes II made king (for one year) killed in his bed
		407	Plato studies philosophy under Socrates
		404	Athens in downfall
	A 2nd Possible date that Joel takes place	404-358	Artaxerxes II ruled Persia
The Silent Period		400	Chinese complete a wall to keep out the Hun people Plato 373 BCE
		356	Alexander The Great is born; leads Greece to a world power
		331	Persia and Egypt falls to Alexander
		323	Alexander dies

INDEX

Complete/Consolidated Index of Persons, Key Words, Depth of Words and Places, and Expanded Help Papers.

Old Testament

Genesis

SCRIPTURE INDEX

Exodus

Leviticus

Numbers

Deuteronomy

Ruth

1 Samuel

1 Kings

SCRIPTURE INDEX

Proverbs

Ecclesiastes

Isaiah

Jeremiah

Ezekiel

Daniel

New Testament

James

1 Peter

1 John

Revelation

NOTES

NOTES